Welfare Reform and Beyond
The Future of the Safety Net

Isabel V. Sawhill, R. Kent Weaver,
Ron Haskins, and Andrea Kane
Editors

Copyright © 2002
THE BROOKINGS INSTITUTION
1775 Massachusetts Avenue, N.W., Washington, D.C. 20036
www.brookings.edu

All rights reserved

Library of Congress Cataloging-in-Publication data is available

ISBN 0-8157-0639-1 (pbk : alk. paper)

Digital printing

The paper used in this publication meets minimum requirements of the
American National Standard for Information Sciences—Permanence of Paper for
Printed Library Materials: ANSI Z39.48-1992.

Typeset in Fairfield

Composition by Sese-Paul Design

WELFARE REFORM AND BEYOND

THE BROOKINGS INSTITUTION

The Brookings Institution is an independent organization devoted to nonpartisan research, education, and publication in economics, government, foreign policy, and the social sciences generally. Its principal purposes are to aid in the development of sound public policies and to promote public understanding of issues of national importance. The Institution was founded on December 8, 1927, to merge the activities of the Institute for Government Research, founded in 1916, the Institute of Economics, founded in 1922, and the Robert Brookings Graduate School of Economics and Government, founded in 1924. The Institution maintains a position of neutrality on issues of public policy to safeguard the intellectual freedom of the staff.

Board of Trustees

James A. Johnson
Chairman

Leonard Abramson
Michael H. Armacost
Elizabeth E. Bailey
Zoë Baird
Alan R. Batkin
James W. Cicconi
Alan M. Dachs
D. Ronald Daniel
Robert A. Day
Lawrence K. Fish
Richard W. Fisher
William Clay Ford Jr.

Cyrus F. Freidheim Jr.
Bart Friedman
Stephen Friedman
Ann M. Fudge
Henry Louis Gates Jr.
Jeffrey W. Greenberg
Brian L. Greenspun
Lee H. Hamilton
William A. Haseltine
Teresa Heinz
Samuel Hellman
Joel Z. Hyatt
Shirley Ann Jackson
Robert L. Johnson
Ann Dibble Jordan

Michael H. Jordan
Marie L. Knowles
David O. Maxwell
Mario M. Morino
Steven Rattner
Rozanne L. Ridgway
Judith Rodin
Warren B. Rudman
Leonard D. Schaeffer
Joan E. Spero
John L. Thornton
Vincent J. Trosino
Stephen M. Wolf
Daniel Yergin

Honorary Trustees

Rex J. Bates
Louis W. Cabot
A. W. Clausen
William T. Coleman Jr.
Lloyd N. Cutler
Bruce B. Dayton
Douglas Dillon
Charles W. Duncan Jr.
Walter Y. Elisha
Robert F. Erburu
Robert D. Haas
Andrew Heiskell
F. Warren Hellman
Robert A. Helman

Roy M. Huffington
Vernon E. Jordan Jr.
Breene M. Kerr
James T. Lynn
Jessica Tuchman Mathews
Donald F. McHenry
Robert S. McNamara
Mary Patterson McPherson
Arjay Miller
Constance Berry Newman
Maconda Brown O'Connor
Donald S. Perkins
Samuel Pisar
J. Woodward Redmond

Charles W. Robinson
James D. Robinson III
Howard D. Samuel
B. Francis Saul II
Ralph S. Saul
Henry B. Schacht
Michael P. Schulhof
Robert Brookings Smith
Morris Tanenbaum
John C. Whitehead
James D. Wolfensohn
Ezra K. Zilkha

Foreword

The Personal Responsibility and Work Opportunity Reconciliation Act (PRWORA) of 1996 led both to dramatic policy changes toward low-income families and to an enormous outpouring of research that attempts to assess the impact of those policy changes. PRWORA imposed stiff new work requirements on Temporary Assistance to Needy Families (TANF) recipients and states, put time limits on the use of federal funds to pay cash benefits to TANF recipients, and gave states expanded discretion in using TANF funds. The legislation also gave increased attention to issues of family formation, strengthened child support enforcement, and placed much stricter limitations on receipt of means-tested benefits by non-citizens.

How have states used their new discretion in setting TANF policies and in spending TANF funds? How have welfare offices changed in response to the new legislation? What has happened to welfare caseloads and why? How have the new policies affected the employment of mothers and the well-being of children? Are some families worse off? Are mothers who have gone to work earning enough to support their families, or are these families still poor? Do they still have access to other means of support such as food stamps, Medicaid, and subsidized child care? These are among the many questions that researchers have addressed in trying to assess the impact of PRWORA.

As Congress begins its debate on reauthorizing the 1996 legislation, legislators and their staffs find themselves inundated by hundreds of reports, articles, monographs, and other research products that have been issued over the past six years. To help busy policymakers come to grips with this flood of information, the Brookings Institution's Welfare Reform & Beyond Initiative began in January 2001 to issue a series of policy briefs, written by leading experts, to synthesize the flood of emerging research in a non-technical, balanced manner.

Most of the chapters in this volume were originally published as part of the Welfare Reform & Beyond series. The first two briefs have been extensively revised to reflect both new developments and the research reviewed in the other briefs and appear in this volume as chapters 2 and 3. The third policy brief in the series, by Isabel Sawhill and Adam Thomas, was omitted from this volume for a different reason: most of its policy recommendations were later incorporated directly into the Economic Growth and Tax Relief Reconciliation Act of 2001. The other policy briefs appear here unchanged, although in a different order from that in which they were originally published.

This volume was edited by Isabel Sawhill and Kent Weaver, co-directors of the Welfare Reform & Beyond Initiative and senior fellows at Brookings; by Andrea Kane, outreach director for the Initiative and a visiting fellow at Brookings; and by Ron Haskins, who was a co-director of the Initiative and Brookings senior fellow until taking a leave of absence from Brookings in February of 2002. Haskins earlier took major responsibility for the editing of the individual briefs. All of

Haskins's writing and editing duties for this volume were performed before he took a leave from Brookings.

This endeavor would not have been possible without the assistance of dedicated people on the Welfare Reform & Beyond team, within Brookings and outside of Brookings. First we would like to thank Bethany Hase for successfully managing the overall production of this volume and the policy brief series, and to Robert Wooley for his assistance in coordinating the editing process. Ron Nessen and Elana Mintz provided excellent editorial advice and helped to steer the individual policy briefs through the Brookings review process. Maria Voles Ferguson and Elana Mintz edited the individual policy briefs that formed the basis for most of the chapters in this volume. Maria Sese-Paul provided the graphic design and layout of the individual briefs as well as for the chapters and the cover of this volume. Brenda Szittya provided her always-expert editing for this volume's three overview chapters on very short notice.

Lawrence Converse of the Brookings Press provided production guidance. Bob Litan reviewed most of the briefs, and both he and Linda Gianessi provided advice and guidance to the project. In addition we would like to thank the following Welfare Reform & Beyond staff members for their assistance: Sara Belz, Molly Fifer, Debra Hevenstone, Maggie Kozak, Catherine McLoughlin, Carly Minner, Shannon Smith, and Adam Thomas.

The editors also thank the funders of the Welfare Reform & Beyond Initiative, including the Annie E. Casey Foundation, the Ford Foundation, the Foundation for Child Development, the Joyce Foundation, the John D. and Catherine T. MacArthur Foundation, the Charles S. Mott Foundation and the David and Lucile Packard Foundation, for their generous support of the Initiative.

The views expressed here are solely those of the authors and should not be attributed to sponsoring foundations or to the trustees, officers, or other staff members of the Brookings Institution.

April 2002
Washington, DC

MICHAEL H. ARMACOST
President, Brookings Institution

Contents

PART I INTRODUCTION AND SUMMARY

1 An Overview 3
Isabel Sawhill, R. Kent Weaver, and Andrea Kane

2 Results to Date 9
Isabel Sawhill, R. Kent Weaver, Ron Haskins, and Andrea Kane

3 Problems and Issues for Reauthorization 20
Isabel Sawhill, R. Kent Weaver, Ron Haskins, and Andrea Kane

PART II STATE RESPONSES

4 State Policy Choices Under Welfare Reform 33
Thomas Gais and R. Kent Weaver

5 Changing Welfare Offices 41
Irene Lurie

6 Sanctions and Welfare Reform 49
Dan Bloom and Don Winstead

PART III RESULTS TO DATE

7 Welfare Reform and Poverty 59
Ron Haskins and Wendell Primus

8 Which Welfare Reforms are Best for Children? 71
Pamela A. Morris and Greg J. Duncan

9 From Welfare to Work: What the Evidence Shows 79
Robert A. Moffitt

PART IV TANF FUNDING AND THE ECONOMY

10 The Structure of the TANF Block Grant 89
R. Kent Weaver

11 Welfare and the Economy 97
Rebecca M. Blank

PART V ENCOURAGING AND REWARDING WORK

12 Welfare Reform and the Work Support System 107
Isabel Sawhill and Ron Haskins

13 The Role of Education and Training in Welfare Reform 120
Judith M. Gueron and Gayle Hamilton

14 Job Retention and Advancement in Welfare Reform 128
Nancye Campbell, John K. Maniha, and Howard Rolston

15 Helping the Hard-to-Employ 135
LaDonna Pavetti

PART VI FAMILY FORMATION

16 Reducing Non-marital Births 145
Paul Offner

17 Fragile Families, Welfare Reform, and Marriage 152
Sara McLanahan, Irwin Garfinkel, and Ronald B. Mincy

18 What Can Be Done to Reduce Teen Pregnancy and Out-of-Wedlock Births? 160
Isabel Sawhill

PART VII RELATED PROGRAMS

19 Food Stamps and Welfare Reform 173
Michael Wiseman

20 Health Insurance, Welfare, and Work 181
Alan Weil and John Holahan

21 Child Care and Welfare Reform 189
Gina Adams and Monica Rohacek

22 Welfare Reform and Housing 197
Rebecca Swartz and Brian Miller

23 Welfare Benefits for Non-citizens 205
Michael Fix and Ron Haskins

Contributors 213

PART I

INTRODUCTION AND SUMMARY

1

ISABEL SAWHILL, R. KENT WEAVER,
AND ANDREA KANE

An Overview

On August 22, 1996, President Bill Clinton signed legislation that transformed the American welfare system. Many of the new law's provisions, including Temporary Assistance for Needy Families (TANF), which replaced Aid to Families with Dependent Children (AFDC), were authorized for six years. By October 1, 2002, the 107th Congress must reauthorize the welfare reform legislation to avoid disrupting the flow of TANF funds to the states.

The 1996 legislation is one of the most closely examined pieces of social legislation in recent decades. The extensive research available on many facets of the law and its implementation has the potential to play a vital role in the reauthorization debate. But research must be synthesized, organized, and shared with policymakers in a form that they can use as a basis for considering changes. This volume of brief essays, most originally published as policy briefs by the Brookings Institution's Welfare Reform & Beyond Initiative, attempts such a synthesis.

The New Law

Enactment of the Personal Responsibility and Work Opportunity Reconciliation Act of 1996 followed decades of complaints about the inadequacies of the existing welfare system and the many attempts to reform it. Some observers charged that the old welfare system left too many families destitute, while others believed it was anti-work and anti-family. These different views reflect an age-old tension between explanations of poverty that emphasize lack of opportunity as the primary cause and those that emphasize lack of personal responsibility. The 1996 law stressed the importance of the latter with an emphasis on encouraging work and reducing out-of-wedlock childbearing.

Although the new law revised many programs—including child care, food stamps, child support, aid for disabled children, and the eligibility of legal immigrants for means-tested benefits—its heart was the TANF program. TANF repealed the individual entitlement to welfare and replaced an open-ended federal payment to the states with a block grant. The funding level of the grant was fixed, but states were given added flexibility in deciding how funds were to be spent. TANF also contained strong work requirements (on states and individuals), sanctions for individuals who failed to comply with the new requirements, and a five-year limit on the use of federal dollars for cash assistance to individual families. Taken together, these five characteristics rendered TANF a radically different program from the AFDC program it replaced.

By the time welfare was reformed, a quiet revolution had already greatly increased the availability of benefits to low-income working families through such programs as the Earned

Income Tax Credit (EITC), Medicaid, and child care. In 1999, working low- and moderate-income families were eligible for $52 billion in assistance from such programs, compared with the $6 billion they would have been eligible for under the 1984 law. If welfare reform was the "stick" encouraging welfare mothers to work, these work support programs were the new "carrot" (chapters 12–15).

State Responses

The first question in considering how the 1996 law has worked is how states have responded (chapters 4–6). Most states have moved not only to implement the provisions of TANF, but to put in place a rich array of both "carrots" (incentives and supports) and "sticks" (penalties) to encourage work by TANF recipients. In 36 states, a family loses their entire welfare benefit if the adult fails to comply with the work requirement (chapter 6). The precise mix of incentives, supports, and penalties chosen varies widely from state to state, however, reflecting differences both in state political environments and in financial resources (chapter 4).

Equally revealing, the spending patterns found in the budgets of state and local offices have changed dramatically. Before welfare reform, state and local offices typically spent around 80 percent of their welfare money on cash benefits, with the rest going to administration, education, training, and child care. Now states often spend 50 percent or less of their funds on cash benefits. Only a few states have reduced their cash assistance benefit levels. Spending on job search, education, training, child care, and other work-related activities has expanded and diversified. If budget is policy, important changes have taken place in the welfare program at the state and local level.

These policy shifts can also be seen in the implementation of welfare reform at the ground level. No longer are local offices simply check-writing operations; they are also agencies that help people prepare for and find jobs (chapter 5). Welfare office personnel have been retrained, and the activities inside welfare offices—which most states have renamed "Work Centers" or a similar term—have expanded to include job-related pursuits.

Results

The major consequences of this emphasis on work have been a big drop in welfare caseloads, increased employment and higher incomes among single mothers, and a decline in child poverty (chapter 2 and chapters 7–9). Some families are worse off, however, and states have only recently focused on how to move the hard-to-employ toward self-sufficiency (chapter 15). Many families have been sanctioned for their failure to comply with work requirements, and little is known about how this group is faring (chapter 6). Moreover, many families have lost the food stamp and Medicaid benefits they had been receiving and to which they remain entitled, primarily because of the difficulty that working families have accessing such benefits (chapters 19 and 20). Legal immigrants—a group that lost eligibility for many benefits in 1996—have been especially affected as their use of TANF, food stamps, Medicaid, and Supplemental Security Income (SSI) have all declined (chapter 23).

Although the great majority of mothers leaving welfare have found jobs, their earnings are quite low, typically around $7–8 an hour (chapter 9). Moreover, few have health insurance coverage through their employers, and many must pay for child care. In fact, despite a large increase in funding for child care since 1996, many states report waiting lists for subsidized care, and working mothers often find it difficult to navigate the child care system or to come up with the co-payments required to get the subsidies (chapter 21). Still, in the end, work pays better than welfare. A mother with no more than three children can escape poverty if she works steadily and full-time at a $7 an hour job and receives the benefits to which she is entitled (chapter 12).

Progress in achieving the family formation goals of the 1996 law has been less evident, but even here several indicators have begun to move in the right direction. Teen pregnancies and births have declined dramatically, the share of children born out of wedlock has leveled off, and the share of children being raised in two-parent families has increased (chapters 16–18). The strong emphasis on parental responsibility in the 1996 law has been followed by large increases in paternity establishment and child support collections.

A major concern of critics of the 1996 law was that it would harm children. So far little evidence of widespread harm has materialized. According to evidence drawn largely from pre-TANF state experiments comparing children whose mothers were required to work with those whose mothers remained on welfare, no consistently significant differences exist between the two groups of children in terms of their health, education, or behavior. Indeed, where the work requirement has been accompanied by extra income for the family (through some type of earnings supplement), elementary-school-aged children appear to be better off (chapter 8). Nor have severe forms of deprivation—such as child abuse and neglect or not having enough food to eat—increased, as some had feared. The only negative findings to date are for teenagers, whose school performance appears to have been adversely affected.

In researching the effects of the 1996 law, scholars have both described the trends in such indicators as caseloads, employment, poverty, and child well-being and attempted to analyze the specific role of welfare reform in explaining these trends. It has proven especially difficult to separate the effects of welfare reform from those of the booming economy or of other policies such as a more generous EITC over this period. Most analysts believe that all three have been important. A careful synthesis of all of the research literature by the RAND Corporation generally found that welfare reform has had few negative effects overall, although problems were identified in some areas (e.g., the declining use of food stamps and Medicaid). Research by the Manpower Demonstration Research Corporation in New York City and the Urban Institute in Washington, D.C., has generally reached similar conclusions.

Although the 1996 law has been far more successful than many people expected, problems remain, and an opportunity exists to further improve the broad range of policies targeted at low-income families. In the remainder of this chapter, we distinguish between issues that Congress is likely to address in reauthorizing the 1996 law and those that will require a more sustained period of research and debate.

Reauthorization Issues

Chapter 3 discusses in some detail many of the issues that Congress is likely to debate when it rewrites the law in 2002. These issues can be grouped into six broad categories: 1) the purposes of TANF, 2) funding levels,

3) family formation and marriage, 4) work supports, 5) access to jobs during a recession, and 6) the treatment of legal immigrants.

Purposes The current TANF program has four goals: providing assistance to needy families with children; promoting work and reducing dependency; preventing non-marital pregnancies; and encouraging the formation and preservation of two-parent families. Controversy is likely to arise over efforts to incorporate two additional objectives into the law: an explicit emphasis on poverty reduction and an increased emphasis on marriage.

Funding Levels Several funding issues will spark controversy in the reauthorization debate. Because the annual TANF block grant is a fixed dollar amount that has not varied since it was established in 1996, its real value has been eroded by inflation. One issue is whether the block grant should continue at its current level, be adjusted upward to reflect inflation between 1996 and 2002 and be indexed thereafter, or be cut to reflect the dramatic drop in caseloads in recent years. Another issue is whether the grant should be adjusted to give states more money during recessions and less in economic good times or continue as a flat amount, as at present. A third concern is the very large disparities in TANF funding per poor child across states, with poorer states generally getting less money from the federal government. Some favor addressing such disparities, while others believe that doing so risks setting off a destructive "formula fight." A final issue is whether to adjust the funding that states must contribute to receive their TANF block grant from the federal government (chapter 10).

Family Formation and Marriage Despite a heavy emphasis in the 1996 law on reducing non-marital births (including teen births) and encouraging marriage, these issues are sure to be front and center during reauthorization. Available data show states are spending less than 1 percent of TANF funds on family formation-related activities. There is considerable interest in helping fathers play a more responsible role in their children's lives by working, paying child support, and having the child support go directly to their children rather than the government (chapter 17). The Administration has proposed dedicating funds to promoting healthy marriages and reducing non-marital births. Others want more emphasis on preventing teen pregnancy, arguing that this is a particularly effective way to reduce non-marital childbearing and increase the prospects for stable family formation (chapter 18). President Bush has called for continuing the abstinence-only grants to states established in the 1996 law and investing additional resources in community-based abstinence programs; others argue that the jury is still out on the effectiveness of this approach and that a premium should be put on state flexibility in such a sensitive area.

In addition to encouraging or requiring states to place greater emphasis on family formation, there is support for eliminating rules that discriminate against two-parent families. Marriage penalties in the EITC were only partially remedied in 2001, and disincentives to marry remain in most means-tested programs, including TANF. Critics of proposals to encourage marriage worry about the diversion of dollars from programs for poor women and children and fear that the emphasis on marriage could lead to more domestic violence. They also question the role of government in these private matters and cite a lack of evidence about what works.

Work Supports With so many former welfare recipients working, but often at very low-wage jobs, a major concern is how to ensure that these families are able to support themselves and move up the economic ladder. One debate will center on how much emphasis to give to education and training and whether to limit states in the amount of education and training they can count toward meeting TANF's work participation goals (chapter 13). Another issue is whether the five-year time limit should apply to welfare recipients who are combining work and welfare. Concerns about the availability, affordability, and quality of existing child care are widespread, and efforts to greatly expand funding for child care have already emerged. Finally, access to food stamps and subsidized health insurance through Medicaid for those who have left welfare are also proving to be major issues.

Access to Jobs Although most welfare recipients were able to find jobs in the fast-growing economy of the late 1990s, finding and retaining jobs during a recession or a period of slower growth may prove more difficult. For this reason, debate may arise about relaxing time limits or work requirements during periods of higher unemployment. Measures to improve access to unemployment insurance benefits or community service jobs for those unable to find work in the private sector may also be debated (chapter 11).

Treatment of Legal Immigrants One of the most controversial aspects of the 1996 law was the denial of most welfare benefits to many immigrants, especially those coming to the United States after 1996 (chapter 23). The Bush administration has now proposed to restore food stamp benefits to legal immigrants who have lived in the country for more than five years, regardless of when they arrived, a proposal that will almost certainly spark a new debate about which groups of immigrants should be eligible for various income-tested benefits.

Longer-term Challenges

Regardless of how the 1996 law is revised, many issues will remain. One piece of legislation, no matter how well crafted, cannot address all the challenges facing policymakers as they seek to improve the lives of lower-income families. Four challenges seem to us to be especially important: 1) how to give more children the opportunity to grow up in a two-parent family, 2) how to make jobs available and make work pay, 3) how to ensure that states and communities adopt the most effective policies and practices for helping low-income families, and 4) how to break the cycle of poverty for young children by family or societal investments in their early care or education.

Making progress on these longer-term challenges seems more possible now than at any time in recent decades. The enactment of welfare reform in 1996 broke a political logjam created by the unwillingness of taxpayers to subsidize people who were not working and who were raising children outside marriage. But the return of federal and state budget deficits will complicate efforts to fund new initiatives in the near term. And many potential next steps in policy toward low-income families involve issues on which public consensus is far less certain than it is on the importance of work.

At present, the debate about what, if anything, the government should do to encourage individuals to bear and raise their children within marriage is especially fierce. The debate revolves around whether the government should intervene in such traditionally personal decisions, whether public policies can accomplish this objective, and which strategies are most promising. Some observers want to focus on preventing unwed births to young women, others on promoting responsible father involvement and encouraging marriage among cohabiting couples who have already had a child, and still others on supporting existing marriages and preventing divorce.

On the employment front, many people believe that much of the good news associated with welfare reform is largely the result of the extraordinarily low unemployment rates that prevailed during the late 1990s. They question whether similar successes can be achieved if the economy should return to the higher unemployment rates of the 1980s and early 1990s. If they are right, more attention may need to be given to strategies that offer community service jobs or some other type of safety net for those unable to find work in the private sector (chapter 15). Equally important is the whole issue of workforce training, job retention, and advancement (chapters 13 and 14). We have few good models for helping low-skilled workers move up the job ladder. And if their earnings remain too low to support a family at some reasonable level—and that level itself will be part of the debate—then the question is how the tax or benefits system can be revised to make work pay (chapter 12) and make child care and health insurance affordable (chapters 20 and 21). Another fundamental issue that needs to be addressed is the role of such non-cash benefits as food stamps and housing assistance and how to make these programs work better for those who are employed (chapters 19 and 22). Despite widespread recognition of the problems posed by multiple systems that are uncoordinated, duplicative, and administratively cumbersome, fundamental structural reform of these systems has always proven difficult.

Because the 1996 welfare law gave substantial flexibility to the states, the effectiveness of any revised law will depend on the policy and spending choices made by states and on implementation practices at the local level. State policy choices have varied widely to date. It remains to be seen, however, whether state choices will remain diverse as state budgets face continuing pressure, or whether competitive pressures to cut either cash or work support benefits such as child care will force a "race to the bottom." The financial capacity of some states to pursue more generous time-limit extension and exemption policies as more recipients hit federal time limits also bears monitoring. In addition, welfare agencies need to develop effective programs and practices to reduce repeat pregnancies among TANF recipients and to encourage job retention and advancement—two areas where local practices have not changed very much (chapter 5).

A final issue that is likely to be debated, and possibly addressed, over the next decade is the early care and education of children. Now that most mothers, including low-income mothers, are working, questions about the availability, affordability, and quality of existing care have been raised. To some, improving the quality of early care and education is a good way to promote school readiness and break the cycle of poverty. To others, such an agenda seems to go beyond what they view as an appropriate role for government. They prefer children to be cared for within their own families. And they question the existing evidence about the effects of child care quality on child development.

These longer-term challenges and debates will not end in 2002. They suggest the need for continuing research, experimentation, and debate as the nation attempts to forge a better policy environment for the future.

2

ISABEL SAWHILL, R. KENT WEAVER, RON HASKINS, AND ANDREA KANE

Results to Date

Executive Summary
The 1996 welfare legislation produced numerous, wide-ranging changes in federal law and in state policies and practices. This chapter summarizes evidence on changing policy outcomes over the past six years and on the extent to which those outcomes can be attributed to the 1996 law. Employment among single mothers, a group that has traditionally been the least likely to work and most likely to be on welfare, is on the rise. Increased employment has led to higher earnings and declining welfare payments to low-income families. Similarly, starting in 1994, overall child poverty fell substantially, and black child poverty saw unprecedented declines. Some of the good news should be attributed to a strong economy. In addition, after increasing for decades, the share of births to unmarried mothers has leveled off; and teen birth rates have declined. Although the evidence of the law's impact on children is incomplete, most researchers conclude that for school-age children, the effects are either neutral or positive in areas such as school behavior and school performance. At the same time, research also points to problems associated with welfare reform. For example, some families are financially worse off, and many families eligible for Medicaid and food stamps are losing those benefits when they leave the welfare rolls. These and other problems merit careful attention.

A combination of administrative data and research has yielded a wealth of information about the effects of the various changes in welfare law. In later chapters in this volume, authors detail the research as it applies to specific issues and programs. Here our intent is to provide a broad overview of the results of the 1996 law. We focus first on changes in state policies and practices, and then examine the effects on caseloads in Temporary Assistance for Needy Families (TANF) and related programs, employment and earnings, total income, poverty, family formation, and the well-being of children.

Many studies suggest that a booming economy has been instrumental in producing the results reviewed below. Thus one should not assume a sputtering or contracting economy would have produced similar results. Indeed, recent increases in TANF caseloads in some states are likely to create new challenges. Similarly, expansions of the Earned Income Tax Credit (EITC), Medicaid, child care, and other benefits that help working families have also played a role in reducing welfare dependency and increasing the well-being of low-income families and their children.

Generally, we take the view that all three

factors—work-oriented welfare reforms, a strong economy, and the nation's growing system of work support benefits—contributed to the observed results. Existing studies do not allow us to pinpoint the relative contribution of each. Demanding work requirements and new supports for the working poor appear to be more or less permanent features of the nation's new approach to fighting welfare dependency and poverty. Whether they will be equally effective in a weaker economy is less certain.

Changes in Caseloads in TANF and Related Programs

One very clear outcome of welfare reform has been a substantial decline in the welfare caseload of every state. Figure 1 shows that by September 2001, the national cash welfare caseload had fallen by nearly 60 percent from its 1994 peak. The rolls have now declined for an unprecedented six consecutive years.

Because the TANF block grant gives states a fixed amount of federal funds each year, the caseload decline leaves the typical state much more money per family left on welfare. We estimate that the total federal funds available per family on cash assistance, including both TANF and the child care block grant, have increased from around $3,500 to almost $8,000. Because states are required to maintain their own spending at no less than 75 percent of what it was in the early 1990s when the caseload was much higher, states also have to spend a substantial amount of their own dollars on poor and low-income families. Data on spending per TANF case are somewhat misleading, however, because many TANF and child care dollars are being spent for services to a broader group of families that includes welfare leavers and the working poor. Moreover, states can use TANF funds to address out-of-wedlock childbearing and promote two-parent families without regard to family income.

As important as the question of how much

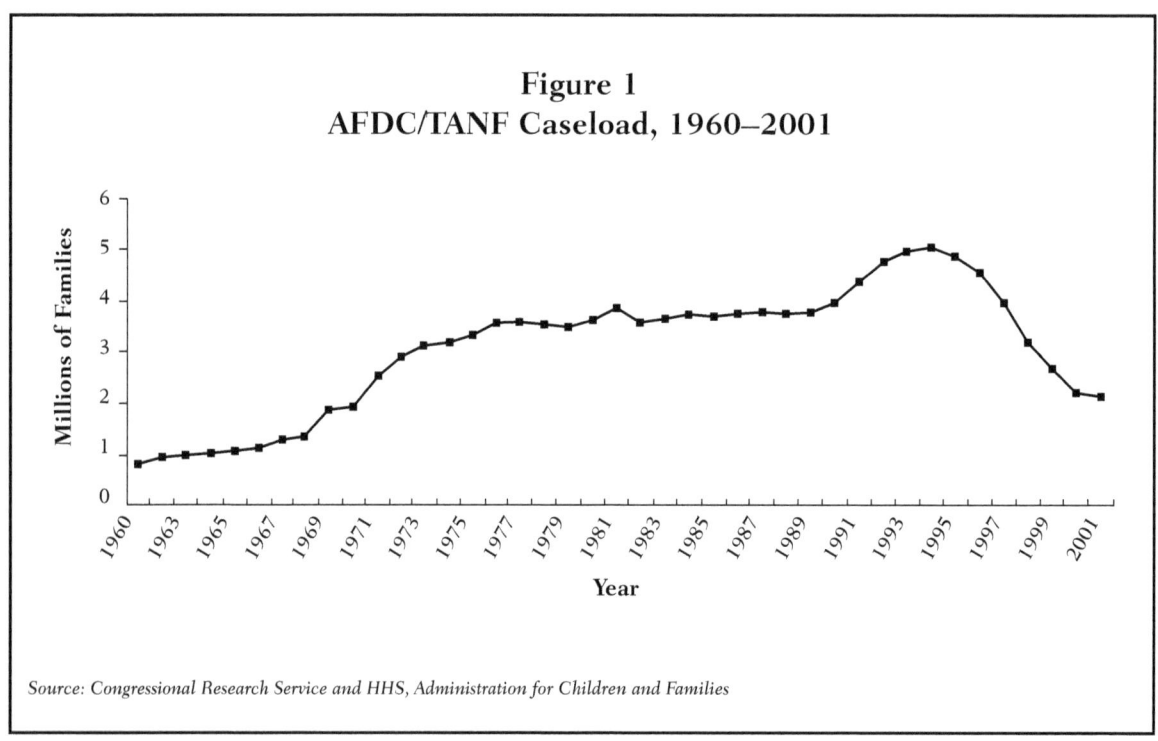

Figure 1
AFDC/TANF Caseload, 1960–2001

Source: Congressional Research Service and HHS, Administration for Children and Families

TANF caseloads have declined is the question of why. If caseloads have fallen because work requirements and incentives have encouraged welfare recipients to enter the labor market and support their families, most observers would count it a success. If, on the other hand, caseload declines primarily reflect a strong economy and are not sustainable during a downturn or result from states' adoption of policies that restrict access to truly needy families, concern would be warranted.

The safest conclusion to draw from recent research would be the following. First, as suggested above, caseload declines result from the interaction of at least three factors: welfare policy changes (especially policies requiring immediate work and sanctioning of those who do not comply), an improved economy, and expansion of policies to "make work pay" (notably an expanded EITC and a higher minimum wage). Second, economic conditions appear to have been more important than welfare policy changes (made by individual states under federal waivers) up to 1996, while policy changes were more decisive after 1996. Third, the relative size of the three factors is the subject of substantial dispute, given their simultaneity and interaction, and probably will never be known with certainty.

It should also be noted that rates of caseload decline have differed dramatically across states (figure 2), ranging from just over 30 percent to around 90 percent. Moreover, caseloads have actually grown in close to half the states in the most recent period for which data are available (figure 3).

As with explanations of trends in national

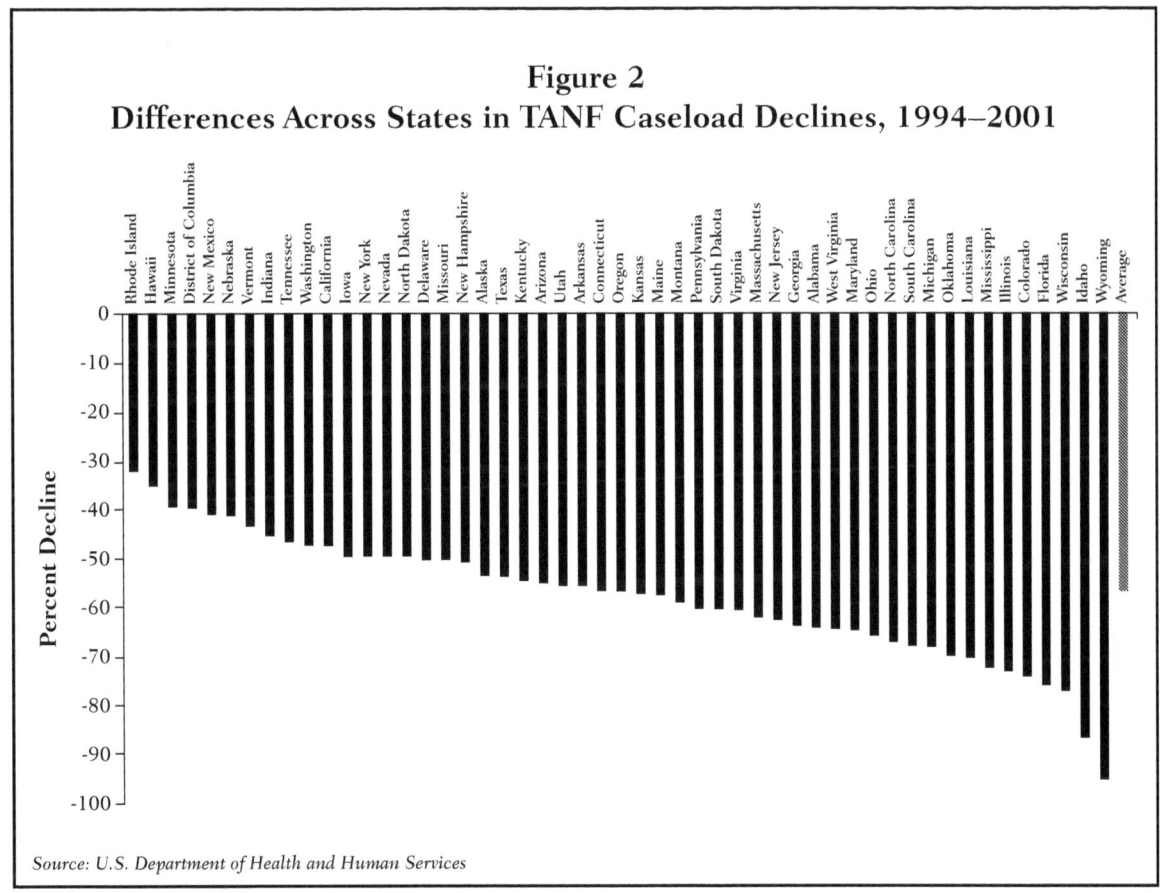

Figure 2
Differences Across States in TANF Caseload Declines, 1994–2001

Source: U.S. Department of Health and Human Services

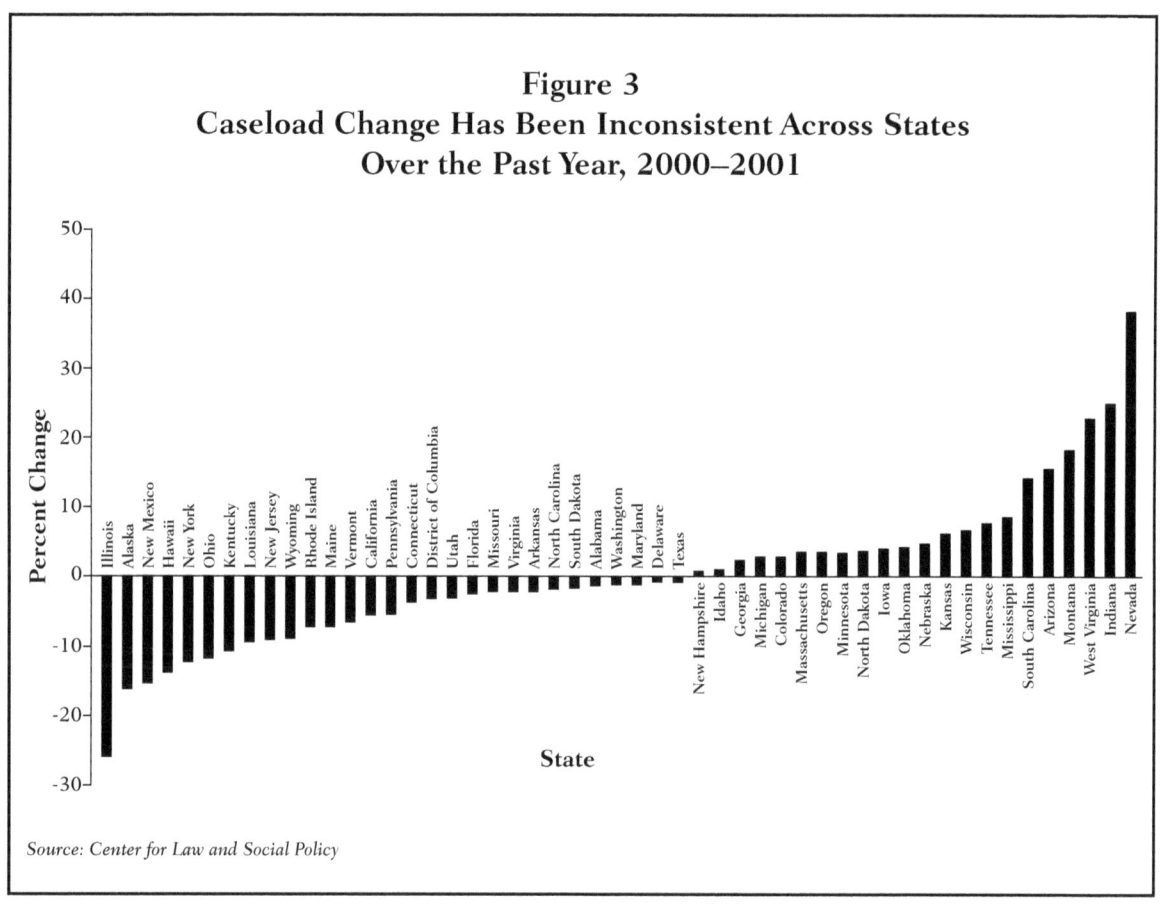

Figure 3
Caseload Change Has Been Inconsistent Across States
Over the Past Year, 2000–2001

Source: Center for Law and Social Policy

caseloads, there is considerable agreement on which factors explain differences across states, but less agreement on their relative importance. Stricter sanctions policies and work requirements (especially immediate work requirements and requiring the mothers of young children to work) appear to contribute to a lowering of caseloads. At the same time, more generous benefit levels and earnings disregards (policies that allow clients to receive partial benefits while working at low wages) inhibit caseload declines because working families who would otherwise be off the caseload are still receiving some benefits. State economic conditions (e.g., unemployment rates and job availability) may also help explain differences in caseload decline, but their effects are more uncertain.

While declines in TANF caseloads have generally been viewed positively, changes in related programs, especially those that assist low-income working families, have evoked more concern. In particular, the number of people receiving food stamps and Medicaid both declined in the immediate wake of welfare reform. Some of these declines were the direct result of the improving economy or of changes in eligibility rules (such as the denial of assistance to many legal immigrants). But even among those still eligible, fewer people were getting the benefits to which they remained entitled.

As noted in chapter 19, several different factors appear to explain the decline in food stamp participation among eligible families with children. Federal administrative policies for food stamps were designed primarily for non-working families, and emphasize minimizing payment errors that are much more common among working than among non-working families. This emphasis on error rates inhibits states from adopting "worker friendly" administrative approaches. Some states, for example, require frequent food stamp recertification to avoid federal sanctions for high error rates. This requirement is much more onerous for working than for non-working families because it means taking time away from a job to sit and wait in a welfare office. In addition, some states "divert" families from assistance at the front door of the welfare office, thereby affecting food stamp as well as TANF participation. And many states do not follow up with families who leave TANF to ensure that those who are still eligible receive benefits.

In chapter 20, the authors note that participation in Medicaid fell for administrative reasons as well, at least up through 1998, and led to an increase in the number of people without health insurance. Subsequent action by the states and the federal government has helped reverse these trends, but many people—adults in particular—still either lack eligibility for health insurance or have difficulty accessing the coverage for which they are eligible.

The availability of child care subsidies among those leaving welfare for work is still another concern. As argued in chapter 21, despite the increased funding for child care contained in the 1996 law and subsequent budgets, many families eligible under federal guidelines receive no assistance. Specifically, only 12 percent of all those eligible for federal child care subsidies are receiving them at the state level. (Federal rules permit subsidies to be provided to families with incomes up to 85 percent of their state's median income—roughly $51,000 in 2000, but most states set eligibility thresholds well below this level.) Surveys suggest that less than half of those leaving welfare for jobs get help with child care expenses. Further, in allocating funds, states give preference to those leaving welfare with the result that low-income working families are less likely to receive subsidies than those who have been on welfare. In addition to relatively low income eligibility limits, states have used a variety of other devices to ration available funds, including high co-payments from parents, low reimbursement rates for providers, and administratively burdensome application processes. Many advocates also remain convinced that the quality of care is inadequate and that more funding is needed not just to extend but also to upgrade available child care.

Finally, concerns have been raised about whether mothers who leave TANF to enter the work force will receive unemployment benefits if they lose their jobs. These women face several barriers to receiving unemployment benefits: they often quit "voluntarily" because of child care problems, illness, or the like; they may lack a sufficiently long work history to qualify (especially since earnings in the most recent quarter are usually not counted in establishing unemployment insurance eligibility); or they may not meet the requirement that they be available for full-time work.

Employment and Earnings

Caseload decline is only one measure of what has happened to families since 1996. It is good that so many families have left welfare, but only if their financial status has not seriously deteriorated and they are moving toward self-sufficiency. Thus, it is important to examine the employment, income, and poverty status of these families.

Two types of information are available to assess whether families leaving welfare are getting jobs. First are studies of mothers who have left welfare. Generally, these studies find that about 60 percent of mothers are employed at the time of the interview and about 75 percent have been employed at some time since leaving welfare. Second are studies of overall changes in women's employment. After a decade of relative stability, the share of single mothers working rose from 58 percent to 74 percent between 1993 and 2000 (figure 4). The increase in the share of never-married mothers who had a job was even greater.

Never-married mothers, who tend to have less education and work experience than other single mothers, are the most likely both to go on welfare and to have long spells on welfare. That these are precisely the mothers who have had the biggest increase in employment in recent years suggests that even poorly educated mothers of the type that used to stay on welfare for long periods are proving themselves capable of productive work in the private sector, at least when unemployment is low. Nevertheless, important questions remain about the employment stability and earnings of those who have left welfare and especially about the circumstances of those who do not have jobs. In the meantime, employment among those still on welfare rose from 11 percent in 1996 to 33 percent in 2000, with many more in unsubsidized employment than in workfare-type programs. All states have met the general work participation standards established in 1996, although most have been heavily aided in this regard by caseload declines.

Total Income

Moving from welfare to work does not guarantee that mothers will be able to lift their families out of poverty. Most mothers leaving welfare receive low wages, on average about $7–8 per hour. Nevertheless, one reason that

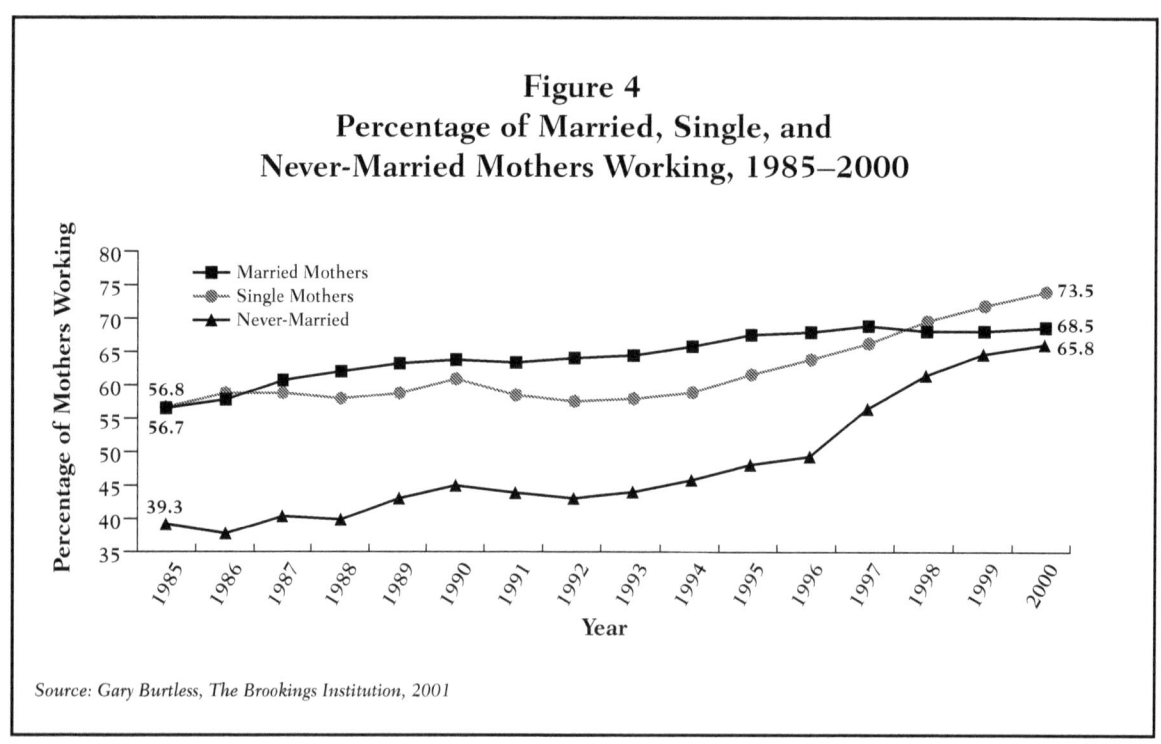

Figure 4
Percentage of Married, Single, and Never-Married Mothers Working, 1985–2000

Source: Gary Burtless, The Brookings Institution, 2001

many families are leaving poverty is that they are earning more money. If we array all mother-headed families from those with the lowest to those with the highest incomes and then divide the distribution into five equal parts, the bottom two-fifths will contain all or nearly all the mothers on welfare and most of the mothers who have left welfare. Comparing the bottom two-fifths of the distribution in 1993 and in 2000, we find that average annual earnings for the bottom fifth increased from $1,377 to $3,148, or nearly 130 percent, while average earnings for the second fifth increased from $4,979 to $11,710, or 135 percent (figures 5 and 6). Logically enough, more work led to increased earnings.

Not surprisingly, mothers in the two bottom fifths lost welfare income. On average, mothers in the bottom fifth lost more than $900 in cash assistance and $360 in food stamps between 1993 and 2000. Even so, because their earnings and their income from the EITC increased so much, the total annual income of these poorest mother-headed families increased by about $1,660 (24 percent) on average

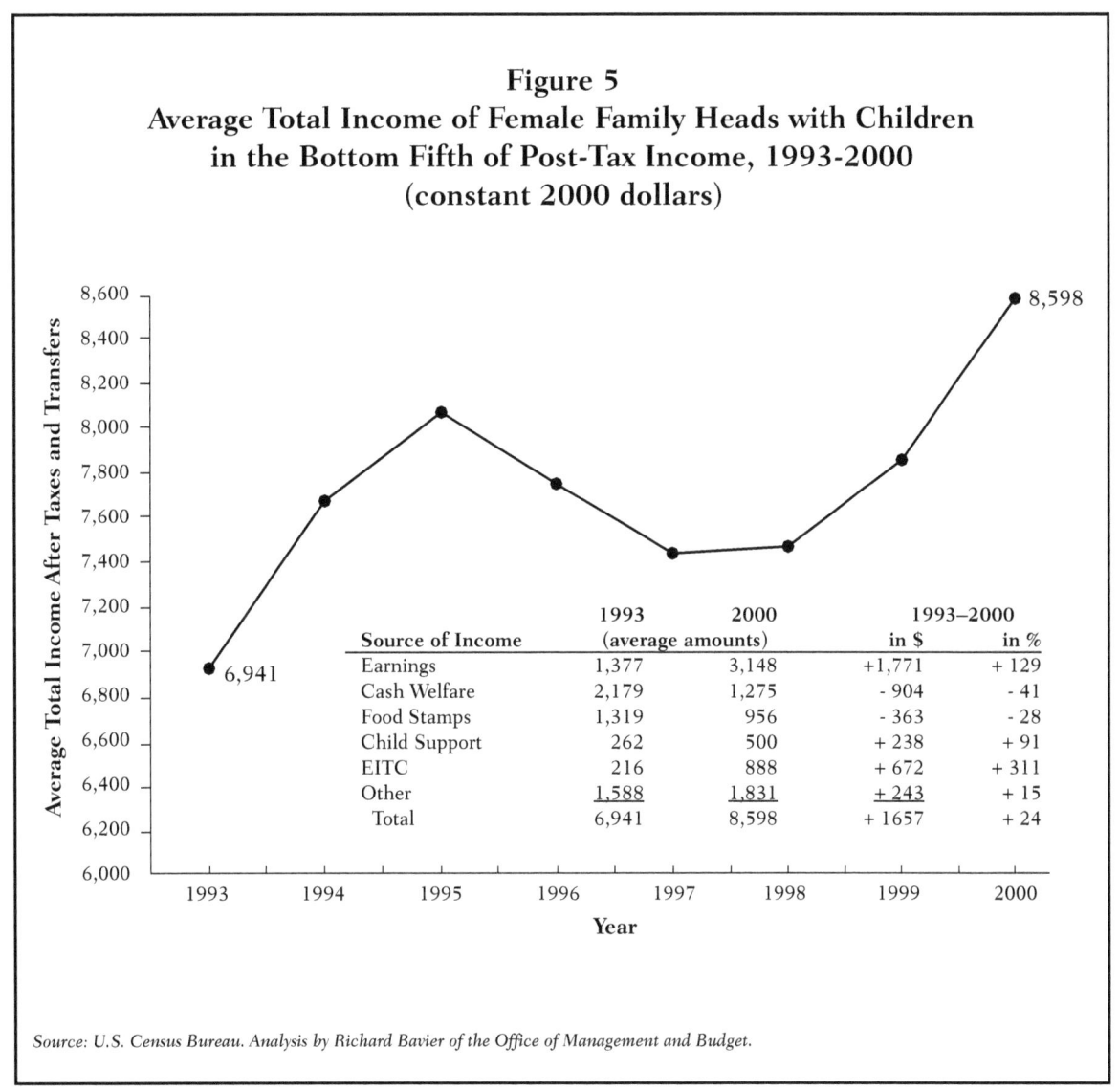

Figure 5
Average Total Income of Female Family Heads with Children in the Bottom Fifth of Post-Tax Income, 1993-2000
(constant 2000 dollars)

Source of Income	1993	2000	1993–2000	
	(average amounts)		in $	in %
Earnings	1,377	3,148	+1,771	+129
Cash Welfare	2,179	1,275	- 904	- 41
Food Stamps	1,319	956	- 363	- 28
Child Support	262	500	+ 238	+ 91
EITC	216	888	+ 672	+ 311
Other	1,588	1,831	+ 243	+ 15
Total	6,941	8,598	+ 1657	+ 24

Source: U.S. Census Bureau. Analysis by Richard Bavier of the Office of Management and Budget.

between 1993 and 2000. Mothers in the second fifth lost even more welfare and food stamps than those in the bottom fifth (more than $3,000, on average), but the combination of earnings and EITC boosted their income by an average of nearly $4,000 per year, or nearly 30 percent.

Although these data are generally favorable, serious concerns remain. Some female-headed families—especially in the bottom 10 percent or 5 percent of the income distribution—appear to be worse off without welfare. In addition, as noted earlier, many families that go to work lose their food stamps or Medicaid, even though they (or their children) remain eligible for them. Finally, Census data do not take adequate account of work expenses, especially child care and transportation, that may leave some families worse off or no better off, despite increased earnings.

Poverty

A major issue is whether those leaving welfare are still poor. Figure 7 shows the annual percentage changes in the TANF caseload, along with changes in poverty

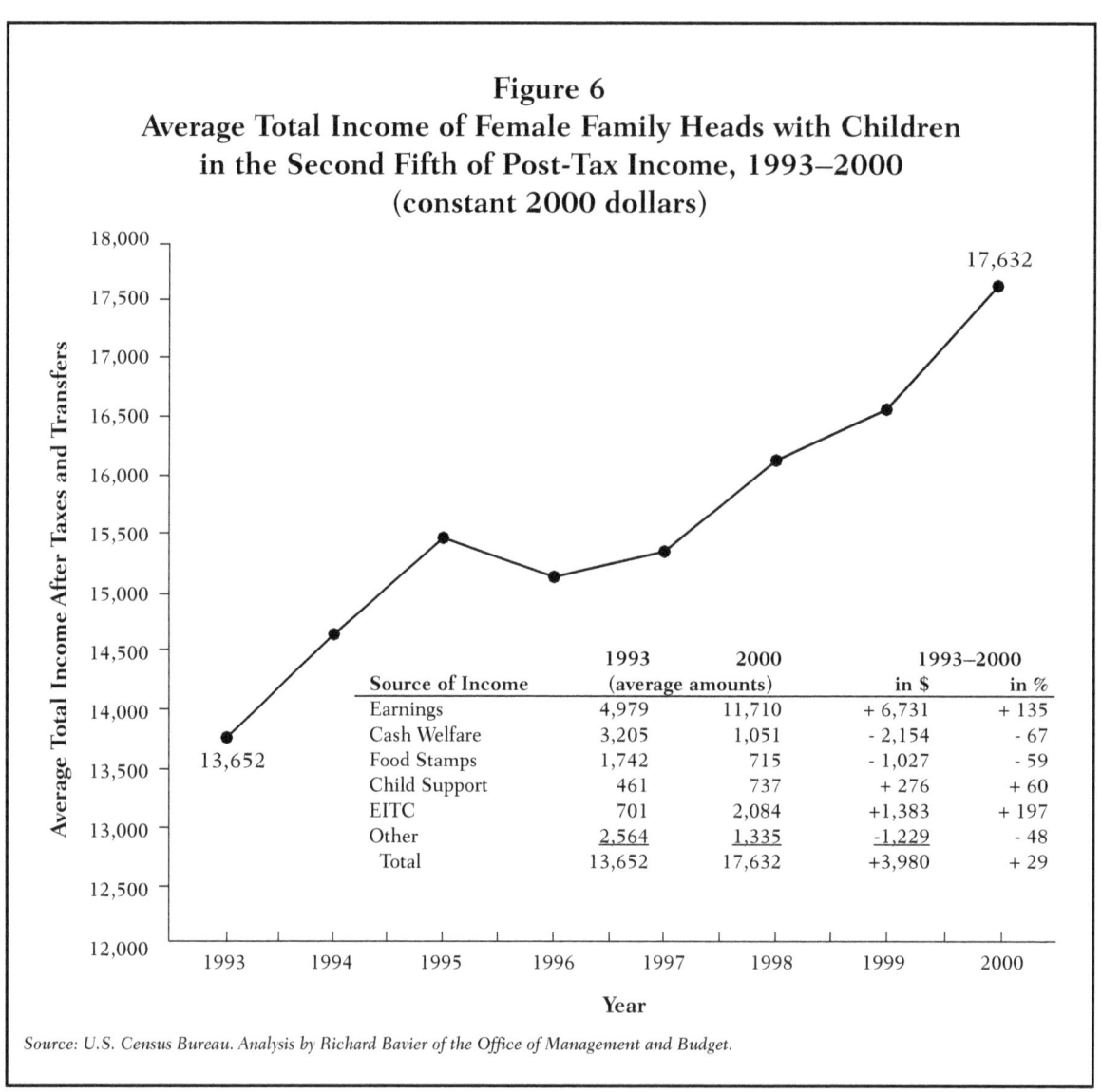

Figure 6
Average Total Income of Female Family Heads with Children in the Second Fifth of Post-Tax Income, 1993–2000
(constant 2000 dollars)

Source of Income	1993	2000	1993–2000	
	(average amounts)		in $	in %
Earnings	4,979	11,710	+ 6,731	+ 135
Cash Welfare	3,205	1,051	- 2,154	- 67
Food Stamps	1,742	715	- 1,027	- 59
Child Support	461	737	+ 276	+ 60
EITC	701	2,084	+1,383	+ 197
Other	2,564	1,335	-1,229	- 48
Total	13,652	17,632	+3,980	+ 29

Source: U.S. Census Bureau. Analysis by Richard Bavier of the Office of Management and Budget.

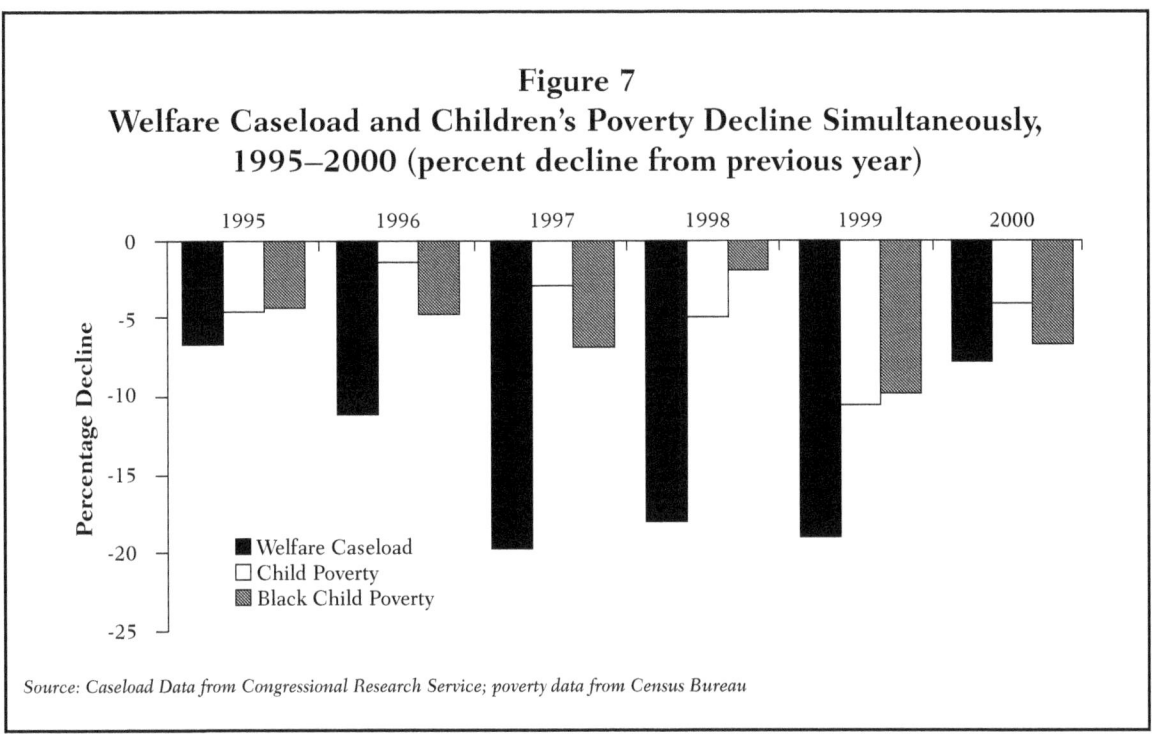

Figure 7
Welfare Caseload and Children's Poverty Decline Simultaneously, 1995–2000 (percent decline from previous year)

Source: Caseload Data from Congressional Research Service; poverty data from Census Bureau

among all children and in poverty among black children between 1995 and 2000. As the caseload has declined each year, so has overall child poverty and black child poverty. In fact, black child poverty reached the lowest level ever recorded in 2000. Similarly, poverty among Hispanic children is at its lowest level since 1979. Overall child poverty also declined substantially and by 1999 was also at its lowest level since 1979. But even where averages are encouraging, the condition of those at the bottom, such as those who leave welfare and do not hold jobs, remains a focus of research and debate. As pointed out in chapter 7, the decline in poverty has not been as steep as the decline in the caseload; and concern about the most disadvantaged families persists.

Family Formation

Because research suggests that children are—on average—better off, both economically and psychologically, in stable two-parent families, one objective of the 1996 law was to reduce the share of children born to unmarried parents. Figure 8 shows three trends in non-marital births since 1940: the number of non-marital births, the rate per thousand women aged 15 to 44, and the percentage of all births to unmarried women.

The pattern is striking: more or less continuous increases, slow at first but picking up steam after the mid-1960s, in all three measures until the mid-1990s, at which point they level off. The trends for teen births are even more striking: after a surge in the 1980s, the rate has declined every year since 1991 and is now the lowest on record. The timing of this decline in teen births suggests that more is at work here than welfare reform, although the rate of decline accelerated after 1995. The teen birth rate has declined because of both increased abstinence among youth and increased use of birth control. The leveling off in non-marital births for all women begins about 1994, the same year that

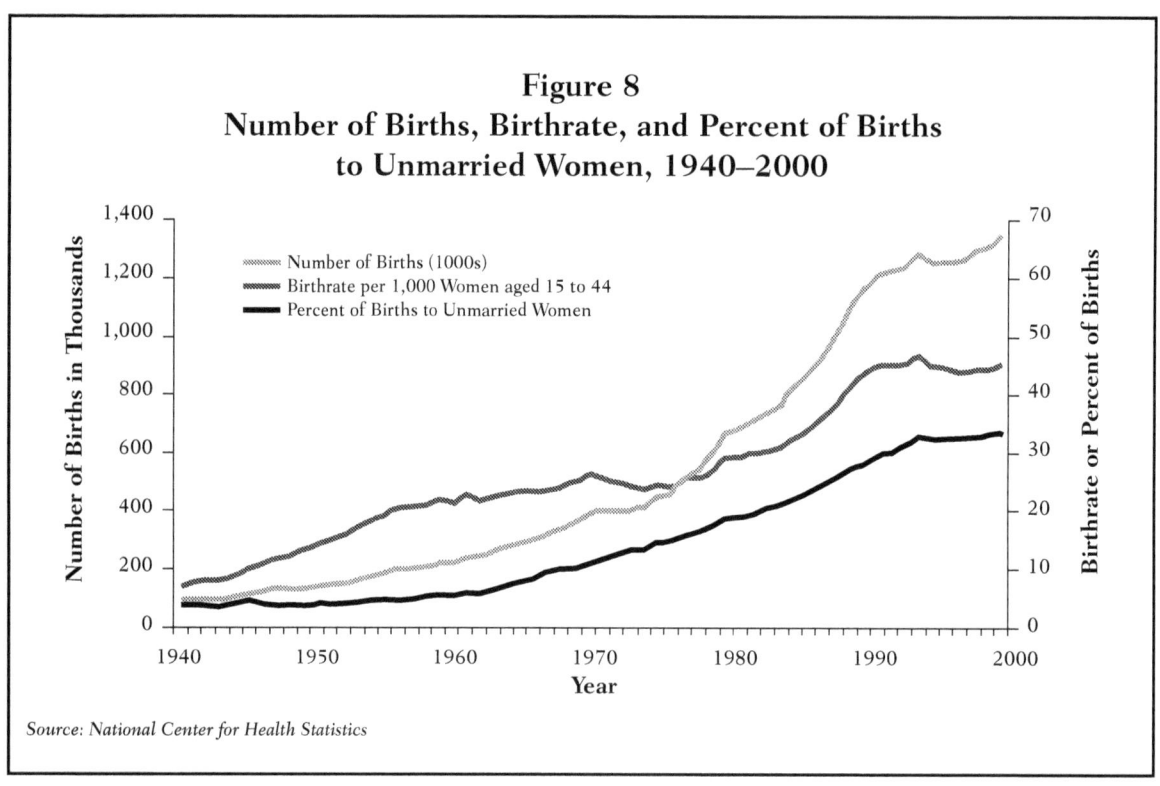

Figure 8
Number of Births, Birthrate, and Percent of Births to Unmarried Women, 1940–2000

Source: National Center for Health Statistics

most states were beginning to implement welfare reform under federal waivers.

As noted in chapter 17, studies suggest that tougher child support enforcement reduces non-marital childbearing. And as shown in chapter 18, the decline in teen pregnancy rates has contributed importantly to the leveling off of non-marital births. Another factor that could have played a role is enhanced supports for work. One study of an experimental program in Minnesota that rewarded work by supplementing wages and treated two-parent families similarly to those with only one parent found that the program increased both entry into marriage and the stability of existing marriages. Still, few studies directly link the various policies contained in the 1996 legislation and reductions in non-marital births.

Well-Being of Children

Children in welfare families could be affected by the 1996 law through changes in income or their mother's employment. Some experts argue that children will be better off once their mothers are working because regular employment will engender a more structured home environment, more work-oriented values, and greater exposure of the children to good quality out-of-home care or education. Others argue that the effects could as easily go in the other direction if mothers fail to find jobs or families have fewer material resources, if the time pressures on mothers lead to greater stress, less adequate parenting, and less child supervision, or if any substitute care provided is of poor quality.

Chapter 8 reviews data from a variety of experiments conducted under waivers before enactment of the 1996 law. The data suggest that the overall effects of work requirements on children are likely to be small. Children seem to be neither positively nor adversely affected by their mother's employment. Where experimental programs have supplemented a parent's earnings and thus increased family income as well as work, researchers have found positive effects on children's academic performance, health, and behavior. Effects for elementary school-age children were the most positive, while teens were more likely to be negatively affected. Not much evidence exists on children under the age of three. As the authors note, the pathways through which these changes in maternal employment and income influence children are harder to discern, but evidence from three of the four earnings supplement programs they reviewed suggests that enrolling children in formal child care or after-school programs is one such possibility.

Conclusion

The overall pattern of welfare and work associated with welfare reform seems clear. The welfare rolls have declined greatly, more mothers than ever are working, the average income of female-headed families is increasing, and poverty has dropped substantially. This pattern suggests that welfare reform, along with the strong economy and supports for working families, has produced some notable successes. However, researchers and advocates have also raised a number of issues and problems that they believe need to be addressed. We turn our attention to these issues in later chapters, especially in chapter 3.

3

ISABEL SAWHILL, R. KENT WEAVER, RON HASKINS, AND ANDREA KANE

Problems and Issues for Reauthorization

Executive Summary
The 107th Congress faces serious controversies as it prepares to reauthorize the 1996 welfare reform legislation. This chapter discusses a series of important issues associated with the law and some of the options that have been proposed for 2002 reauthorization. The issues include: the purposes of the law; the level and allocation of funding of the Temporary Assistance for Needy Families (TANF) block grant; a growing concern that some families are worse off as a result of sanctions or time limits or because they failed to find or retain jobs after leaving welfare; the degree of flexibility to give states regarding work requirements; and the rising number of children being reared by single mothers. Also at issue is whether the current policy for recessions is adequate, whether to increase funding for child care, how to improve the child support system, whether to provide more assistance to working poor families, how to better serve the hard-to-employ, whether to do more to help mothers qualify for better jobs, how to make the Food Stamp Program and Medicaid more accessible, and whether to restore benefits to non-citizens.

Reauthorizing the 1996 welfare legislation will be a major issue for the Bush administration and Congress during 2002. The Bush administration unveiled its welfare reform proposal in late February, at about the same time that leading members of Congress introduced their own bills. Both House and Senate committees have held hearings on reauthorization, and the House Ways and Means Committee put reauthorization on a fast track for movement through the House by late spring or early summer. The Senate will probably pass its own reauthorization bill in the summer. A House/Senate conference committee is likely to fashion the final bill in the fall of 2002.

Debate is likely to be vigorous. Governors will certainly want a seat at the table. Many of the interest groups that played important roles in the debate over the initial 1996 legislation will seek to be actively involved.

Debate will address a broad range of issues, including the purposes of reform, the structure of the TANF block grant, provisions requiring work and limiting benefit receipt, support for work and job advancement, family formation, and benefits for non-citizens. Later chapters discuss specific issues in detail; this chapter provides a brief overview of some of the issues likely to receive the most attention.

Purposes of the 1996 Reforms

One question that will pervade the reauthorization debate is the purpose of the TANF program. As stated in the 1996 legislation, the goals of TANF were to assist needy families, fight welfare dependency by promoting work and marriage, reduce non-marital births, and encourage the formation and maintenance of two-parent families.

Debate over TANF's goals will continue as Congress considers reauthorization. The Bush administration has proposed adding "improving the well-being of children" as the overarching goal of TANF, from which the other objectives follow. It would also revise the fourth current TANF goal to focus on two-parent *married* families and responsible fatherhood. Many conservatives share the president's emphasis on increasing attention to marriage. Many liberals support giving more emphasis to ensuring an adequate income for needy families by making poverty reduction an explicit goal of TANF.

The Size of the TANF Block Grant

The TANF block grant was established as an essentially fixed sum of $16.5 billion per year through fiscal year 2002. Increased spending for the war on terrorism in the wake of September 11th, together with competing budget priorities, will make it difficult to increase or even maintain spending on TANF especially since not all of the key provisions are included in the budget baseline (see table 1 at the end of this chapter). As detailed in chapter 10, several issues related to the TANF block grant are likely to be debated during reauthorization.

A first area of potential conflict is the overall size of the block grant. Fiscal conservatives prefer to keep spending constant, noting that TANF block grant funding levels were set when welfare caseloads were much higher than they are now. Moreover, some states did not use their full TANF block grant allocations in the early years of the program, although almost all states are now using their full complement of TANF funds, and many are drawing down surpluses from past years.

Others argue that current funding is inadequate, observing that the program has taken on the new task of providing support to the working poor, which requires services geared toward a much broader clientele than solely recipients of cash assistance. They also note that because the block grant was not adjusted for inflation, it declined in real terms by about 12 percent between 1996 and 2002. Moreover, stiffer work requirements proposed by the Bush administration and some Democrats would lead to increased costs for the states.

Several options are likely to be on the table. The Bush administration's welfare reform proposal, for example, calls for keeping funding at its current nominal level for fiscal years 2003–2007, meaning that it would continue to decline in real value. Other proposals suggest adjusting funding levels for future inflation or for both past and future inflation.

Allocating the TANF Block Grant Among States

A second potentially contentious area is the formula for allocating the TANF block grant among states. The share apportioned to each state is based on its historical allocation of federal Aid to Families with Dependent Children (AFDC) funds. Largely because of differing state choices regarding benefit levels under AFDC, poorer states generally receive far fewer federal TANF dollars per poor child than do wealthier states. Critics argue that poor states should not be punished for long-ago policy choices by being denied funds needed to help move today's low-income families to self-sufficiency. Defenders of the status quo argue that whatever the shortcomings of the current allocation formula, reopening the issue is likely to fragment support for TANF. The Bush administration has proposed continuing both the current TANF block grant allocations and the TANF provision that allocates additional funds to states that have high levels of poverty or high population growth rates. A total of 17 states have received money from this supplemental fund. But the fund makes only a tiny dent in funding inequities across states (chapter 10). And the funding inequities will become even more important if the stiffer work requirements proposed by the Bush administration and some members of Congress are adopted, because states receiving less generous block grants will not be able to afford expensive work support and work experience programs.

Policy for Recessions

As in 1996, there is bound to be extensive discussion of what will happen to mothers who leave welfare for jobs in a slowing economy. Many advocates fear that layoffs will disproportionately affect former welfare mothers because of their limited skills and experience. Moreover, most mothers who lose jobs do not qualify for unemployment insurance because they have not worked enough hours to qualify or because they left their job "voluntarily" (often because of illness or difficulties in securing child care or transportation).

Unlike AFDC, under TANF additional funds do not automatically flow to the states when recessions cause more families to rely on welfare. The 1996 legislation contained a fund from which states could borrow money as well as a contingency fund that provided modest sums to states that suffered high unemployment or similar signs of economic distress. Neither fund was used by states during 2001. There appears to be a bipartisan interest in continuing the contingency fund with improvements that will make it more accessible to states during recessions.

Supporting Working Families

Assistance for the working poor has increased dramatically since the early 1980s, with expansions of the Earned Income Tax Credit (EITC) being the most prominent example. But reauthorization will almost inevitably catalyze a debate about whether parents who have moved into the low-wage job market have enough income to adequately support their families.

Those who believe that enough has been done to make work pay for such families point to the many benefits already available, including the EITC, child care, food stamps, Medicaid, and enhanced child support. Further expansions are likely to be expensive and could lead to permanent dependence on government support. Others will press for more assistance in the form of a higher minimum wage indexed for inflation, an expanded EITC, greater subsidization of child care and health care, more money for education and training, or other work supports. Advocates of increased spending for work supports will argue that in the absence of such assistance, high rates of poverty among working families are likely to continue.

Education, Job Retention, Job Advancement

Three issues in this area are likely to receive attention during the 2002 reauthorization debate. First, during the debate on the 1996 law, some Democrats expressed great concern that the law placed too little emphasis on education and training. At a minimum, these same Democrats have already proposed to expand the amount of education that can count toward fulfilling the work requirement. Some Republicans may oppose these amendments on grounds that welfare mothers can currently combine work and education and that states already have sufficient flexibility. Moreover, because of the rapid decline in the welfare rolls, states have much more money available for education than they had before welfare reform. The Bush administration appears to recognize the need for some additional flexibility on this issue and would allow three months of full-time training every two years to count toward the work requirement. In addition, the administration proposes counting up to 16 hours per week of any activity that promotes self-sufficiency.

Second, research shows clearly that mothers who leave welfare for work often lose or leave their jobs in a few weeks or months. Program operators and researchers believe that special efforts are needed to help mothers retain their jobs longer or find new ones quickly. Several studies of model programs that attempt to help mothers succeed in the workplace and retain their jobs are now under way, and Congress may wish to fund more demonstration projects. The administration proposes that states give special attention to this issue as well as to career advancement in the plans they submit to the federal government, which will then reward their performance in achieving specific employment-related goals.

A third issue is how to improve cooperation at the local level between TANF and the other federal and state programs designed to promote work. The Bush administration has proposed giving states broad waivers to better align rules across different programs. Whether Congress will provide this authority in the face of likely opposition from advocates supporting each individual program remains uncertain.

Requiring Work

The vision of those who supported work requirements in 1996 was that every state would have an increasing share of its caseload actively involved in work programs for 20–30 hours per week. Because caseload reductions can be used to meet the state work participation requirement (50 percent in 2002), states have largely met this requirement by placing welfare recipients in unsubsidized employment, rather than by creating large-scale programs in which welfare recipients work in exchange for their benefits.

The Bush administration's welfare reform proposal would dramatically ratchet up work requirements for individuals and work participation rates for states. Beginning in 2003, parents in TANF families would have to be engaged directly in work (either paid employment or community service jobs) at least 24 hours per week. In addition, they would have to participate another 16 hours—for a total of 40 hours per week—in work-related activities (which could be defined by the states) to be counted toward meeting their state's work participation rate. At least 70 percent of a state's caseload would have to meet these higher work requirements by 2007. The Bush administration would also phase out the caseload reduction credit and replace it with a credit that would count the first three months that welfare recipients are employed toward meeting the higher work participation standard.

Supporters of this proposal argue that adults on welfare should work, that properly designed work programs provide valuable work experience, and that having work experience positions available is especially important during recessions. States can be expected to vigorously oppose additional work participation mandates, citing increased programmatic and child care costs to engage more recipients in work activities. These added costs would be especially onerous for states with less generous block grants. Another concern about these tougher work requirements is that they would shift TANF resources toward ensuring that adults on TANF are working, thereby diverting resources away from helping them leave welfare. This resource shift could also lower state investment in activities such as helping former recipients stay off assistance and move up the job ladder, preventing teen pregnancy, and providing substance abuse or mental health services. For all these reasons, states are likely to argue for increased flexibility in deciding how to move recipients toward self-sufficiency and in defining what should count as a work activity.

Five-Year Time Limit

The five-year time limit on use of federal dollars to provide cash assistance to any adult was one of the more controversial features of the 1996 law. Moreover, states are allowed to set even shorter time limits, and 40 percent of them have chosen to do so. Most recipients leave the rolls before the time limit hits, even when the limit is less than five years. Nevertheless, more than 200,000 families have hit time limits imposed by the states, and many will hit the five-year time limit in 2002 and every year thereafter.

States now have the flexibility to provide federally financed benefits beyond the five-year limit for up to 20 percent of their caseload and can use their own funds for families that have passed the time limit. But whether this will be enough flexibility to help all affected families is an open question. Time limits are especially problematic in states like California that have relatively high benefits and that allow clients to receive partial benefits while working at low wages. In those states, many recipients have been on TANF rolls almost continuously while working.

One policy reform that is bound to receive attention in the reauthorization debate is whether states should be allowed to stop the federal time-limit clock for recipients who are working a significant number of hours per week—perhaps 25 or 30. A similar alternative would be to define income supplements to families reaching this level of work engagement as something other than cash assistance.

Sanctions

Requiring states to impose financial sanctions against families when an adult does not comply with program requirements was also extremely controversial in 1996. States vary widely in their use of sanctions, as noted in chapter 6. Many states impose sanctions routinely, while others try to avoid them. In some states, as many as a third of the caseload are under sanction or have received a sanction, and 36 states use full-family sanctions, meaning they can end the entire cash welfare benefit of families that fail to meet requirements. Research suggests that some families do not understand why they are being sanctioned, that sanctions are sometimes applied inequitably, and that sanctioned families tend to be more disadvantaged.

Congress may want to examine these issues. Some lawmakers are likely to try to restrict the circumstances under which full-family sanctions can be applied, require assessment of barriers that may prevent recipients from complying with program requirements, and address issues such as adequate notice and due process rights. Representative Patsy Mink has introduced a bill that would forbid states to impose full-family sanctions, while some conservatives favor requiring all states to impose full-family sanctions.

The Hard-to-Employ

Another serious complication is that a subset of families has not responded well to the new welfare requirements. Before 1996, hard-to-employ adults could stay on welfare year after year without having to meet any work or training requirements and without having their barriers to employment addressed. Today most families are being subjected to such requirements, and some families are unable to meet them. Studies of mothers leaving welfare show that around one in five goes through long periods without work and many more are without jobs from time to time. Census Bureau data suggest that many of these mothers are likely to live with others—either relatives or boyfriends—who have income, but the stability of these arrangements is unclear.

As noted in chapter 15, these families often have multiple barriers to employment, including addictions, disabled children, emotional illness, domestic violence, lack of work experience, and low levels of education. Several states are now developing strategies to help these families, but most are expensive to implement and uncertain in result. The question that looms is whether such families will need cash welfare for more than five years.

Congress is likely to consider directing research funds to learn how to help adults with multiple barriers hold jobs and become less dependent on welfare. For example, the Bush administration, and some Democrats as well, has proposed allowing limited substance abuse treatment and other services addressing employment barriers to count toward the work requirement. Congress may also consider loosening the five-year time limit for these families.

Family Formation

There are several reasons why so many children are growing up in poor, single-parent families. The most important is the continuing high rates of non-marital births, including teen births. Concern about this problem animated Republicans during debate on the 1996 legislation, and the law included many provisions to address it. Although all measures of non-marital births have leveled off for the first time in half a century and the birthrate among teens has dropped every year for a decade, U.S. rates are still among the highest in the industrial world. As mentioned in chapter 18, although the number of states with teen pregnancy prevention programs has grown and the effectiveness of some of these prevention programs has been documented, states are still spending far less on prevention than they should, given the savings that effective programs could offer taxpayers. Several researchers, including the author of chapter 5, have reported a reluctance among welfare caseworkers to broach issues of sex or marriage with clients. The President has emphasized the importance of abstinence and proposed to increase funding for programs that promote abstinence outside marriage.

A related reason for the growth of poor single-parent families is the precipitous decline in marriage, especially in poor communities. In the past, both the federal government and the states have been reluctant to become deeply involved in promoting marriage, in part because of the fear of stigmatizing single parents. However, in recent years several states, including Oklahoma and Arizona, have made promoting marriage a goal. President Bush has proposed investing up to $300 million in federal and state funds for research, demonstration, technical assistance, and matching grants for states interested in marriage education, mentoring, and counseling programs.

Lastly, the growth of poor single-parent families could be attributed to deteriorating economic prospects among low-income fathers. As welfare reform and the strong economy lured millions of poor mothers into the workforce, many of the fathers of their children remained jobless. Indeed, Census Bureau data show that between 1992 and 2001, as the economy boomed and the labor force participation of 20- to 24-year-old black females increased from roughly 60 percent to more than 70 percent, the participation of comparable black males declined from more than 75 percent to less than 70 percent. By 2001, young black females had a higher employment rate than young black males. Legislators have already signaled their interest in this issue by considering (but not passing) legislation in the last Congress to fund a national network of programs to promote marriage, better parenting, and employment among poor fathers. The 107th Congress will almost certainly return to this issue as part of the reauthorization debate.

Child Support Enforcement

The child support enforcement program appears to be improving steadily. However, as demonstrated by a 405 to 18 vote in the House during the 106th Congress, many members of Congress, and both conservative and liberal advocacy groups, believe more child support collections should be paid to families. Under current law, state and federal governments can retain all child support payments to welfare mothers and even after mothers leave welfare, the government retains around half the payments on overdue child support. Agreement seems to be widespread that all payments on overdue child support should go to mothers, not the government, once mothers leave welfare. Many also agree that mothers should receive at least part of the fathers' payment while they are still on welfare. The administration has offered proposals along these lines, and powerful members of Congress from both parties will make this issue part of welfare reauthorization.

Access to Food Stamps and Medicaid

As discussed in chapters 19 and 20, many families who are eligible for food stamps and Medicaid are not receiving these benefits. This problem has several roots. Under AFDC, families that applied for welfare were automatically given food stamps and Medicaid. But under TANF, some applicants are diverted from the welfare program into work and never appear on the rolls, thereby missing out on food stamps and Medicaid. Others lose these benefits when they leave welfare—not because they are not eligible, but because they fail to apply. Studies show that once a family leaves AFDC or TANF, participation in food stamps and Medicaid declines, perhaps because families have not been informed that they retain eligibility. In addition, working families may find it too difficult and time consuming to report to welfare offices to establish their eligibility.

The TANF high-performance bonus available to states has been revised to include measures of receipt of food stamps and Medicaid by eligible families, but other steps are also possible. Several food stamp reforms may be approved this year as part of the farm bill. The Bush administration has also proposed reforms, including simplifying program rules, putting more emphasis on access and less on error rates, and excluding one vehicle per adult from program asset limits.

Child Care

The 1996 reforms created a child care block grant with about $4.5 billion more available for child care during 1997–2002 than under previous law. States were also allowed to transfer up to 30 percent of their TANF block grant funds to the child care program and to spend TANF funds directly on child care. Regulating the quality of care was left to states and localities. Although less than half the families leaving TANF for employment use child care funds, states nonetheless have used all the federal and state dollars in the child care block grant and have now used nearly $4 billion of their TANF funds for child care.

Two child care issues will receive extensive attention during reauthorization: whether states have enough money to pay for care and whether available care is of sufficient quality. Despite increased child care block grant funding and substantial use of TANF dollars for child care, critics believe that even more federal spending is necessary. Currently families leaving welfare are often provided with child care subsidies while similar low-income families that did not go on welfare often do not receive them. Additional funding is necessary to serve both groups. A widely cited estimate from the Department of Health and Human Services suggests that existing child care block grant funding provides enough money to serve only 12 percent of all federally eligible low-income children. (Children are eligible if family income is less than 85 percent of state median income—about $51,000.) Concern also continues about the quality of care and the federal role in promoting better care either through federal or state regulation or through increased funding to states. Some legislators may press for an increase in set-asides within the child care block grant aimed at improving quality. Controversy over increasing resources for child care is likely to be especially strong if work requirements are stiffened.

Benefits for Non-citizens

One of the most contentious features of the 1996 law was the sweeping restriction on access to public welfare benefits for legal immigrants, including TANF, food stamps, Medicaid and Supplemental Security Income. Although the cuts were extremely complex, one broad new rule emerged: non-citizens who legally enter the country after 1996 face a five-year ban on some public benefits and permanent bans on others (chapter 23). Despite partial restoration of some benefits for some groups of immigrants in 1997 and 1998, there have been sharp declines in most public benefits received by legal immigrants as well as by citizen children of immigrant parents. Congress is certain to debate whether, and to what extent, to restore benefit eligibility for legal immigrants. The Bush administration has proposed restoring food stamp eligibility for legal immigrants who have been in the United States for at least five years. Serious consideration of whether to expand TANF eligibility is likely to be debated as well.

The Political Environment for TANF Reauthorization

Congress must act on TANF and related programs before October 2002. But changes as far-reaching as those enacted in 1996 are unlikely. The political impetus for dramatic reform has been tempered both by the 1996 law, which abolished the extremely unpopular AFDC program, and by striking declines in caseloads since the early 1990s. The very tight margins of party control in Congress mean that neither conservatives nor liberals will have strong leverage for enacting their preferred reforms. The general satisfaction of the states with the status quo also weakens the impetus for reform.

Substantial uncertainties remain, however. The biggest unknown is the state of the economy. If the U.S. economy fails to recover quickly, if there is evidence that mothers who have left TANF are having greater difficulty getting and keeping jobs, and if fiscally strapped states are having trouble meeting their TANF spending commitments, some key members of Congress are likely to seek more fundamental changes to the law, including making the TANF block grant sensitive to economic conditions.

Table 1
Overview of TANF Provisions for Reauthorization

Provision	Description	Funding	In Baseline?
Basic TANF Grant	Block grant to states to help needy children, to reduce non-marital births, and for other purposes	$16.5 billion annually, FY1996–FY2002	Yes
Illegitimacy Bonus	Bonus grant to reward up to five states for greatest reduction in out-of-wedlock birth rates	$100 million annually, FY1999–FY2002	Yes
Performance Bonus	Bonus grant to reward high performance by states for attaining goals of TANF	$1 billion for FY1999–FY2003; Average annual bonus grants are $200 million	Yes
Population and Poverty Adjustor	Supplemental grants for 17 qualifying states with above-average population growth and low welfare spending per poor person	Up to a total of $800 million for FY1998–FY2001 (extended through FY2002)	No
Contingency Fund	Matching grants for needy states	$2 billion for FY1997–FY2001 (extended through FY2002)	No

Table 1, continued

Provision	Description	Funding	In Baseline?
Indian Tribes	Grants for tribal work activities programs	$7.6 million annually, FY1997–FY2002	Yes
	Funds transferred from state block grants to tribes that operate TANF	Approximately $86 million annually (included in $16.5 billion above)	
Territories	Grants to territories for TANF, foster care, adoption assistance programs, and other programs	About $116 million, FY1997 grants FY2002, for TANF, Title IV-E, and aid to the aged and disabled	Yes
Loan Fund	Interest-bearing loans for state welfare programs	Total amount of loans outstanding may not exceed $1.7 billion	N/A
Medicaid for Families Leaving Welfare	Federal payments to provide up to 12 months of Medicaid for families leaving welfare	About $.5 billion per year, FY1997–FY2001 (extended through FY2002)	Yes
Additional Medicaid Administrative Costs	Funds provided to compensate for increased costs of computing Medicaid eligibility	$500 million total without fiscal year limit	No
Research: Census Bureau	Census Bureau study to evaluate impact of TANF on national sample of low-income families	$10 million annually, FY1996–FY2002 (plus supplementals)	No
Research by HHS on effects, costs, and benefits of state TANF programs	Funds for DHHS to use to evaluate and conduct research on welfare reform	$15 million annually, FY1997–FY2002	No
Abstinence education	Funds for states to operate programs stressing the importance of sexual abstinence to healthy development	$50 million annually, FY1998–FY2002	No

Note: If TANF provision is in the baseline, then Congress will not need to find a funding mechanism (either a tax increase or a program cut) to reauthorize the provision. If funding is not in the baseline, Congress must find a funding mechanism. For example, if Congress decides to reauthorize the Census Bureau study for five years, it will need to find $50 million in funding offsets.

PART II

STATE RESPONSES

4

THOMAS GAIS AND R. KENT WEAVER

State Policy Choices Under Welfare Reform

Executive Summary
The 1996 welfare reform law increased state flexibility over a range of policy choices, while imposing a new set of mandates and incentives to move in specific policy directions. States have used their discretion to adopt a number of policies designed to lower barriers to work, such as disregarding more income in calculating benefit levels and easing limits on the value of autos and financial assets. Many states have also adopted policies that restrict access to benefits, such as imposing stiffer sanctions for recipients who do not cooperate with work requirements and shorter time limits than those mandated by the federal government. The packages of policy choices vary widely across states. States that receive higher block grants per low-income child are more likely to pursue generous income supplementation policies, while the political characteristics of a state are more closely related to policies intended to restrict access to Temporary Assistance to Needy Families (TANF). There is little evidence thus far of an overall "race to the bottom" in TANF policies.

The 1996 federal welfare reform law joined two approaches to changing welfare policy in the United States. The law put in place many policies reflecting a conservative approach to the goals of work, independence, and marriage. These included time limits on assistance, stricter work requirements, and demands that teen mothers live with their parents and finish school. The law also strengthened requirements that clients cooperate with child support enforcement efforts and established stronger sanctions for noncompliance.

However, the law also created a block grant giving states flexibility in fashioning their own policy and administrative strategies to achieve the goals of the law. State innovation and experimentation are seen as critical ingredients of policy change. Federal time limits and work requirements apply only to cash assistance funded by the federal block grant, Temporary Assistance to Needy Families (TANF). States can, however, devise programs without time limits or work requirements when they use their own money, spending state funds under TANF's "maintenance of effort" provision, which requires states to spend 75 percent of the state dollars they spent in 1994. States can even use federal TANF funds to provide benefits to low-income families without time limits if those benefits help pay the costs of working, such as child care or transportation. States can impose stricter work requirements or shorter time limits. They can change many other eligibility requirements for cash assistance, including

Table 1
Selected Policy Changes Adopted in States by 2000

Number of states adopting	Policies enhancing access to supports	Policies restricting access to supports
Most frequently adopted (40-51 states)	Increased asset disregards for cars (51) Enhanced earned income disregards (47) Increased financial asset disregards (44) Ended 100 hr work limit for 2 parent families (40)	Required work activity in less than 24 months (43)
Frequently adopted (26-39 states)	Ended 30 day waiting period for 2 parents (30) Ended work history requirement for 2 parents (28)	Required immediate work activity (38) Decreased or ended child support pass-through (34) Limited post-secondary education as allowable activity to less than two years full-time (26)
Less frequently adopted (12-25 states)	State earned income tax credits (16)	Adopted family caps (23) Limited General Education Development (GED) or English as a Second Language (ESL) as allowable first activities (22) Enforced worst-case sanctions equal to 100% of benefits for 3 or more months (21) Reduced food stamps or Medicaid through sanctions (22) Decreased age of child exempting mothers from work to less than 12 months (22) Enforced sanctions equal to 100% of benefits for first-time violations (17) Introduced intermittent time limits (14) Imposed state residency requirements (13, but struck down by courts)
Least frequently adopted (0-11 states)	Extended transitional Medicaid past 12 months (11)	Reduced lifetime time limit to less than 60 months (6) Ended all cash benefits to teen parents (0)

Source: Authors' analysis of data from a variety of sources: the Green Book 2000; unpublished Center on Budget and Policy Priorities data; the Urban Institute's Welfare Rules Database; the Center for Law and Social Policy & the Center on Budget and Policy Priorities State Policy Documentation Project; the DHHS 2000 TANF Annual Report to Congress; and the Welfare Information Network's State Plan Database.
Note: The District of Columbia is counted as a state in this table.

asset and earnings disregards. They determine the services to be offered to low-income families and define who is eligible for such services. And they have wide discretion over which providers—public or private, secular or religious—carry out their programs.

This combination of work-focused policy mandates and increased state discretion raises several questions. Have states used their flexibility—and, if so, how? Have they advanced the philosophy of the federal legislation, or have they introduced different elements? Have states "raced to the bottom," competing with one another to make their policies more punitive and less attractive to low-income families? Or have they developed diverse approaches to welfare reform, responding to different economic conditions and political climates? And what do state choices suggest about changes that Congress may want to consider in reauthorizing TANF?

State Policy Choices

Initial evidence on the differences and similarities in state policies comes from an examination of choices states made under TANF. Table 1 summarizes several decisions and the number of states selecting them. The left column includes policy choices that use positive incentives to encourage the work, marriage, and childbearing objectives of the 1996 federal law. These policies tend to enhance access to services and income supports. The right column contains work, marriage, and childbearing policies that use negative incentives—typically, restrictions on benefits or supports—to meet the same objectives.

The policy choices listed in table 1 reflect the broad support that states have given to the employment goals of the federal legislation. Most states accepted the premise in TANF that assistance should be temporary. Six states have reduced the limits on payment of cash assistance below the 60 months in the federal law while fourteen states have introduced "intermittent" time limits (e.g., available for only 36 out of 60 months). Only a few states have chosen to eliminate the 60-month time limit, but several states have announced that they will apply time limits only to adults, apply broad exemptions, or otherwise limit the effects of time limits (not shown).

By 2000, forty-three states had strengthened the federal work requirements by demanding that caregivers engage in a work activity before the TANF-imposed deadline of twenty-four months; thirty-eight required adults to do so immediately. States also endorsed the federal law's emphasis on "work first" over education and training: the number of states counting full-time post-secondary education as an allowable work activity for two years dropped to twenty-six in 2000. The number of states extending the coverage of the work requirements to parents of children less than one year old rose from six states in 1996 to twenty-two states in 2000.

Other changes reduced assistance to people who failed to meet the new obligations. TANF did not require states to cut off all benefits to a noncompliant household, but seventeen states now levy 100 percent sanctions for first-time violations, and twenty-one states impose 100 percent sanctions for at least three months as an ultimate sanction. Twenty-two states also reduce or eliminate Medicaid and/or food stamp benefits if sanctions are imposed for violations of TANF work requirements. Twenty-three states have adopted family caps, which means that children born or conceived while a family receives welfare are not counted in determining cash benefits. Finally, thirty-four states have ended or reduced the "pass through" to families on welfare of $50 per month of child support collections that was required under the old Aid to Families with Dependent Children (AFDC) program.

Two other highly restrictive options are not now in effect in any state. By 1998, thirteen states had reduced or delayed assistance to new residents coming from other states. Such laws, however, were struck down by the U.S. Supreme Court as unconstitutional in 1999, so they no longer apply. And no state adopted a policy favored by the most conservative advocates of federal welfare reform in 1996—barring all cash benefits to teen parents.

Overall, however, states accepted and often strengthened the restrictions on assistance found in the federal law. Few of these policies were adopted by a majority of the states, but most states adopted at least one such policy.

At the same time, several policies increasing access to services or supports became quite widespread. Earnings disregards were liberalized in forty-seven states compared to AFDC standards. Families with earnings were allowed to keep more assistance than before, thereby increasing the incentive to work. Sixteen states strengthened positive incentives by creating a state Earned Income Tax Credit for low-income families with earnings and children. However, these credits can be used only to lower tax liability rather than being received as a cash income supplement in five states.

Nearly all states increased their asset disregards—limits on what a family could save or own and remain eligible for assistance. All states increased their vehicle disregards, primarily because the $1,500 ceiling for an automobile under AFDC was viewed as a barrier to employment for people who needed a reliable car for work. A large majority of states also made it easier for two-parent families to get cash assistance. For example, AFDC restricted eligibility for two-parent families by limiting how many hours the parents could work in a month, but forty states had eliminated those restrictions by 2000.

Taken together, the changes in disregards and the elimination of restrictions on two-parent families have expanded the range of working families eligible for cash assistance. One indicator of this shift is a substantial increase in "break even" points for families on assistance— the income recipients may earn before losing eligibility.

By contrast, states have not made major changes in their maximum cash assistance levels; i.e., the money families receive if they have no other income. Indeed, the most common pattern is a continuation of the pre-1996 pattern of real benefit levels being eroded by inflation. Between 1994 and 2000, twenty-nine states made no change in the nominal value of the benefit a family with no earnings receives; benefits in these states lost about 14 percent of their real value. Fifteen states increased their nominal maximum benefits, though only three of these states increased their real value; seven states cut their nominal benefits.

The increasing disregards and the declining real value of maximum benefits for families with no other income shifted the distribution of cash benefits away from persons without income and toward those with earnings. However, there is substantial diversity across states. In 2000, thirty-nine states offered some benefits to persons working 35 hours a week at the minimum wage, at least initially. But in eighteen states, a three-person family with one minimum wage worker who worked 35 hours a week would get no TANF benefits in their fourth month; in another ten states they would get less than $100. In short, only in a minority of states does TANF provide major wage supplements for workers working full-time even at minimum wage. Wage supplementation is even more modest for workers earning $8 per hour or more. Because maximum benefits remain low in most states, even generous disregards whittle down assistance to small sums as parents increase their earnings.

In short, states generally accepted the "sticks" elements in TANF, those provisions that punish noncompliance with work requirements. Many states used their discretion to stiffen work requirements or

Table 2
Predictors of State Policy Choices

	State Benefits under Five Wage Scenarios plus State Earned Income Tax Credit	Sanctions Scale	Time Limits Scale	Family Caps	Immediate Activity Requirement
Type of regression	linear	linear	linear	logistic	logistic
R Square	0.623	0.345	0.351	0.320	0.233
% of caseload that is African American	−	−	−	−	
% of caseload that is Hispanic			−		
% popular vote for Clinton in 1996		+	+		+
% Republican state legislators		−			
Republican governor					+
TANF $/ children in low-income household	+				−
Unemployment rate					
State per capita income	+				
Welfare dependency (peak caseload as percentage of state population)			+		
Statewide non-marital birthrate					

- (lightest shading) = significant between the 5 and 10% levels
- (medium shading) = significant between the 1 and 5 % levels
- (darkest shading) = significant between the 0 and 1% levels

+ = more generous policy (i.e., more generous state benefits, weaker sanctions, less strict time limits, no family caps, and no immediate activity requirement)
− = more restrictive policy (i.e., less state benefits, harsher sanctions, stricter time limits, etc.)

Source: Authors' analysis of data from a variety of sources: the Green Book 2000; unpublished Center on Budget and Policy Priorities data; the Urban Institute's Welfare Rules Database; the Center for Law and Social Policy & the Center on Budget and Policy Priorities State Policy Documentation Project; the DHHS 2000 TANF Annual Report to Congress; and the Welfare Information Network's State Plan Database.

penalties for non-work over those in federal law. A majority of states adopted stiffer initial work requirements, and a large minority of states strengthened the federal sanction policies and cut the time limits. Yet the vast majority of states also adopted "carrot" policies—those aimed at rewarding work by enhancing access to certain benefits or supports, especially by eliminating provisions that discouraged work. As table 1 shows, however, most policy choices, especially those that restrict access to benefits, are in the two intermediate categories in terms of breadth of diffusion, having been adopted in more than ten but fewer than forty states.

States engaged in substantial innovation in both access-enhancing and access-restricting policies before 1998 and in some cases before 1996 (through AFDC waivers prior to passage of the federal legislation). A leveling off of innovation occurred thereafter. In some cases, the leveling off occurred because policies had been adopted by almost every state (eased auto asset limits, for example). In other cases, the apparent political limits of the policy had been reached (notably family caps). Instead of a "race to the bottom"—a continuing expansion of restrictive policies and little or

Giving more states the resources to pay for income supplements and child care might push TANF to become a stronger work support program.

no expansion in access-enhancing policies—many states adopted both types of policies. Yet states have differed dramatically both in their overall degrees of policy change and in their mix of "carrot" and "stick" policies. Rather than an emerging homogeneity, either around a "race to the bottom" or a consensus set of "best practices," there remains substantial heterogeneity in packages of state choices.

Factors Related to State Variations

Why do states differ in their policy choices? To explain variation across states in their policy choices under TANF, we used statistical techniques designed to find the relationship between characteristics of states and the policies they choose, while controlling for other attributes of those states. Table 2 summarizes our analyses of five policy choices: family caps, time limits shorter than those required under TANF, immediate work activity requirements, stronger sanctions than required under TANF, and the generosity of work supplements for working families. In the cells of table 2, a "+" means that the variable or factor is associated with a policy choice that is comparatively "liberal"; i.e., makes assistance more widely available or more generous. A "–" sign means that the variable is estimated to have a "conservative" impact on the dependent variable; i.e., constrains access to public assistance. Several points emerge from this analysis.

First, ideological factors are correlated with policies restricting cash assistance. Stronger sanction policies, shorter time limits, and immediate activity requirements are more common in conservative states than in liberal states (liberalism is measured here by the percent of the state's popular vote going to Bill Clinton in the 1996 presidential election, but other measures of state public opinion produce similar results).

Second, policies restricting cash assistance—such as shorter time limits, more severe sanctions, and family caps—are also more common among states that have a high percentage of African Americans on the caseload. Having a high percentage of Hispanics in a state's caseload is associated only with stiffer time limits.

Third, a state's resources under the TANF block grant are strongly related to policy choices regarding income supplements through earnings disregards and state earned income tax credits. Earned income disregards are more generous in states that were given relatively large grants per needy person—here, measured as the size of the TANF grant per child living in a low-income household. Because the formula for distributing federal TANF funds was based on state and federal spending in 1994, states that spent a lot on a per-case basis then got a comparatively large block grant under TANF and now have greater resources to spend on each of their families.

Fourth, policy decisions among the states were generally not statistically related to the severity of social problems in the states once other factors are controlled for. Out-of-wedlock birth rates, welfare dependency (measured by the percentage of the population on welfare at its highest point in the early 1990s), and unemployment showed weak marginal effects on state policy choices.

Policies that restrict assistance are thus most responsive to factors likely to affect a state's politics, particularly in the area of social policy, such as its electoral tendencies and the racial and ethnic composition of the caseload. Policies offering positive incentives to work, by contrast, are most strongly affected by a state's resources, especially the resources per needy family member provided through the TANF block grants.

Implications for TANF Reauthorization

Most states responded to the federal TANF program by endorsing both the employment goal and the means to achieve it, including time limits and work requirements. Perhaps the most surprising finding is the large expansion of eligibility for cash assistance among working families. States increased the rewards of work and lowered barriers to employment by increasing earnings and asset disregards, by eliminating anti-work regulations aimed at two-parent families, and by increasing their funding for child care and other services that directly support employment.

Expanded access to assistance for working families was in no way mandated by TANF. It emerged out of the new flexibility accorded to the states. Some aspects of TANF may have encouraged this tendency, including the block grant funding formula, the performance requirements, and the political popularity of the law's employment goals. The strong economy may also have been a factor. Although employment levels were not significant in accounting for differences among the states in their earnings disregards, it is still possible that the general prosperity of the late 1990s made policymakers willing to spread benefits to a wider range of working families.

However, there were important differences among state responses. States that were politically conservative and those that had large numbers of African Americans on their welfare rolls tended to adopt policies—such as stricter time limits, work requirements, and sanctions— that made assistance less attractive and less widely available. Contrary to the hopes of some welfare reform proponents, the new welfare law does not seem to have dissipated the image of the program as disproportionately aiding minorities, or the negative impact that this image has on support for the program in many states.

Several implications flow from this analysis. First, the absence of evidence that a "race to the bottom" in state policy choices is under way weakens the case for tightening federal limits on the range of state choice. But it should be noted that the good economic conditions that have existed until recently are those least likely to produce a "race to the bottom."

Another issue for reauthorization is whether differences in policy choices across states are problematic and, if so, what can be done about them. If one finds the divide between states that rely heavily on "sticks" and those that put greater emphasis on "carrots" to be troubling, it may be necessary to increase the funding levels per poor family in the states that had smaller relative grants in the first years of TANF. Giving more states the resources to pay for income supplements and child care might push TANF to become a stronger work support program in a larger number of states, not just in the traditional high-benefit states.

Encouraging work could also be addressed by maintaining or increasing the required work participation rates while revising the caseload reduction credit in calculating state performance levels. One possible revision might be to transform the caseload reduction credit into an employment credit for former TANF recipients who are in the work force.

Increasing hours of work required for individuals as well as state work participation rates is another option, with its own distinct challenges. Income supplements for families with full-time workers remain small or non-existent in most states—even when they earn only the minimum wage. Since work participation rates are based on the number of families on assistance who work the required hours, basing those rates only on full-time workers would make it difficult for most states to increase or even maintain their work participation rates.

It is still unclear, moreover, how states will respond to new challenges. What policies will they develop in dealing with timed-out families? How will they react when and if they have to meet 50 or 70 percent work participation rates year after year, especially if they face higher caseloads in a weakened economy? Evidence from the first five years of the TANF program suggests that there could be wide variation in state responses.

Additional Reading

Gais, Thomas L., and others. 2001. "Implementation of the Personal Responsibility Act of 1996." In *The New World of Welfare,* edited by Rebecca M. Blank and Ron Haskins. Washington, D.C.: Brookings.

Pavetti, LaDonna, and Dan Bloom. 2001. "State Sanctions and Time Limits," In *The New World of Welfare,* edited by Rebecca M. Blank and Ron Haskins. Washington, D.C.: Brookings.

Soss, Joe, and others. 2001. "Setting the Terms of Relief: Explaining State Policy Choices in the Devolution Revolution." *American Journal of Political Science,* 45(2): 378-395.

5

IRENE LURIE

Changing Welfare Offices

Executive Summary
The 1996 welfare reform law that established the Temporary Assistance for Needy Families (TANF) program gave states increased discretion in providing benefits and setting program rules. In response, states have dramatically changed their policies and practices for handling welfare applications. Many welfare offices have adopted "work first" policies that require recipients to engage in job search or other work-related activities while they apply for cash assistance, and some offices have initiated policies that try to divert applicants from monthly cash assistance. However, fewer offices have created effective mechanisms for informing diverted applicants and recipients leaving welfare about the availability of food stamps, Medicaid, and other benefits. Welfare offices in many states have been haphazard in linking clients to pregnancy prevention and other family formation services, particularly where state policy gives them little or no support. In addition, they have only recently made job retention and advancement a high priority. Improving the performance of welfare offices would be facilitated by removing conflicting requirements across programs as well as by improving the training of workers and coordination across human services agencies.

The implementation of the Temporary Assistance for Needy Families (TANF) program occurs at thousands of welfare offices where staff talk with people who are applying for assistance or already receiving it. At this point of service delivery, the TANF legislation, state laws and regulations, agreements between agencies that serve TANF clients, and the many other arrangements and procedures needed to run the program are brought to life.

To understand how TANF has unfolded, and how welfare caseloads have been cut so sharply, we must look at what happens inside welfare offices. How are the new rules in the TANF legislation conveyed to welfare applicants and recipients? How are the rules enforced? How are people referred to the services arranged for them or selected by them? Studies of program implementation show that changes in policy do not automatically translate into changes in treatment of recipients. Formal rules promulgated by legislatures or administrative agencies may be unknown or misunderstood by frontline workers. These workers may not have the skills, resources, or motivation to explain and apply the rules correctly. In addition, when rules cannot be written in sufficient detail to specify all the aspects of the services that program designers envision, workers must exercise discretion in serving their clients.

TANF programs exhibit great diversity both among and within states. Because TANF increased the states' authority to design their own welfare programs, state programs now differ much more than they did under the Aid to Families with Dependent Children (AFDC) program. Under TANF, states devolve many functions and decisions to counties and specialized local agencies. But despite this diversity, there are similarities in the direction of change. One of the most striking changes has occurred in the welfare application process: families entering the front door of the welfare agency now encounter a more rigorous application process than they did under AFDC.

Changes at the Front Door of the Welfare Agency

Under AFDC, states were required to give anyone the opportunity to apply for aid, to act on the application with reasonable promptness, and to give aid to all eligible individuals. With the end of welfare entitlement and these procedural rules, each state now designs its own application process to certify or deny eligibility for assistance. This process is a primary vehicle for conveying the new rules of the TANF program. Almost all welfare offices use the application process to send a strong signal to TANF applicants that employment is now expected. Frontline workers generally believe welfare recipients should work and they support this change in orientation.

Many states use a variant of "work first," which requires that individuals cooperate with work requirements while applying for welfare. Frontline workers generally have little or no discretion to exempt applicants from work first activities, and must make referrals to work first agencies before assistance can be authorized. Before becoming eligible for welfare, recipients may be required to engage in a job search for a period of time, attend a workshop on how to search for work, or attend a work agency orientation on employment services and supportive services such as child care and transportation.

State and local administrators report that the work first model serves several functions beyond the obvious one of promoting immediate employment. Sending people to job search can help the agency assess applicants' skills and their need for education and training. Work first requirements can send a clear message to welfare applicants that they will need to take a job or do unpaid work as a condition of receiving welfare, a prospect that discourages some people from continuing their application. Finally, requiring people to search for work or attend a workshop can identify people who cannot fulfill these requirements because they are already working, but not reporting their earnings to the welfare agency.

Because welfare agencies no longer need to give everyone the opportunity to apply for assistance, agencies can now use strategies designed explicitly to divert applicants from joining the welfare rolls. One diversionary approach used by agencies is to give applicants a one-time payment instead of providing continuing assistance. For example, if someone comes to a welfare agency after losing her job because her car broke down, she can be given a lump-sum payment for car repairs. The agency pays her enough to resolve her immediate emergency but does not formally accept her as a welfare recipient. Nearly half the states give short-term assistance if, in exchange, the applicant foregoes assistance for some specified period of time. A second diversion strategy is to refer applicants immediately to resources in the community, like housing programs, food pantries, and charities.

Short-term diversion payments are advantageous for people who prefer to avoid going on welfare, but they can also have negative consequences. In New York City, for example, a new eligibility process led frontline workers to discourage people from applying for benefits on their first visit to the welfare office, and instead encouraged them to look elsewhere for support, such as among family members or within the community. Because eligibility for TANF, food stamps, and Medicaid are determined jointly using the same application, these diverted families did not have the opportunity to apply for food stamps and Medicaid, although both programs remain legal entitlements and must be offered on the first visit to a welfare office. These practices were challenged in court, and the city was placed under a court injunction to redesign its eligibility process.

Greater use of computerized information systems has also made the welfare application process more rigorous. Computerized systems give offices information about applicants that was not available before the revolution in information technology. Finger-imaging systems used in New York and Texas enable offices to reduce welfare fraud by comparing an applicant's fingerprints with the fingerprints of people already receiving benefits. Other desktop computer systems enable workers to verify the information that applicants provide as well as discover unreported information.

In addition to these high-tech systems, some welfare agencies are returning to the old practice of sending workers to visit the homes of applicants and recipients. Home visits yield information about the family's lifestyle that may uncover unreported household members, income, or assets, and may also reveal problems such as disability and domestic violence that call for additional services.

Because applications for welfare have not declined as dramatically as welfare caseloads, the workload at the frontlines of welfare agencies remains heavy. New and improved computer systems do not necessarily reduce the time needed to process a case. The volumes of information to be gathered and conveyed leave little time to problem-solve with clients and give them information that might promote self-sufficiency.

Pursuing TANF's Goals Inside the Front Door

One of the specific goals of the TANF legislation is to promote greater personal responsibility among welfare recipients regarding work, marriage, and childbearing. However, differences in political culture, personal values, economic and fiscal conditions, welfare benefit levels, and the unique characteristics of the adults and children in TANF families often result in varied state and local policies and practices to promote personal responsibility.

A common characteristic among state programs is an increase in the percentage of welfare recipients who work in regular jobs, as opposed to participating in post-secondary education and vocational training. In the late 1980s, federal law encouraged states to enroll recipients in educational activities. As a result, 39 percent of participants engaged in work-related activities were actually in school (almost half in higher education), and not working in regular jobs. Emphasizing education, however, was a long-term investment strategy that did not immediately move people into the labor force and may even have led them to stay on welfare longer. So in 1996, the TANF legislation encouraged recipients to find regular work by limiting the amount of education and training that counted toward meeting states' work requirements.

States have clearly responded to these changes in federal law: by 1999, according to GAO, 27.7 percent of TANF adults worked either full-time or part-time in unsubsidized employment, while only 6.1 percent of TANF adults were engaged in education or training. More recently, some states have altered this trend by allowing TANF recipients greater access to post-secondary education.

The treatment of TANF adults who are not engaged in regular employment varies widely among the states, but the treatment still signals the importance of work. Job search, the next most common work activity after regular employment, was an activity for 5.9 percent of adults in 1999. Work experience, in which recipients work in exchange for their welfare benefits, was an activity for only 3.7 percent of adults. But where work experience is used heavily, as in New York City, Ohio, and Wisconsin, it conveys a strong message about the expectation of work and reduces the attractiveness of welfare.

Welfare offices tend to convey information about the financial rewards from work in a haphazard manner. The Rockefeller Institute's Frontline Management and Practice Study, for example, found that frontline workers rarely mentioned the fact that states will ignore part of earnings when computing the welfare benefit, a widespread practice that increases the incentive to work. Workers also rarely mentioned the federal Earned Income Tax Credit, a program that pays up to $4,000 per year to low-income working families with children. Even when workers did explain these important policies, they did not always describe them fully and accurately. Similarly, a recent study by the Manpower Demonstration Research Corporation (MDRC) found that

While states decide the amount of the sanctions, the decision to impose or lift a sanction is inevitably at the discretion of the frontline worker.

workers frequently did not mention the continued availability of food stamp and Medicaid benefits after leaving welfare. In recognition of these problems, several advocacy groups and welfare agencies have designed attractive and colorful brochures with specific examples of the full range of benefits available to working families.

To meet TANF's goals regarding parental behavior, all states have adopted a policy of requiring people to sign a personal responsibility agreement (PRA) as a condition of receiving assistance. PRAs require workers to be more paternalistic toward welfare recipients. Depending on the state, workers can ask recipients to attend classes on parenting, money management, life skills, family planning and counseling, or substance abuse counseling and treatment. Workers can also require parents to take their children for regular medical checkups and immunizations, make their children attend school regularly, and refrain from alcohol abuse. States may also test recipients for the use of controlled substances. Requiring recipients to cooperate with authorities to establish paternity and obtain child support was federal law under AFDC and continues to be under TANF. To the extent that workers monitor compliance with a PRA and make it clear that noncompliance will be costly to the recipient, PRAs can reduce the attractiveness of welfare and discourage welfare dependency.

TANF substantially strengthens the ability of states to enforce their rules on work and personal responsibility. Federal law now requires states to sanction welfare recipients by reducing the benefits of those who do not meet work requirements and child support obligations. TANF goes further than the former AFDC program by permitting states to increase the severity of sanctions and even end benefits completely, usually after repeated noncompliance with the rules. Changes in food stamp rules have also increased the severity of TANF sanctions because food stamp benefits no longer rise automatically when welfare benefits are cut. While states decide the amount of the sanctions, the decision to impose or lift a sanction is inevitably at the discretion of the frontline worker, perhaps with oversight by a supervisor. How hard the worker tries to understand the client's position, encourage different behavior, make referrals to additional services, or realize the client is truly unable to comply, is ultimately up to the individual worker. For these reasons, the actual frequency with which sanctions are imposed for a given rule violation varies among states, offices, and individual workers. According to the U.S. General Accounting Office, 5.1 percent of TANF families were under a sanction during an average month in 1998. By far the most common reason for the sanction was noncompliance with work requirements. However, less than 1 percent of TANF families experienced a termination of all cash benefits.

Sanctions for failure to comply with other components of the PRA are less frequent, in part because monitoring compliance is costly in terms of workers' time and requires methods of tracking the client's behavior. The extent to which workers actually monitor compliance with all the items in the PRA varies among offices, which makes the PRA more meaningful in some places than others. Clients must sign numerous forms in order to establish and maintain their eligibility for assistance, but observations during the Rockefeller Institute's Frontline Management and Practice Study suggest that they often sign after hearing little or no explanation of the form and without reading it.

Efforts to change behavior regarding out-of-wedlock childbearing and marriage have been implemented more slowly and with less force than policies to encourage work, perhaps a reflection of divided public opinion on these issues and less clarity about which policies are likely to be effective. To discourage childbearing by women already on welfare, some states have introduced a "family cap," which means that welfare benefits do not increase with the birth of another child. A family cap is easy to administer because it requires no action or discretion by the welfare office.

Linking welfare recipients to family planning and pregnancy prevention programs has been far more problematic, however. Public health workers or family planning nurses are on site in only a small minority of welfare offices. In some offices, welfare workers say they are prohibited from mentioning family planning to their clients. Even where workers are instructed to refer clients to family planning services, they may fail to do so because of personal beliefs, embarrassment, lack of time, or oversight during a crowded application process. While some workers may discuss marriage with their unmarried clients or try to repair relationships between married couples, few have had training in marital counseling.

Frontline Workers: Combining New and Old Roles

Many welfare agencies are trying to broaden the duties of frontline workers. Once limited to impersonal clerical functions related to determining eligibility and benefits, frontline workers are now being asked to engage in more personalized conversations about their clients' lives, behaviors, and financial problems. Most agencies have changed the titles of their frontline workers from names like "eligibility specialist" to the more professional "case manager," which implies a broader set of duties. Many states have also trained their workers to involve clients in finding solutions to the problems that keep them on welfare. But frontline workers typically do not have an educational background in social work, and they often feel unprepared and reluctant to get involved with their clients' personal problems.

Although states are adding additional responsibilities to the welfare office worker's role, they have done little to reduce the time that workers must devote to determining eligibility and benefits. A continuing focus on welfare payment accuracy requires workers to spend a great deal of time collecting and verifying documents. Financial accountability is still important to welfare agencies, in part because workers collect information for both the TANF and food stamp programs, and the food stamp program continues to penalize states that make errors.

Frontline workers must still collect documents to verify family relationships and residence, income and assets, expenses, and other personal matters such as immunizations for children or school registration. Thus, the continuing focus on welfare payment accuracy requires workers to spend a great deal of time collecting and verifying documents.

Changes at the Back Door: Helping Recipients Leave and Stay Off Welfare

Families that succeed in working their way off welfare often continue to be eligible for child care assistance, Medicaid, and food stamps—all of which are important supplements to the earnings of low-income families. But many recipients do not inform workers that they are leaving welfare and simply fail to appear at a recertification appointment. When recipients exit the system in this way, welfare agencies do not have the opportunity to inform them of their continued eligibility for these supplements. In addition, some agencies require recipients who leave welfare to reapply for child care assistance, a step that is not always taken. As a result, people leaving assistance often do not take full advantage of the important supplements that may be available to them. Of families leaving welfare, but with incomes below the eligibility cut-off for food stamps, only about 40 percent continued to receive food stamps, according to a recent national survey by Sheila Zedlewski of the Urban Institute. Unfortunately, most agencies have not yet developed processes and practices at the back door that match the rigor of the eligibility determination process.

After moving many applicants and recipients into jobs, the next step for some welfare agencies is to help people retain and upgrade their jobs. People with low skills, little job experience, and child care responsibilities frequently do not retain their jobs and even if they do, they may earn too little to leave welfare. They may cycle on and off welfare as they take jobs and then hit snags that throw them back on the rolls. Although job retention services are less developed than work first services, states are beginning to turn their attention to the task of supporting stable employment, re-employing people who have lost jobs, and advancing the careers of people beyond low-wage, entry-level jobs. With the TANF time limit affecting families in all states as of summer 2002, some states are also using their own funds to supplement the earnings of welfare families that are working but approaching the time limit for TANF-funded assistance.

Issues and Challenges for Welfare Agencies

Welfare offices are recognizing that their primary strategy for reducing caseloads—diverting applicants and requiring and supporting work—may be insufficient for recipients who still are not working or who work but earn too little to leave welfare. Families that exhibit physical or mental health problems and disabilities, dysfunctional behavior, or the inability to speak English and perform other basic job functions, need a wide and flexible array of services. Welfare offices cannot be expected to provide all these services themselves, particularly specialized services for narrow populations such as drug addicts. Nor can welfare offices be expected to bear the sole responsibility for reducing out-of-wedlock childbearing and encouraging marriage, both of which require a broader response from society.

Welfare agencies have always drawn on the expertise and capacity of many public and private organizations. Departments of labor, workforce agencies, non-profit community-based agencies, and for-profit firms deliver employment and training services for welfare recipients; schools and colleges offer education programs; and public and private agencies coordinate child care, provide mental health and substance abuse treatment, and offer family planning services. The "charitable choice" provision of the 1996 welfare reform law permitted states to purchase services for TANF clients from faith-based organizations. This controversial provision has yet to be used on a widespread basis, but it offers yet another group of potential partners for welfare agencies.

In order to serve the families that remain on the rolls, welfare agencies must have the capacity to draw further on the expertise and resources of community partners, and all partners must operate together as an integrated system that can serve families with multiple problems. Too often, families go from one agency to another for specific services without a coordinated plan. One way for welfare offices to coordinate services is to locate them in the same physical space with other agencies so staff can communicate directly with each other. Another approach is a case manager system that allows one person to assess the family comprehensively, develop a single plan, and coordinate the efforts of all agencies involved in the case.

Frontline workers need training to develop the skills necessary to recognize and understand client problems, make the appropriate referrals to specialized agencies when necessary, and establish a continuing personal connection with the clients they serve. Many states have not invested sufficiently in the training needed to prepare frontline workers for these additional tasks, nor have they hired more highly skilled people. The reluctance to increase the size of the welfare bureaucracy—expressed in the cap on administrative costs in the TANF legislation and caps in state legislation—limits funds for both training and hiring. In recognition of the service-intensive nature of the current TANF program, Congress and the states may want to consider relaxing or removing these caps.

Welfare agencies also need sufficient resources to obtain a supply of services for their clients, particularly families with multiple problems. Sufficient funds to finance child care for parents who are expected to work, including low-income parents who are not on welfare, will be a continuing need.

At the federal level, TANF and other programs should be designed to facilitate service integration. Barriers to effective service integration include program-to-program differences in goals, outcome measures, performance standards, eligibility rules, income and asset limits, target groups, and geographic boundaries. The state and local administrators who manage these programs, and the frontline workers who implement them, see many of these differences as impediments to serving their clients. The upcoming reauthorization debate provides an opportunity to refine these program features so they operate as a more coordinated system.

Additional Reading

Leibschutz, Sarah F., ed. 2000. *Managing Welfare Reform in Five States: The Challenge of Devolution.* Albany: Nelson A. Rockefeller Institute of Government.

Mead, Lawrence M., ed. 1997. *The New Paternalism.* Washington, D.C.: The Brookings Institution.

Quint, Janet, et al. 2001. *Post-TANF Food Stamp and Medicaid Benefits: Factors That Aid or Impede Their Receipt.* New York: Manpower Demonstration Research Corporation.

Weissert, Carol S., ed. 2000. *Learning from Leaders: Welfare Reform Politics and Policy in Five Midwestern States.* Albany: Nelson A. Rockefeller Institute of Government.

6

DAN BLOOM AND DON WINSTEAD

Sanctions and Welfare Reform

Executive Summary

Financial sanctions have long been used to enforce work requirements in the welfare system, but more frequent and severe sanctions have been a central feature of the welfare reforms of the 1990s. Sanctions will be an important discussion topic in 2002 when Congress debates reauthorization of the 1996 welfare reform law. Some will argue that states should be required to use "full-family" sanctions that terminate the entire cash benefit, while others will push for restrictions on completely terminating cash benefits and new requirements for states to reach out to noncompliant families before imposing complete termination. There is little hard evidence to inform this debate. Studies have found that welfare recipients who are sanctioned are a diverse group but, on average, face more barriers to employment than other recipients; they are also less likely to work after leaving welfare. Studies have also found that enforcing work requirements is important, but it is not clear whether complete termination of benefits is more effective than partial termination. We believe states should continue to have flexibility in setting sanction policies. To reduce inappropriate sanctions, Congress could expand the types of work activities for disadvantaged recipients, and require states to describe both how they will inform recipients about exemptions from work requirements and what is required to remove a sanction.

Sanctions are financial penalties for failing to comply with work or other requirements of state welfare programs. They have been a central feature of the welfare reforms of the 1990s. Although time limits may receive more attention in the media, many more families have been directly affected by sanctions, and sanctions have arguably played a greater role in reshaping welfare recipients' day-to-day experiences.

Sanctions will be an important topic of discussion when Congress considers the reauthorization of the Temporary Assistance for Needy Families (TANF) block grant in 2002. Some participants in the reauthorization debate will argue that Congress should require all states to use "full-family sanctions" in which a family's entire cash welfare grant is terminated rather than the partial sanctions in place in some states today. Others will contend that sanctions disproportionately affect the most vulnerable families and that Congress should restrict the use of full-family sanctions and require states to reach out to families before and after reducing or terminating benefits to try to resolve the problems that lead to noncompliance.

The Evolution of Sanction Policies

Financial sanctions have long been used to enforce work-related requirements for welfare recipients. What changed in the 1990s was the severity of the penalties and the frequency of their use.

Until the early 1990s, sanctions did not involve terminating a family's entire Aid to Families with Dependent Children (AFDC) grant. Rather, the individual who failed to comply (usually the parent) was removed from the grant calculation, resulting in a lower grant and reflecting the view that children should not be punished for their parent's noncompliance. At the same time, however, noncompliance with eligibility-related requirements (for example, failure to appear for a redetermination interview at the welfare office) did result in closing the case and terminating benefits.

Some welfare staff and administrators complained that sanctions under AFDC were too small to effectively induce recipients to comply with work requirements. In addition, when a family's AFDC grant was reduced owing to a sanction, the family's food stamp benefits were generally increased, partly offsetting the cash sanction. Critics also contended that recipients often abused the conciliation process, a federally required procedure intended to resolve participation problems before sanctions were imposed.

In the early 1990s, the federal government began granting waivers of AFDC rules, including waivers that allowed states to impose full-family sanctions. By mid-1996, nearly half the states had received such a waiver. Then the 1996 welfare reforms required states to terminate or reduce benefits "pro rata" when recipients failed to comply with work requirements, but the amount and duration of sanctions were not otherwise specified. The act also changed the food stamp rules so that benefits are no longer increased when the cash grant is cut, and required states to reduce (or, at state option, eliminate) the food stamp grant when a TANF sanction is imposed. Finally, the law eliminated the requirement for states to have a conciliation process.

What States Are Doing

There is great variation in state sanction policies today, although most states have policies that are more stringent than required

---

Several states with large TANF caseloads, such as California, New York, and Texas, do not use full-family sanctions; thus, a substantial proportion of TANF recipients nationwide are not subject to such sanctions.

---

by federal law. According to the State Policy Documentation Project operated by the Center for Law and Social Policy in Washington, D.C., 36 states use full-family sanctions and 18 of these impose full-family sanctions on the first instance of noncompliance. In the other 18 states, partial sanctions can escalate to full-family sanctions with repeated or continued noncompliance. In most states, repeated noncompliance triggers a sanction that remains in place for at least a minimum period—typically three or six months—even if the individual agrees to comply earlier. In seven states, repeated or continued noncompliance can result in lifetime ineligibility for benefits. It is important to note, however, that several states with large TANF caseloads, such as California, New York, and Texas, do not use full-family sanctions; thus, a substantial proportion of TANF recipients nationwide are not subject to such sanctions.

Most states have procedures to resolve disputes before sanctions are imposed but, in many states, the process is less extensive than the AFDC conciliation process. Almost all states have specific criteria that constitute "good cause" for failing to comply with work mandates. Federal law prohibits states from sanctioning single custodial parents with preschool children if they cannot find child care. Most states also grant good cause exemptions when a recipient is ill or incapacitated, is caring for an incapacitated family member, or lacks transportation.

Although some information on state sanction policies is available, there is little systematic data on how, and how often, sanctions are imposed. One point is clear, however; during the 1990s most states extended work requirements to a greater share of the welfare caseload and began to enforce the requirements more aggressively. These trends were bound to generate more sanctioning.

The most comprehensive national study of sanctioning, conducted by the U.S. General Accounting Office (GAO) in 2000, estimated that 136,000 families (5 percent of the national TANF caseload at the time) received reduced benefits or no benefits due to sanctions in a typical month in 1998. However, GAO counted recipients as being subject to a full-family sanction only in the month when the sanction was imposed, even though sanctions cause many families to remain off assistance for more than one month. Thus, GAO's 5 percent estimate is low.

If one simply projects GAO's monthly estimates over several years, it is easy to conclude that well over half a million families have had their cases closed due to full-family sanctions (although there is no way to know how many families are counted more than once in this total). This compares to perhaps 85,000 families who have had their cases closed because of time limits.

There are anecdotal reports that sanctions are often imposed on clients who do not understand the program rules or who have good cause for their failure to comply, but it is impossible to determine how often this happens. Data from a Connecticut program that assists certain families who are terminated from welfare due to noncompliance show that a significant proportion are allowed to return to welfare, often because the individual qualifies for a medical exemption. A recent study by Wisconsin's Legislative Audit Bureau found evidence that some new mothers were sanctioned in error. A detailed study of eight states conducted by the Inspector General of the Department of Health and Human Services (DHHS) found that, while the states usually explained sanctions clearly, most of the TANF clients who were interviewed did not understand the sanction rules. In addition, the study found that the sanction notices mailed to clients who failed to comply were often confusing or inaccurate.

Other studies have found that caseworkers often have substantial discretion in imposing sanctions and interpret good cause criteria differently; thus, clients who engage in the same behavior are not equally likely to be sanctioned.

A number of states and localities have developed special pre-sanction review procedures to evaluate the circumstances of noncompliant families before sanctions are imposed. These reviews are sometimes conducted by contracted service providers, and may involve home visits. A review process that precedes case closures in Tennessee results in a substantial fraction of proposed sanctions being rescinded, either because the recipient comes into compliance or because the sanction was erroneous. State officials report that the fraction of closures overturned in this manner has dropped over time, in part because the review process has helped staff better understand program policies. Other states and counties have developed post-sanction outreach programs to check on the well-being of sanctioned families and their children, identify obstacles to participation, and try to reengage clients in work activities.

Who is Being Sanctioned and How are They Faring?

A number of states have examined the characteristics of recipients who are sanctioned. Sanctioned clients are a diverse group, but the studies have consistently found that, on average, sanctioned clients have lower levels of education and are more likely than other recipients to face barriers to employment such as physical and mental health problems. This finding may be attributable to the fact that such families tend to remain on assistance longer, increasing the odds that they will be sanctioned.

States that have used administrative records or surveys to follow sanctioned families after they left welfare have also found some consistent results; notably, that sanctioned welfare leavers have lower employment rates and earnings than individuals who left welfare for other reasons.

Fewer studies have examined the material well-being of sanctioned families that are off welfare, and it is difficult to decide on the most appropriate benchmark for assessing their circumstances. One can compare families' circumstances before and after leaving welfare, but it is not possible to definitively attribute changes to the sanctions. Several studies have compared sanctioned welfare leavers to individuals who left welfare "voluntarily," but the meaning of this comparison is not always clear.

One of the most comprehensive studies, conducted by Thomas Fraker and his colleagues at Mathematica and published in 1997, surveyed families in Iowa that were in the midst of a 6-month period of ineligibility for benefits. This study confirms that sanctioned families are a diverse group: about 40 percent had higher income than while they were on welfare, while 49 percent had lower income. Even among the latter group, however, there was little evidence of extreme deprivation such as homelessness.

Similarly, studies that have compared the circumstances of sanctioned leavers with those of other leavers have found that sanctioned families report lower income, but not necessarily higher levels of material hardship (e.g., housing problems, food insufficiency). Such hardships are common among all categories of leavers.

Do Sanctions Work?

Most people would agree that sanctions are not designed to reduce welfare caseloads, but rather are intended to persuade recipients to comply with work requirements and to find jobs. Do they achieve this goal?

It is inherently difficult to answer this question because many people respond to the threat of sanctions and never actually experience them. Findings from the National Evaluation of Welfare-to-Work Strategies conducted by the Manpower Demonstration Research Corporation and published in 2001 suggest that programs need to enforce work-

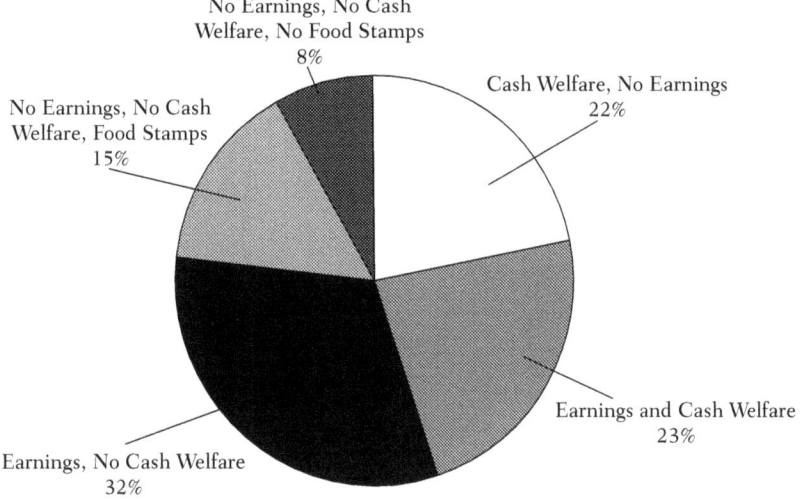

Figure 1
What Happens to Recipients Who Receive Full-Family Sanctions

- No Earnings, No Cash Welfare, No Food Stamps: 8%
- No Earnings, No Cash Welfare, Food Stamps: 15%
- Earnings, No Cash Welfare: 32%
- Earnings and Cash Welfare: 23%
- Cash Welfare, No Earnings: 22%

Note: Number of cases is 3,367; recipients were sanctioned in June 2000 and followed for six months. Data from Florida administrative records.

related mandates in order to obtain high rates of participation in employment activities. In programs that did not closely monitor attendance and rarely imposed sanctions, participation rates were only slightly higher for adults in the group subject to work mandates than for adults in the control group that faced no mandates. Among the programs that enforced mandates, however, higher sanction rates were not associated with higher participation rates. Some observers contend that programs that do a good job of communicating expectations to recipients do not need to sanction as often.

Another way to examine the utility of sanctions is to see how recipients respond after they are sanctioned. Staff from the Florida Department of Children and Families used administrative data to examine more than 3,000 cases that were closed due to sanctions in June 2000. About 45 percent received cash assistance in the subsequent 6 months, probably by coming into compliance with program rules (many of these clients also worked during the period). Another 32 percent worked but did not receive any cash assistance (in fact, most of these people also worked in the quarter before the sanction was imposed). The remaining 23 percent neither worked nor received cash assistance during the 6 months after they were sanctioned, although a majority of them received food stamps (figure 1).

These results provide further evidence that there are distinct subgroups within the sanctioned population. Some people respond to sanctions by coming into compliance. Others respond by finding jobs—or continue to work in jobs they had before they were sanctioned. In such cases, the sanction may have allowed for early identification of individuals who had already found jobs and stopped communicating with the welfare office. Ten years ago, when there were fewer work-related requirements, recipients' first scheduled appointment after accepting a job would more likely have been a redetermination interview and the welfare exit might have been classified as eligibility-related. But simply taking a job and leaving welfare without notifying the welfare office now often results in losing food stamps, Medicaid, and other transitional benefits.

The people who neither worked nor returned to welfare may have had other income not captured in the administrative data. Even so, they are a cause for concern. Among those who worked and did not receive welfare in the second quarter after exit, nearly 40 percent earned less than $1,500, suggesting that they were working part-time or were unsteadily employed. The two categories of nonworkers and part-time workers account for a substantial minority of the sanctioned clients, and add to the evidence cited above which suggests that some portion of sanctioned clients may face barriers to steady employment. Caseworkers interviewed by the Office of the Inspector General reported that sanctions are very effective for certain groups of recipients (e.g., those who are working off the books), but usually do not provide motivation for clients facing multiple barriers to employment.

Do Full-Family Sanctions Work Better Than Partial Sanctions?

It is not clear whether full-family sanctions generate larger changes in recipients' behavior than partial sanctions. It may be that most of the recipients who are able to follow the rules are induced to do so by partial sanctions. If that were true, full-family sanctions could end up imposing greater penalties on people who are unable to comply.

Some analysts have argued that full-family sanctions are particularly important in the context of time limits: when clients do not respond to partial sanctions, they often end up exhausting their months of eligibility without obtaining needed employment services. Others argue that full-family sanctions increase the likelihood that families with the most serious employment barriers will simply exit from welfare without receiving needed services.

Unfortunately, there is very little direct evidence to inform this debate. Many welfare-to-work programs using partial sanctions have generated high rates of participation in employment activities—and substantial increases in employment and reductions in welfare use—but there have been very few comparable evaluations of programs using full-family sanctions.

One study by Robert Rector and Sara Youssef of the Heritage Foundation in Washington, D.C. found that states with strong work requirements and full-family sanctions have experienced much larger welfare caseload reductions than other states. This seems plausible, since full-family sanctions result in more case closures, but the study does not address whether the sanctions induced more people to work. On the other hand, a study by Sandra Hofferth, Stephen Stanhope, and Kathleen Harris of the University of Maryland did not find an association between stricter sanction policies implemented under waivers and work-related welfare exits (stronger work requirements were associated with work exits).

Despite strong views on both sides, at this point there is not enough solid evidence to draw firm conclusions about the relative effectiveness of full-family and partial sanctions.

Implications for TANF Reauthorization

Advocates will likely push for two kinds of changes in federal sanction policy when

Congress debates the reauthorization of TANF. Some on the right will argue that all states should be required to use full-family sanctions. From the left will come a push for new restrictions on the use of full-family sanctions and new federal rules designed to reduce erroneous sanctions and increase outreach and assistance both before and after sanctions are imposed. Our view is that Congress should not impose new restrictions on state flexibility unless there is reasonably strong evidence of problems.

Although many administrators believe that full-family sanctions play a critical role in creating a work-focused welfare system, some states believe that such sanctions are not necessary to achieve this goal. Given the potential risks associated with full-family sanctions and the lack of definitive evidence on this issue, it seems reasonable to allow states to proceed with partial sanctions if they can achieve the outcomes required under the law (e.g., high work participation rates).

By the same token, there does not seem to be sufficient evidence to restrict the use of full-family sanctions. Because state programs include a mix of policies related to payment amounts, earnings disregards, employment strategies, and so forth, states should continue to have flexibility to set the sanction policy that works best in their program.

The question of new federal requirements for pre- and post-sanction outreach efforts is more difficult. The evidence suggests that there is some cause for concern; namely, that families with serious barriers to employment may constitute a significant minority of those sanctioned, but the knowledge base is still very thin. Moreover, extensive procedural requirements from the federal government can make it difficult for states to enforce work requirements.

One of the most effective ways to reduce inappropriate sanctions is to expand the set of work-related activities that count toward a state's participation rate, particularly for recipients who have impairments that limit their ability to work or who need to combine work activities with treatment or rehabilitation. With more options available, states would be better able to devise employment plans that fit the needs of particularly disadvantaged clients and thereby avoid the need for sanctions.

Congress should also consider requiring states to describe, in their TANF state plan, what safeguards they will implement to assure that individuals who are subject to sanctions have information on potential exemptions and on what they must do to have the sanction lifted. This policy would send a signal that Congress is concerned about inappropriate sanctions without significantly restricting state flexibility. DHHS could study various review and outreach procedures and provide states with guidance on which appear to be most efficient and effective.

One of the most effective approaches would be to target outreach efforts on situations in which full-family sanctions have a minimum duration. Full-family sanctions that can be lifted as soon as recipients come into compliance are not substantially different from the case closures for eligibility reasons that always existed in the old AFDC program. Sanctions with a minimum duration, on the other hand, can cause considerable harm if they are imposed on families that have serious problems that limit employability, but these problems are not known to the welfare agency. In this case, the family would remain off welfare for a mandatory period without being offered services designed to eliminate or reduce their work barriers.

Finally, additional research on sanctions should be encouraged. For example, a random assignment study could compare the effects of full-family and partial sanctions (or, perhaps, other strategies for increasing engagement in work activities), examining participation rates, employment and earnings, duration and amount of welfare payments, family income, and child well-being. This type of study, along with other research on the implementation of sanctions, would provide a firmer base of evidence to inform the ongoing policy refinements of states as well as the next reauthorization debate.

Additional Reading

Fraker, Thomas, and others. 1997. *Iowa's Limited Benefit Plan: Summary Report*. Washington, D.C.: Mathematica Policy Research.

Goldberg, Heidi, and Liz Schott. 2000. *A Compliance-Oriented Approach to Sacntions in State and County TANF Programs*. Washington, D.C.: Center on Budget and Policy Priorities.

Hofferth, Sandra L., and others. 2001. "Exiting Welfare in the 1990s: Did Public Policy Influence Recipients' Behavior?" (Unpublished manuscript). College Park: Department of Family Studies, University of Maryland.

Office of the Inspector General, U.S. Department of Health and Human Services. 1999. *Temporary Assistance for Needy Families: Educating Clients About Sanctions*.

Office of the Inspector General, U.S. Department of Health and Human Services. 1999. *Temporary Assistance for Needy Families: Improving Client Sanction Notices*.

Pavetti, LaDonna, and Dan Bloom. 2001. "State Sanctions and Time Limits." In *The New World of Welfare*, edited by Rebecca M. Blank and Ron Haskins. Washington, D.C.: Brookings.

Rector, Robert, and Sarah Youssef. 1999. *The Determinants of Welfare Caseload Decline*. Washington, D.C.: Heritage Foundation.

Wisconsin Legislature Audit Bureau. 2001. *Audit Summary: Wisconsin Works (W-2) Program* (Report 01-7).

Neither the Florida Department for Children and Families nor the Department of Health and Human Services is responsible for the views expressed in this chapter.

PART III

RESULTS TO DATE

7

RON HASKINS AND WENDELL PRIMUS

Welfare Reform and Poverty

Executive Summary
Congress must reauthorize the 1996 welfare reform legislation by October 1, 2002, and child poverty is expected to be a major issue. This policy brief reviews important facts about child poverty and examines several policies that could reduce child poverty. Child poverty declined in the late 1960s but then drifted generally upward between the early 1970s and the early 1990s. However, child poverty has now declined every year since 1993 and has reached its lowest level since 1979; poverty among black children has reached its lowest level ever. The 1996 welfare reforms that emphasized work and the dramatic increase in work by single mothers that resulted, a hot economy, and increased government benefits that support working families all contributed to the sharp decline in poverty. However, many analysts argue that child poverty would have fallen even more if working families were allowed to retain more of their cash welfare and food stamp benefits when they entered the labor force. Policies that are likely to receive attention during the reauthorization debate include taking steps to ensure that qualified working families receive food stamps, focusing programs on ways to help families with many obstacles to work, promoting marriage, and making poverty reduction an explicit goal of federal policy.

Child poverty will be an important issue as the welfare reform reauthorization debate heats up in the 107th Congress. Since the federal government adopted a standard definition of poverty in the 1960s, scholars, politicians, the media, and the public have used poverty as a measure of the strength and success of government policy and the economy. Having a standard definition of poverty, however, does not prevent disputes on many issues related to poverty. Thus, it comes as no surprise that reauthorization will spark debates about whether the federal government is primarily responsible for poverty reduction, about whether welfare reform has led to adequate reductions in poverty, and about the specific actions government should take to further reduce poverty. We begin this brief with a rendition of the facts about poverty on which there is broad agreement. After that, we address a number of policies aimed at reducing child poverty that we expect to dominate the reauthorization debate.

Evidence on Children's Poverty
Several key pieces of information provide what we believe is a solid base of knowledge about child poverty for the reauthorization debate. The first piece of information is how the federal government measures poverty. The Census Bureau, the official scorekeeper for federal poverty measures, computes poverty by comparing individual or family income from

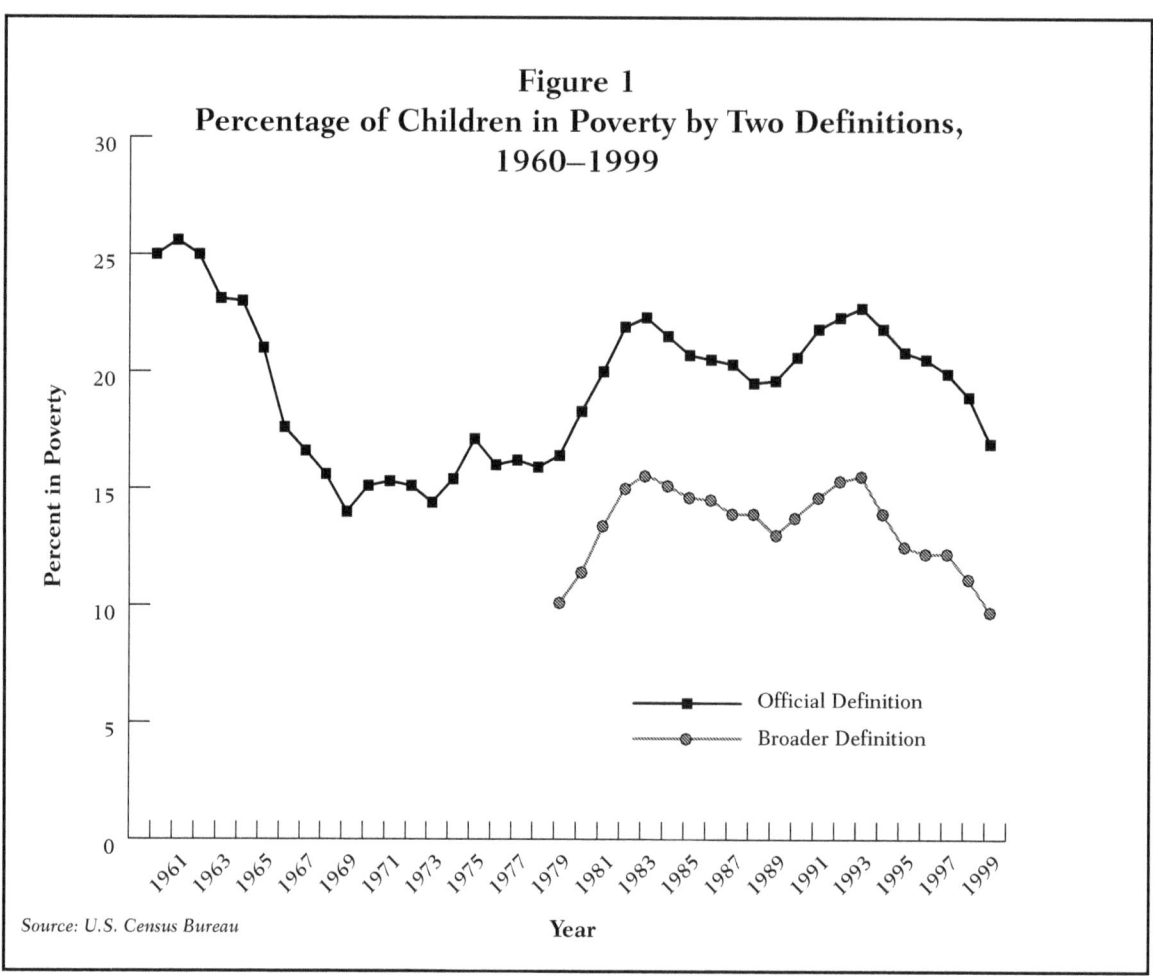

Figure 1
Percentage of Children in Poverty by Two Definitions, 1960–1999

Source: U.S. Census Bureau

earnings, cash government payments, and a few other sources to a criterion income level, adjusted for family size and inflation, that represents a minimally adequate standard of living. In 2001, the criterion income, or poverty line, was about $14,600 for a family of three.

Both the definition of income and the poverty line criterion are controversial. One criticism of the Census Bureau's official measure of poverty is that not all sources of family income are included. Non-cash government benefits, such as food stamps and housing, as well as cash income provided to families through the tax code, are omitted. A mother with two children earning $10,000 is eligible for over $2,000 in food stamps and nearly $4,000 from the Earned Income Tax Credit (EITC). Both of these sources of income are, however, ignored by the official definition. The official definition is also criticized because it ignores work expenses such as transportation and child care. In addition, many observers believe the poverty line is too low.

The official approach to defining income is especially unfortunate in the new world of welfare reform because more mothers are now working and eligible for food stamps, the EITC, and other benefits that are not counted as income. In response to this concern, the Census Bureau in recent years began computing a broader poverty measure that includes food stamps, the EITC, and several other government benefits in the calculation of income.

The second set of information that provides essential background for the upcoming debate over child poverty is Census Bureau data on the course of child poverty in recent decades. Figure 1 shows changes in the Census Bureau's official measure of child poverty from 1960 to 1999 and the broader measure from 1979 (the earliest year for which it was computed) to 1999. The top line in figure 1 shows that progress against child poverty under the official definition was rapid during the 1960s. Then, after a brief period of stability in the early 1970s, child poverty drifted generally upwards until the early 1990s, as shown by the fact that as compared with an average of about 15 percent in the early 1970s, child poverty seldom fell below 20 percent in the years after 1980. Although poverty did decline during the economic expansion of the 1980s, it moved back up again and reached the 20 percent level in the late 1980s and early 1990s. Thus, in the quarter century before the welfare reform movement that began in the states in the early 1990s and culminated in the federal welfare reform legislation of 1996, child poverty was rising modestly but noticeably.

Recent trends, however, are more encouraging. As shown in an earlier policy brief in this series (chapter 2), welfare rolls, overall child poverty, and poverty among black children have all been declining rapidly since 1993. At that time, states began aggressively implementing welfare-to-work programs under waivers from federal law, the EITC and other "make work pay" policies were expanded, and the economy started growing rapidly. By 1999, the child poverty rate had fallen to its lowest level since 1979 and poverty among black children to its lowest level ever, although their rate was still well above the rate for white children. The rate for Hispanic children was also declining rapidly and by 1999 had reached its lowest level since 1979.

A third type of background information illuminates what is surely the most important demographic correlate of poverty; namely, the proportion of children in female-headed families. This proportion is important in accounting for poverty because children in these families are much more likely to be poor than children in two-parent families. Thus, it is unfortunate that the percentage of children in female-headed families increased steadily from 8 percent in 1960 to over 20 percent in 1983 (figure 2). It has remained above 20 percent ever since. The figures for black children are even more dramatic. As compared with about 20 percent in the mid-1960s, by the mid-1980s about 50 percent of black children were in female-headed families and the percentage has remained above 50, although in recent years there has been a slight upturn in the percentage of black children living in married-couple families.

Not all female-headed families are created equal. The type of female-headed family most likely to be poor and stay poor for long periods is never-married female-headed families. The percentage of single parent families headed by never-married mothers increased from less than 1 percent in 1960 to about 31 percent in 1995, an increase of immense proportions and the single most important factor contributing to high and growing child poverty rates.

Given the unfortunate correlation between families headed by women and poverty, and the increases in the percentage of children living in female-headed families—especially those headed by a never-married mother—progress against poverty depends to a substantial degree on improving the financial status of female-headed families. Until

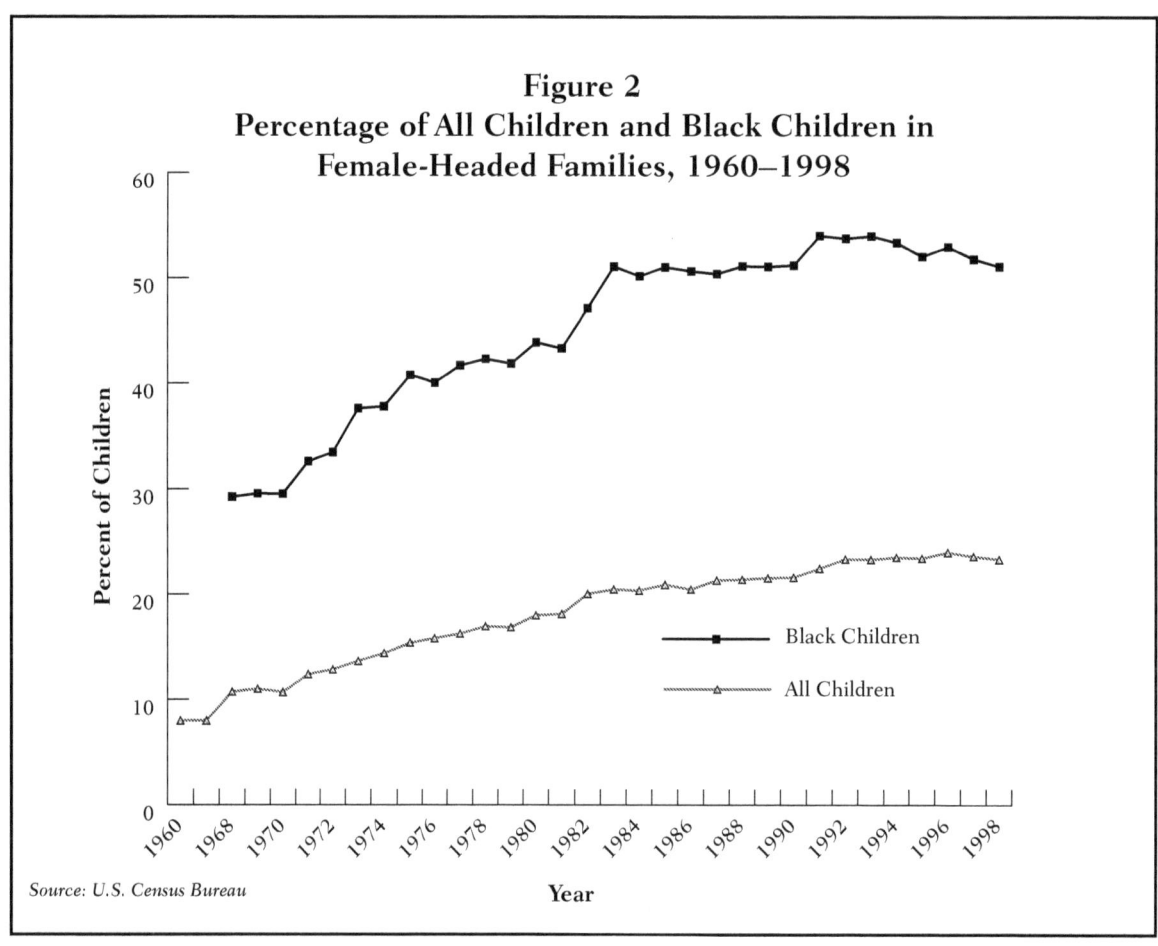

Figure 2
Percentage of All Children and Black Children in Female-Headed Families, 1960–1998
Source: U.S. Census Bureau

recently, the primary means by which federal and state policy tried to achieve this goal was providing welfare benefits.

Beginning in the mid-1960s, federal and state governments developed new programs and spent more money to assist poor, especially female-headed, families. The 1960s saw a substantial decline in poverty among female-headed families from over 50 percent to 38 percent in 1970, perhaps because of both new government welfare programs and a strong economy (figure 3). Progress for black female-headed families was especially notable, with the poverty rate falling from about 70 percent in 1960 to under 60 percent in 1970. In the quarter century between 1970 and 1994, however, little progress was made and the poverty rate for female-headed families was virtually stagnant, averaging nearly 39 percent. But then the rate began to fall again in 1995 and reached 30.4 percent in 1999, the lowest level ever. To a substantial degree, the recent progress against child poverty is associated with the rapid reductions in poverty among female-headed families.

A fourth background fact about poverty uses the broader measure of poverty discussed above to compare relative progress against poverty during the economic recovery of the 1980s with that during the economic recovery of the 1990s. As shown by the bottom line in figure 1, this broader measure consistently shows a much lower level of child poverty than the level shown by the official measure. But an even more interesting insight from the

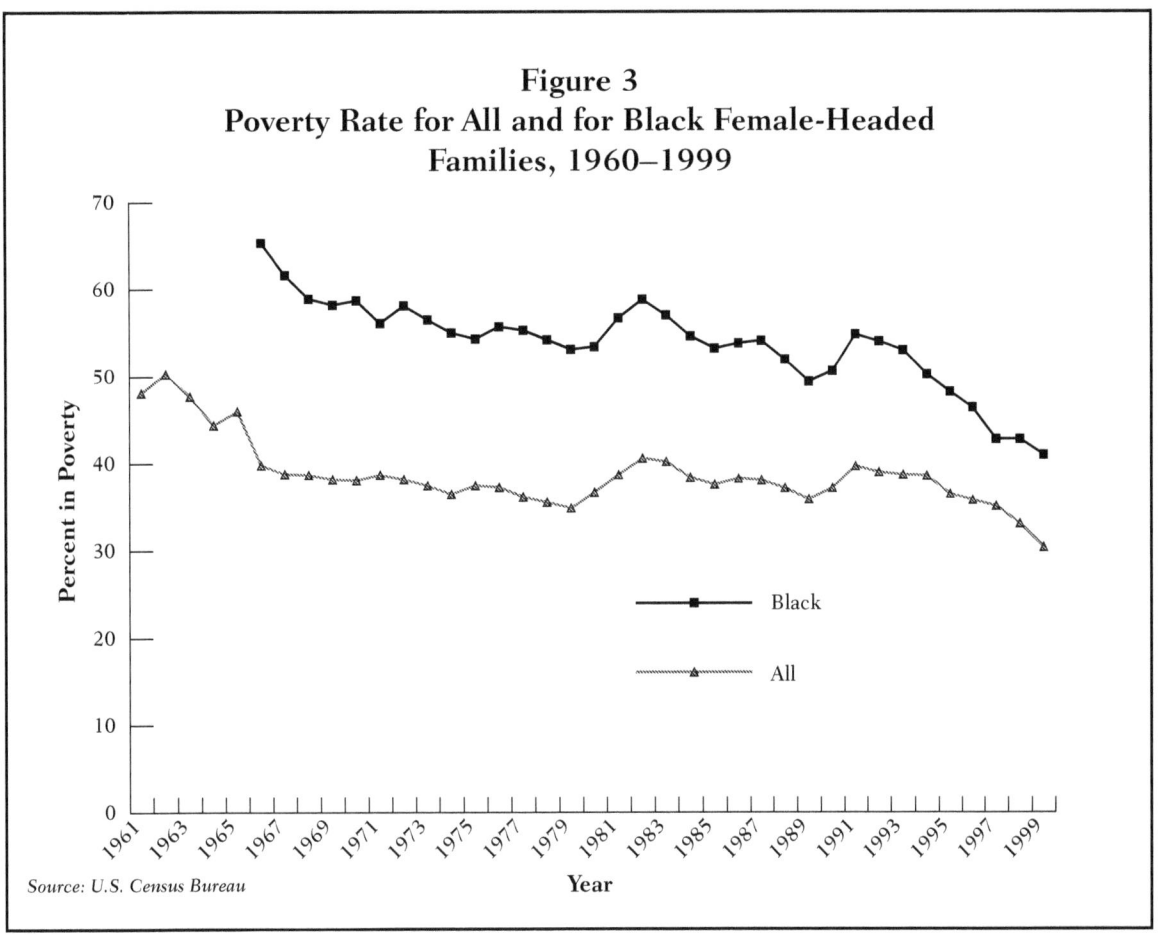

Figure 3
Poverty Rate for All and for Black Female-Headed Families, 1960–1999

Source: U.S. Census Bureau

broader measure is that poverty declined by only 15.5 percent during the expansion of the 1980s as compared with 35.5 percent—more than twice as much—during the expansion of the 1990s. The gains against child poverty during the 1990s under the broader measure are comparable to the impressive gains of the 1960s.

There is wide agreement in the research community both on the accuracy of this basic picture of steep declines in child poverty in recent years and greater declines in the 1990s than at any other time since the 1960s. There is also agreement on the major causes of these trends. Employment among mothers who head families, and especially those who have never married, has increased greatly since the early 1990s and today has reached its highest level ever. Although there are undoubtedly many factors related to this remarkable increase in employment by single mothers, welfare reform, recent increases in the EITC, and a booming economy are the most important factors. Second, real wages of low-income workers increased between 1994 and 1999. Third, the often-modest earnings of these female heads are augmented by public benefits enacted by Congress to help working families. These benefits include the EITC, food stamps, Medicaid, the child tax credit, child care, and other benefits. Many of these programs, along with the minimum wage, were created by Congress or have been expanded by Congress since roughly the mid-1980s. It is the combination of increased earnings from work and the system of public

Table 1
Impact of Government Programs on Children's Poverty Gap

Poverty Gap Based On:	Year					
	1979	1983	1989	1993	1995	1999
Cash Income Before Transfers	33.9	45.0	41.2	51.7	46.1	34.8
Plus Social Insurance	28.5	37.9	35.8	44.7	39.9	29.5
Plus Means-Tested and Non-Cash	12.7	18.8	17.2	21.3	19.9	17.6
Plus Federal Taxes	12.8	19.4	17.2	20.8	17.2	15.2
Total Reduction (%)	62.4	56.9	58.4	59.8	62.7	56.3

Note: Figures in billions of 1999 dollars. Poverty gap is the amount of money that would be required in a given year to bring all children to the poverty line. Federal taxes include the EITC.
Source: Computations performed by the Department of Health and Human Services and the Congressional Budget Office based on Current Population Survey data.

subsidies for low-wage workers, both occurring in a rapidly expanding economy, which constitutes the most parsimonious explanation of the substantial progress against poverty in recent years. Working families do not always receive all the benefits for which they are qualified under these programs, but the programs still play a major role in reducing child poverty.

Not All the Poverty Data Are Favorable

Although there is broad agreement that these facts about poverty reduction are correct, many analysts think the reduction in child poverty should have been much greater given the remarkable increases in employment and earnings by low-income mothers. They emphasize data on the poverty gap (the amount of money required to bring every poor family to the poverty line) to argue that the true picture of poverty is not as bright as the one painted above. Data on the poverty gap are especially important because they take into account not only the frequency of poverty, but also its depth. Figures in the first row of table 1 show that the market economy has become much more effective in reducing the poverty gap in recent years. Thus, based only on earnings and other non-governmental income, the poverty gap reached a whopping $51.7 billion in 1993 and $46.1 billion in 1995, but then fell to $34.8 billion in 1999, lower than in any year since 1979. This positive development is consistent with the employment and poverty data reviewed above. The substantial increase in work by mothers has greatly reduced the poverty gap before any government transfers.

However, given the relatively low level of poverty after market income, one might expect that government programs would have a major impact in reducing the poverty gap even more. Unfortunately, this is clearly not the case. Consider the data for 1993 and 1999: based just on market income (before any government transfers), the poverty gap was $51.7 billion in 1993 but only $34.8 billion in 1999. Adding income from social insurance programs (such as Social Security) reduced the poverty gap in both years, but by $7 billion in 1993 as compared with only $5.3 billion in 1999. Even more revealing, means-tested cash and non-cash programs (government programs that provide benefits to families whose income is less than a given amount) reduced the poverty gap by $23.4 billion in 1993, but only $11.9 billion in 1999. Despite improvement in the role of the EITC in reducing the poverty gap (see fourth row of table 1), on the whole, government means-tested programs were much less effective in reducing poverty after 1993.

If we turn from figures on reducing the poverty gap to simple measures of the income of mother-headed families issued by the Census Bureau, we find this same pattern of increased earnings before taxes and transfers but big offsetting losses of welfare income. The poorest 40 percent of single-mother families increased their earnings by about $2,300 per family on average between 1995 and 1999. But their disposable income increased on average only $292. Once again, increased earnings are not translating into greater disposable income because these families are losing most of their cash welfare income and much of their food stamp income as well. There is some evidence that underreporting of welfare income increased over this period, but more families are also encountering substantial work expenses.

Thus, although there is broad agreement that child poverty has fallen substantially under the 1996 welfare reforms, many liberals are dissatisfied with the degree of poverty reduction. Based on data from the Current Population Survey, Wendell Primus has estimated that in 1999 there were 700,000 families that were worse off than their counterparts before welfare reform. The primary reason is that the substantial earnings increases by mothers have not been matched by the ability of government programs to remove them from poverty as effectively as in the past. In short, liberals believe that government programs are letting these families down.

These findings about family income are especially troubling in light of recent evidence from the Manpower Development Research Corporation (MDRC) that increased income—and not just employment—has a positive impact on children. The MDRC study examined five experiments covering 11 different welfare reform programs and found that increased employment among the parents in a family did not by itself significantly improve their children's lives. It was only in programs in which increased employment was accompanied by increased income that there were positive effects, such as increased school achievement for elementary-aged children. These results lead to the conclusion that boosting income, especially by ensuring that working families actually receive the work support benefits for which they are qualified, is a major issue and should receive careful attention from Congress during reauthorization.

Policies to Reduce Child Poverty

As might be expected, there is little consensus on steps Congress should take during reauthorization to address child poverty. Since welfare reform began in the states, the general pattern of income by poor and low-income mothers has consisted of two very clear trends: increased income from earnings and the EITC, and decreased income from cash welfare and food stamps. Conservatives generally believe this is a desirable pattern because it shows declining dependency by welfare mothers. Most liberals agree that the increases in work and earnings are desirable, but also believe that the decreased income from cash assistance and food stamps is a troubling indicator because those decreases greatly exceed the declines in poverty.

Both liberals and conservatives are likely to agree that it is necessary to maintain substantial work incentive by ensuring financial rewards for work. Most liberals and at least some conservatives are also sympathetic to the view that providing work subsidies to help working families escape poverty is a worthy goal of welfare reform. However, conservatives emphasize the importance of time limits and work requirements. If recipients do not meet work requirements, they must be subject to strong penalties, including benefit termination. Thus, the new welfare system has both increased financial incentives and powerful new limits on welfare. Most conservatives see these limits as the heart of the new reforms and a major reason for declining welfare rolls, increasing work, and declining poverty among female-headed families. Even when the limits on welfare increase the odds of poverty for some individual families, many conservatives are willing to accept this unfortunate result as a cost of maintaining a system of authoritative emphasis on work, especially because most adults who lose benefits and increase their risk of poverty are doing so on the basis of their own choices. Nonetheless, most conservatives are willing to make investments to reduce poverty—as long as the benefits are tied to work and the discipline of work is maintained.

Food Stamp Reforms Because fewer than half the mothers leaving welfare continue to receive the food stamps to which they are entitled, Congress should carefully examine food stamps to ensure that eligible children and parents have every opportunity to receive these entitlement benefits. Several changes in food stamp policy could boost participation among the working poor. The federal quality control system, designed to control fraud and abuse, should be modified because it has led many states to take administrative actions that reduce participation among working families. The food stamp program itself should be simplified. Asset tests, in particular, should be revisited, because current tests make the program hard to administer and make too many low-income working families ineligible. The adequacy of the food stamp benefit structure also warrants reexamination, particularly in light of the cuts in benefits enacted in 1996. Another reform supported by many conservatives would be to provide states with a food stamp block grant and then allow them to solve coordination issues without interference from the federal government.

One of the major reasons low-income working families have not improved their financial situation more than they have is that many of them do not receive the food stamp benefits to which they are entitled. Fixing this food stamp problem would have a major impact on the poverty gap figures reviewed above and would substantially reduce child poverty.

Medicaid Reforms Changes in Medicaid are also needed to address the problem of eligible children not receiving the benefit. Typically, a parent in a family of three loses Medicaid eligibility when her income surpasses 67 percent of the poverty line (about $9,800 for a family of three in 2001). Research has shown that expanding state Medicaid programs to cover parents also increases the number of low-income children who receive coverage, apparently because parents are more likely to apply if they themselves receive coverage. An additional option is to expand funding for the State Children's Health Insurance Program (SCHIP) and allow states to use the funds to extend coverage either through their Medicaid or SCHIP programs to low-income working parents and their children. Some liberals would also allow non-custodial parents who are supporting their children to be covered by Medicaid or SCHIP.

Expansion of Tax Code Benefits There are a host of tax code changes that could help reduce poverty. One change on which there appears to be broad agreement is to reduce the marriage penalty in the EITC by starting the phase-out range (the income at which the benefit begins to fall) at a higher income for married families. Another option is to make the child tax credit partially refundable (meaning that, in a kind of negative income tax, low-income families without tax liability would be given a cash return equal to the amount of the credit). One approach outlined in an earlier brief in this series is to provide a significant credit to parents who work full time by phasing in the credit as earnings increase. The recent tax bill signed into law by President Bush in June 2001 adopted this approach and included modifications of the EITC to reduce the marriage penalty. Another tax policy that favors low-income families would add another tier to the EITC that would provide higher benefits for families with three or more children. All of these policies would significantly reduce child poverty.

Help for Floundering Families According to one study, 44 percent of TANF recipients reported at least two significant obstacles to work, such as low education, no recent work experience, language barriers, mental or physical health problems and disabilities, and lack of transportation or child care. This study also showed that the share of recipients reporting no work activity increased steadily with the number of significant obstacles. Research also indicates that families that fail to meet work requirements (and have their welfare benefit reduced as a result) have greater obstacles to employment than other families receiving welfare. Providing services and accommodations appropriate to the greater needs of such floundering families, while maintaining the emphasis on work, should enable more of these parents to succeed in the workplace. Some states have been able to help many families that initially failed to comply with work requirements, rather than simply sanctioning them and setting them adrift. All states should be encouraged to follow this policy. Congress should also provide incentive funding to states that are willing to design and conduct demonstration programs (including careful evaluations) aimed at developing new ways to help these families work toward self-sufficiency.

The Five-Year Time Limit Most liberals and conservatives disagree sharply on the fairness and efficacy of welfare time limits. Most liberals would favor dropping time limits altogether because they believe work requirements and sanctions are sufficient measures to address the issue of dependency. However, recognizing the low political probability of eliminating time limits, they would expand the share of participating families that states may exempt from time limits—now 20 percent of caseload—to at least 30 percent. Today, the exemption covers many fewer people than was envisioned when the law was passed because current caseload size is much smaller than anyone expected (and 20 percent applied to a smaller number yields fewer exemptions). Many conservatives oppose this reform.

By contrast, another modification of time limits appears to enjoy considerable bipartisan support. In many states, work requirements and earnings disregards encourage welfare recipients to make the transition to work by combining earnings with a wage supplement in the form of cash assistance payments. But working adults who receive these wage supplements risk using up their five years of TANF eligibility because federal law requires states to count every month adults receive assistance from the TANF program as a month of welfare use, even if the adult is working full-time. Thus, liberals would require states to stop the five-year clock whenever parents are working. Many conservatives would support this policy if it were a state option and applied only to parents working at least 25 or 30 hours per week.

Child Support and Supporting Non-Custodial Parents   Non-custodial parents (most of whom are fathers) should be encouraged to provide for their children both financially and emotionally. Child support, for poor families that receive it, is the second largest source of family income—about $2,000 or more than one-quarter of income on average. Since only about 35 percent of poor families receive child support, child poverty could be greatly reduced if a higher percentage of poor families were to receive $2,000 or so in child support payments.

Another way to increase the anti-poverty impact of child support, even without increasing child support payments by fathers, would be to ensure that all child support payments are given to mothers and children. In the case of families that have been on welfare in the past, the government keeps nearly $1 billion per year of the support that fathers pay as reimbursement for welfare costs. Ending this "welfare cost recovery" focus of the current child support system would substantially reduce child poverty. It would also eliminate a major disincentive for fathers to pay child support because it would result in even more of the fathers' payments going to their children.

States could go further and build on the proven success and cost-effectiveness of the EITC by creating similar financial incentives for payment of child support. For example, states could be encouraged to use funds from their welfare block grant or state dollars to supplement low-income fathers' child support payments so that fathers would have additional incentive to pay child support and mothers and children would receive more than the amount paid by fathers. The size of the supplemental payment could vary with the father's income and gradually phase out as income increases.

Congress could increase the capacity of low-income fathers to pay child support by providing employment services and work supports. Many of these fathers do not pay child support regularly because they are unemployed or under-employed and have only a limited income from which to make payments. Welfare reform required and helped more low-income mothers enter the workplace so they could better support their children. Now states should be encouraged or required to help low-income fathers increase their employment and earnings and to address some of their difficulties with the child support system, including child support orders that are high relative to their income and large accumulated child support debts owed to states.

Promoting Marriage   As shown above, living in a female-headed family greatly increases a child's chances of living in poverty, especially if the female-headed family was created by a non-marital birth. Living in a married-couple family, in addition to reducing poverty, confers a host of other benefits on both children and adults. It follows that promoting marriage would be a good way to reduce child poverty and to promote child and adult well-being more generally. Early indications are that the Bush administration and Republicans will emphasize marriage during the reauthorization debate.

According to recent research, about half of the children born outside marriage live with both biological parents at birth. As times goes by, however, these fragile families tend to break apart. Policymakers need to find ways to help these families stay together and move toward marriage. A large-scale study in Minnesota conducted by the Manpower Demonstration Research Corporation produced results that suggest one way to promote marriage. The study found that the combination of work requirements, an income supplement, and work supports such as child care substantially increased the marriage rate. This outcome was caused primarily by the fact that two-parent families that had both the work requirement and work supports were almost 40 percent less likely to separate or divorce than two-parent welfare families that did not have the work requirement and work supports. Because two-parent families participate in food stamps, Medicaid, and cash welfare assistance at a lower rate than single-parent families, even when their incomes are similar, states should eliminate any remaining barriers or eligibility restrictions that apply to two-parent families. The federal government should encourage states to actively seek to serve larger proportions of eligible two-parent families through their welfare programs, thus giving them access to employment services and other work support programs.

Despite the evidence on marriage from the Minnesota experiment and a very small number of similar experiments, little is known about how to promote marriage. Last year, the House (but not the Senate) passed legislation by a vote of 405-18 that would have appropriated about $160 million over five years to fund community-based (including faith-based) projects to help poor and low-income fathers marry the mother of their children, become better parents, and improve their employment and income. Although there are now no programs that have proven they can achieve these goals, the nation is fortunate to have a growing number of programs that are trying. It would be a prudent investment of public funds to stimulate the growth of these programs and to carefully evaluate their effects.

Some liberals have suggested that the federal government should declare its responsibility for poverty reduction and set the goal of reducing child poverty by at least half within 10 years. Most conservatives oppose making poverty reduction an official goal of federal policy.

Making Poverty Reduction Official Federal Policy Prime Minister Tony Blair has recently set the official goal of eliminating child poverty in Great Britain within 20 years. The Blair government plans to achieve this goal, in part, by using the same means the United States is now successfully using to reduce poverty—namely, stressing the importance of work and finding ways to supplement income.

Many liberals in the United States would like to follow Blair's lead and use the reauthorization debate to prompt a discussion about the federal government's responsibility for reducing child poverty, both to make the responsibility more explicit and to set a specific target for child poverty. Some liberals have suggested that the federal government should declare its responsibility for poverty reduction and set the goal of reducing child poverty by at least half within 10 years. Most conservatives oppose making poverty reduction an official goal of federal policy both because they reject the federal responsibility for poverty reduction and because they believe that liberals would use the goal as leverage to increase government spending on social programs that may or may not reduce poverty.

Conclusion

Further reductions in child poverty, like those achieved in recent years, can be realized through a mixture of federal and state policies that encourage individual effort and then subsidize work and perhaps marriage. An aggressive pursuit of some of the policies outlined above would constitute an expanded battle against poverty and would in all likelihood have the effect of reducing child poverty even below the remarkably low levels achieved since enactment of the 1996 reforms.

Additional Reading

Bos, Johannes, and others. 1999. *New Hope for People with Low Incomes: Two-Year Results of a Program to Reduce Poverty and Reform Welfare.* New York: Manpower Demonstration Research Corporation.

Citro, Constance R., and Robert T. Michael, eds. 1995. *Measuring Poverty: A New Approach.* Washington, D.C.: National Academy Press.

Gennetian, Lisa, and Cynthia Miller. 2000. *Reforming Welfare and Rewarding Work: Final Report on the Minnesota Family Investment Program, Volume 2: Effects on Children.* New York: Manpower Demonstration Research Corporation.

Jencks, Christopher. 1993. *Rethinking Social Policy: Race, Poverty, and the Underclass.* HarperTrade.

U.S. Census Bureau. 2000. *Poverty in the United States (Series P60-210).* U.S. Government Printing Office.

PAMELA A. MORRIS AND GREG J. DUNCAN

Which Welfare Reforms are Best for Children?

Executive Summary
This policy brief summarizes the effects on children of 11 welfare experiments aimed at increasing the self-sufficiency of low-income parents. Contrary to the concerns of some, the experiments show that efforts to increase single parents' employment through mandates neither harmed nor benefited elementary school-aged children. On the other hand, welfare policies aimed at both increasing parents' employment and supplementing their income appear to benefit elementary school-aged children, particularly their school achievement. Results for adolescent children suggest that welfare policies may be less positive for older children. Implications of these findings are twofold. First, they suggest that welfare policies can be designed in ways that increase parental employment without affecting elementary school-aged children's development. Second, they suggest that welfare policies can also be designed to improve the well-being of elementary school-aged children if the federal government and states fashion welfare reforms that include financial supplements to earnings.

The Temporary Assistance for Needy Families (TANF) program, the centerpiece of the 1996 federal welfare reform law, imposed time limits and work requirements on welfare recipients in all states. TANF also freed states to formulate a variety of sanction and incentive packages, some of which have been relatively generous. In this policy brief, we summarize results from a synthesis of nearly a dozen welfare experiments to identify which ones are most favorable for children.

How Might Child Well-Being Be Affected by Reforms?

Over the past 30 years, policymakers have struggled to devise a welfare system that would simultaneously protect children and encourage parents' self-sufficiency. Until recently, however, there has been precious little information to inform our understanding of the effects of welfare reform policies on children. Proponents of changes in welfare policy have argued that parental employment benefits children by providing them with family role models who work and are self-sufficient, by introducing a regular schedule into the family routine, and perhaps by increasing the income available to families. But critics have argued that employment may also create stress in the family by reducing parents' opportunities to spend time with their children and interfering with parents' monitoring of their children's activities, particularly in single-parent families. And for families unable or unwilling to comply with work mandates, work requirements may actually increase poverty.

Policymakers have tried a number of approaches to increase employment among single parents on welfare. One of the earliest of these were coercive policies, like those that required single parents to participate in employment-related activities as a condition of receiving their welfare benefits. Even those who believed in the importance of such requirements were concerned about the harmful effects of "forcing" single mothers to participate in activities away from their children, particularly very young children. Accordingly, parents with children under the age of three were exempted from these policies when they were first considered as part of the Family Support Act of 1988.

While these programs were effective in moving parents into employment, the jobs welfare recipients found paid very little, leaving parents only slightly better off financially than when they were receiving welfare benefits. This motivated a second approach to increasing the self-sufficiency of welfare recipients: supplementing the earnings of those who moved from welfare into employment, or in effect, increasing the incentive to go to work. Unlike policies mandating participation, there was little reason to predict any negative effects of these policies on children. The thinking was that the positive effects of increased income might counteract any negative effects of maternal employment, protecting and perhaps even improving the well-being of children.

More recently, policymakers have instituted time limits on the receipt of welfare. Critics of this approach feared that parents would not be able to find work and support their families without the safety net of welfare. The families least able to make the transition into employment could experience pronounced income loss, which ultimately might harm children. As with programs requiring participation, however, proponents of time limits hoped for better role modeling, higher maternal self-esteem, more stable family routines, and higher family incomes as parents relied more on employment than on the welfare system.

The Experimental Evidence

Five large-scale studies collectively examined the effects on children of 11 different employment-based welfare and anti-poverty programs aimed primarily at single-parent families. Although most of the studies were under way by 1996, they were designed to test the effects of many program features that have been implemented by the states since the federal welfare law of 1996 was passed.

These programs tested three basic approaches that are currently being used in many state welfare policies to increase the self-sufficiency of welfare recipients: earnings supplements, mandatory employment services, and time limits. Four of the programs offered generous earnings supplements designed to make work more financially rewarding by providing families with monthly cash supplements or by increasing the amount welfare recipients could keep when they went to work. Six of the programs provided only mandatory employment services—such as education, training, or immediate job searches—in which parents were required to participate to be eligible for cash welfare benefits. One of the programs put time limits on families' eligibility for welfare benefits, restricting

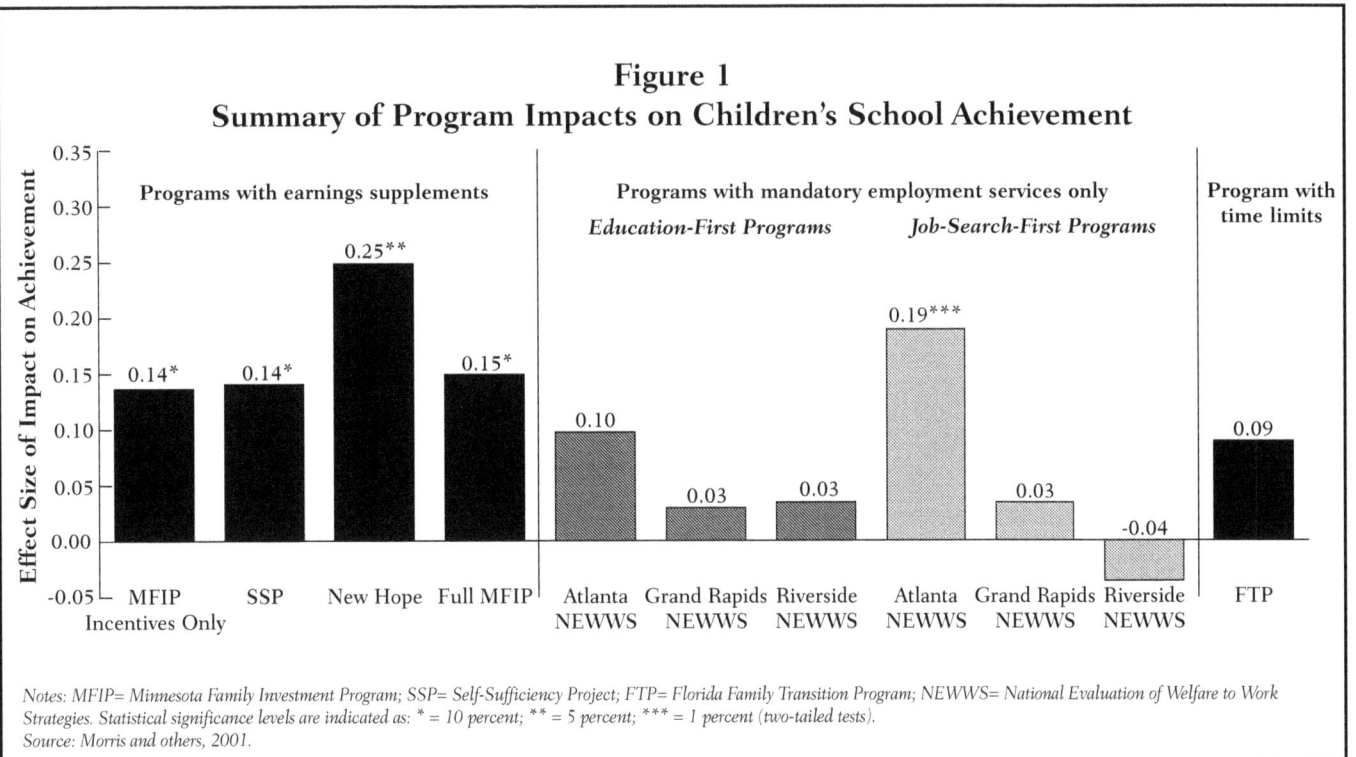

Figure 1
Summary of Program Impacts on Children's School Achievement

Notes: MFIP= Minnesota Family Investment Program; SSP= Self-Sufficiency Project; FTP= Florida Family Transition Program; NEWWS= National Evaluation of Welfare to Work Strategies. Statistical significance levels are indicated as: * = 10 percent; ** = 5 percent; *** = 1 percent (two-tailed tests).
Source: Morris and others, 2001.

eligibility to a certain number of months in a specified period.

A great virtue of these experiments is that participants were randomly assigned to a "program group" that received the welfare reform package or to a "control group" that continued to live under the old Aid to Families with Dependent Children (AFDC) rules. Random assignment provides a strong basis for assessing causal impacts of the reform packages relative to the old AFDC system.

Relying on evidence from experiments has its limitations, however. The treatments in these experiments represent neither the full range of TANF programs implemented by states nor of the macroeconomic conditions—both good and bad—that states currently face or are likely to face in the next decade. Furthermore, because the experiments followed families for only a short period of time, they probably detected few of the longer-term changes in norms and expectations regarding work and childbearing that might accompany these programs.

The Effects on Elementary School-Age Children

In order to understand how various welfare policies may affect children, we classified programs into the three categories described earlier (mandatory employment services, earnings supplements, and time limits) and then examined the impact on children for each category.

In figure 1, we focus on program impacts on school achievement outcomes for younger children, most of whom were preschool and elementary school-aged when these programs started, and in elementary school when the achievement outcomes were assessed. Mothers reported most of the measures, and others were drawn from standardized tests and surveys conducted with both teachers and the children themselves.

Figure 1 shows program impacts—the standardized differences in the school achievement of the children in both program and control groups—for each category of program. Each bar represents the effect of a single program, and bars above the horizontal axis indicate that the program had a positive effect on that outcome. Bars below the axis indicate that the program had a negative effect on that outcome. Stars on top of the bars indicate program effects that are large enough to be statistically significant.

As figure 1 shows, programs that offer the most generous earnings supplements appear to have more consistently positive impacts on children than programs without these supplements. In all four of the programs that provided earnings supplements, children in the program group had significantly higher academic achievement than children in the control group. (These impacts are about the same size as moving the children from the 25th percentile to the 30th percentile on a standardized IQ test.) In comparison, just one of the six programs that provided only mandatory employment services had such positive effects and the single time-limited program had no effect on children's school achievement.

Although less consistently than for the achievement outcomes, programs with earnings supplements appear to benefit children's behavior and health outcomes as well, with beneficial impacts found for some of the programs with earnings supplements (not shown in figure 1). By comparison, programs with mandatory employment services or time limits had few effects across children's behavioral and health outcomes, and the effects that were found were sometimes positive and sometimes negative.

While there are several negative effects on children's behavior and health outcomes across all three types of programs, the positive and neutral effects are far more common than the negative effects, suggesting little evidence

The positive effects of the earnings supplement programs show that certain welfare policies, when designed in ways that increase both parents' employment and income, can benefit children.

of the harm that critics feared. Concerns that the development of young children, especially elementary school-aged children, might be compromised by the stresses and disruptions wrought by welfare-to-work transitions receive virtually no support from these studies. This is the case even in the single study of Florida's time-limited welfare program. Even so, it is important to recognize that in Florida, welfare officials bundled time limits together with intensive case management, a practice that many states do not follow. Moreover, the findings occurred only shortly after recipients began reaching the time limit, so we do not know what the long-term effects of such a program may be. Finally, there was little evidence of income loss from this program; a time-limited program that results in a loss of income to families may have very different effects on children.

At the same time, the positive effects of the earnings supplement programs show that certain welfare policies, when designed in ways that increase both parents' employment and income, can benefit children. These programs benefited children's school achievement, and sometimes benefited their behavior and health as well.

Children in Generous Programs Remain at Considerable Risk

The positive evidence of favorable program impacts on elementary school-aged children in several studies does not indicate that all the children lucky enough to be in the most generous programs are now doing well. Among children in the four earnings supplement programs, a little more than 10 percent of children had repeated a grade, and 15-20 percent had received special education in the two- to four-year period of these studies. A much smaller proportion of children in this age group had a reportedly "high" level of behavioral and emotional problems, however. One-third of the children scored in the bottom 25th percentile on a nationally standardized test of language skills, and almost 40 percent of children had long-term health problems, although most of the parents reported that their children were in very good or excellent health. Thus, even in families offered generous work supports, there were many children with school or health-related problems.

What Changes in Family Functioning May Account for Changes in Child Well-Being?

We look now at the evidence of which components of family functioning appeared to have caused the beneficial changes in child well-being in the earnings supplement programs. While we know that these programs caused the effects on children, the design of the experiments does not allow us to know exactly how these effects occurred, and therefore the conclusions here are somewhat tenuous.

First, we know that all of the generous programs increased both employment and income. What is not clear, however, is whether it was the increased income alone or the combination of increased income and employment that brought about the benefits to children.

In three of the four earnings supplement programs, mothers in the program groups were more likely to enroll their children in formal child care programs or after-school programs and extracurricular activities than were mothers in the control group. Thus, evidence from three of the programs suggests that structured programs outside of the home may be one of the pathways by which the beneficial effects to children occurred.

Surprisingly, effects on parenting behavior (including parental warmth, control, and cognitive stimulation) were remarkably limited. Also, contrary to the hopes of many welfare reformers, work preparation or employment itself did little to improve the mothers' mental health, as there were only scattered impacts on depression and stress across these programs. A likely reason for the general lack of improvement in parenting and mental health is the difficulties inherent in combining child rearing with employment in the context of economic hardship.

These findings point to parents putting their children in formal child care or after-school activities as one important way earnings supplement programs may have affected the well-being of children. However, one study puts this conclusion into question because it found that the benefits to children and increases in formal child care were

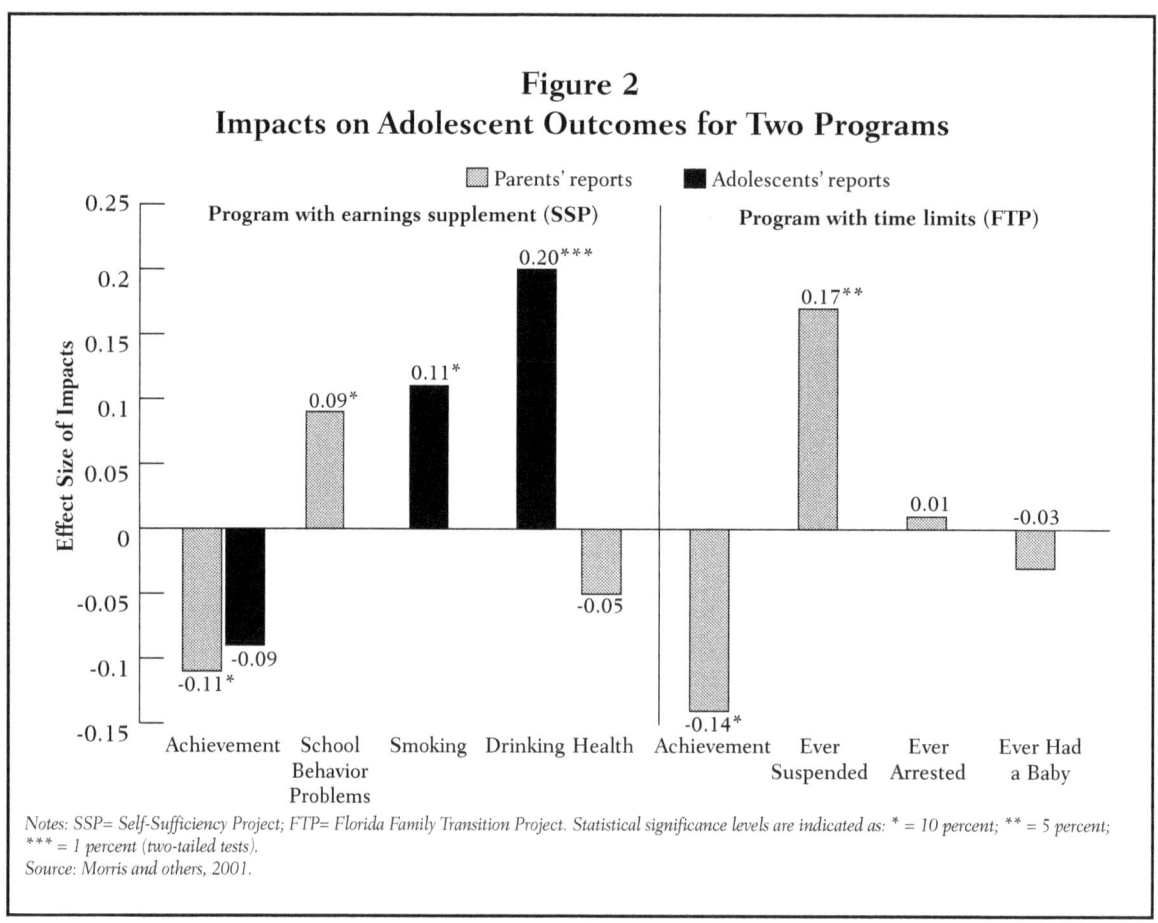

caused by different policy dimensions (the former by earnings supplements, the latter by mandatory employment services). If the benefits to children were a result of increases in formal child care, we would have expected both to be caused by the same policy approach. Further research is currently being conducted to help us better understand the pathways to improved child well-being in these programs.

Impacts on Very Young Children and Adolescents

How do these programs affect infants and toddlers? Only one of the earnings supplement programs assessed impacts on very young children (in this case children aged 0-2) at the time of program enrollment. In contrast to the favorable picture for elementary school children, no impacts were found on young children's achievement and behavior. It is unwise to generalize from a single source of data, although it seems plausible that the positive effects of increased income may have canceled out any negative effects of full-time maternal employment in this study. Some non-experimental studies have shown that very young children may be more vulnerable to the ill effects of an employment-induced separation from their mothers than older children, although the evidence here is limited. Increases in income as a result of welfare reforms are probably more important for very young children given their greater sensitivity to spells of economic deprivation and the significance of the early years for healthy development later on.

As we turn from young children to adolescents, the pattern of impacts changes for the worse. Two of the programs (one with earnings supplements and one with time limits) included assessments of adolescent well-being (see figure 2). The earnings supplement program showed that adolescent self-reports of drinking and smoking, as well as parental reports of school achievement and problem behavior, were significantly worse in the program group relative to the control group. Notably, not as many teens participated in the surveys as one would like to be truly confident in the findings. In the time-limited welfare program, parents in the program group reported lower levels of achievement and more suspensions than did parents in the control group, but no differences were found in adolescents' fertility or involvement with police. Thus, there is some experimental evidence indicating that adolescents may be more at risk with welfare reforms that increase the self-sufficiency of welfare recipients. However, more than two studies are needed before more definitive conclusions can be made about the effects of welfare policies on adolescent children.

What Do These Findings Mean for Policy?

A key finding from the experiments is that impacts on child achievement and behavior were consistently more positive in programs that provided financial and in-kind supports (earnings supplements) for work than in those that did not. The packages of work supports were quite diverse, ranging from generous earnings supplements provided alone to more comprehensive packages of earnings supplements, child care assistance, health insurance, and even temporary community service jobs.

Although more costly than the "work first" approach taken by the programs with mandatory employment services only, two of the programs with earnings supplements had costs within the range of some of the actual welfare reform packages implemented by states in response to the 1996 legislation. Relative to the AFDC program, the average yearly cost for a participant in a program with mandatory employment services ranged from savings of $255 to a cost of $1,595. The annual costs per participant of the earnings supplement programs ranged from $2,000 to $4,000 above the costs of the AFDC program.

These findings suggest that policymakers face a choice when deciding which welfare reforms are best for children. They can increase parental self-sufficiency, provide few benefits to children, and save government money with mandatory employment service programs. Or they can increase parental employment, raise family income, provide benefits to children, and increase government spending with earnings supplement programs. Clearly, welfare policies can affect and improve the well-being of children if states or the federal government choose to spend additional money on work supports in the context of their welfare programs.

Potential ways to expand federal policies to include work supports are providing additional funds for the child care block grant, expanding health insurance coverage and participation for children, expanding participation in the food stamp program, and expanding the Earned Income Tax Credit (EITC). Notably, in three of the programs with earnings supplements, benefits to children were found even though the EITC was available for both the program and control groups. This implies that even if the EITC does have some similar positive effects on children, there is room for further improvement for families through additional work supports or through expansion of existing programs. For states that wish to increase their work supports, the challenge is how to use TANF and other dollars to fashion support packages that best meet the needs and concerns of local populations, labor markets, and policymakers.

Another policy implication of these findings is that states should be aware of the potentially differential consequences of their policies among children of different ages. Many critics have suspected that time limits, sanctions, and categorical restrictions may be more detrimental to families with very young children, as may participation requirements for mothers in the first months of their children's lives. But the findings summarized here are the first to suggest that adolescents may experience negative effects when parents increase their self-sufficiency. If the findings hold when additional welfare reform efforts are examined, states may want to consider after-school and community-based programs for adolescents to help support working parents' efforts to keep their children focused on school achievement and positive behavior.

With the reauthorization of TANF in 2002, policymakers will face some other difficult questions. One key question will be whether to maintain the same amount of money in the block grants that states received in 1996, given the sharp decline in welfare caseloads. For states with an interest in supporting working families, the research here suggests that those funds could be effectively used to supplement the earnings of low-income workers, increase employment among welfare recipients, and give children a better start in school.

Additional Reading

Bloom, Dan, and others. 2000. *The Family Transition Program: Final Report on Florida's Initial Time-Limited Welfare Program.* New York: Manpower Demonstration Research Corporation.

Bos, Johannes, and others. 1999. *New Hope for People with Low Incomes: Two-Year Results of a Program to Reduce Poverty and Reform Welfare.* New York: Manpower Demonstration Research Corporation.

Gennetian, Lisa, and Cynthia Miller. 2000. *Reforming Welfare and Rewarding Work: Final Report on the Minnesota Family Investment Program: Volume 2: Effects on Children.* New York: Manpower Demonstration Research Corporation.

McGroder, Sharon, and others. 2000. *National Evaluation of Welfare-to-Work Strategies: Impacts on Young Children and Their Families Two Years After Enrollment: Findings from the Child Outcomes Study.* Washington, D.C.: U.S. Department of Health and Human Services and U.S. Department of Education.

Morris, Pamela, and Charles Michalopoulos. 2000. *The Self-Sufficiency Project at 36 Months: Effects on Children of a Program That Increased Parental Employment and Income.* Ottawa: Social Research and Demonstration Corporation.

Morris, Pamela, and others. 2001. *How Welfare and Work Policies Affect Children: A Synthesis of Research.* New York: Manpower Demonstration Research Corporation.

9

ROBERT A. MOFFITT

From Welfare to Work: What the Evidence Shows

Executive Summary
The great transformation of the welfare system set off by state reforms in the early 1990s and by the 1996 federal welfare reform law had as its primary goal the encouragement of work by mothers on welfare. This goal has been achieved to a much greater degree than anyone expected. Employment rates among single mothers have increased dramatically; former welfare recipients have experienced average employment levels of around 60 to 75 percent, far higher than anticipated and much greater than their work levels while on welfare. While a strong economy and expanded work incentive programs (especially in the tax code) have helped fuel these employment gains, the welfare reforms of the 1990s have produced significant progress in meeting the primary goal of encouraging mothers on welfare to work. However, there remain two sources of concern. While incomes of single mothers as a whole have risen, incomes of women leaving welfare are only slightly above what they were when the women were on welfare. Additional ways of increasing the incomes of such women need to be found. Second, there is a significant group of very disadvantaged women, many no longer on welfare, who have major difficulties with employment because of poor job skills, poor physical and mental health, and other problems. Special policies also need to be directed toward this group.

The American public has made clear that work by welfare recipients is a defining goal of state and federal welfare laws, the pursuit of which deserves the highest priority in social welfare policy. One of the four goals listed by Congress in the 1996 welfare reform legislation was to encourage job preparation and work. Work among welfare recipients is widely regarded as part of the social contract—a quid pro quo for the provision of income support—as well as a source of self-esteem and self-reliance among single mothers. This in turn is thought to increase the mothers' chances for long-term economic improvement for themselves and their children.

Now that five years have passed since the 1996 reforms were enacted, the evidence shows that while much success has been attained, there are remaining concerns that Congress should debate during reauthorization. This policy brief reviews both the evidence and the concerns.

Employment Among Single Mothers Has Increased

The overriding single piece of evidence showing that progress has been made on the agenda of helping mothers on welfare work is

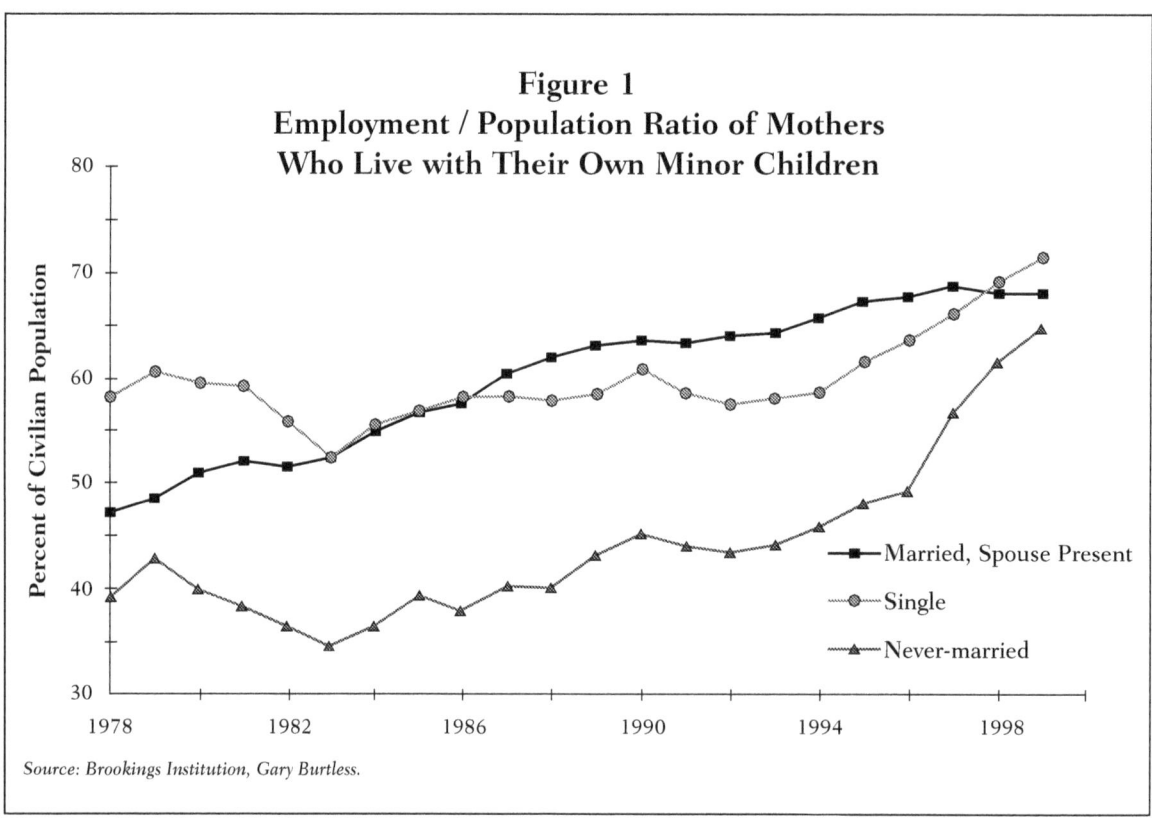

Figure 1
Employment / Population Ratio of Mothers Who Live with Their Own Minor Children

Source: Brookings Institution, Gary Burtless.

the dramatic increase in employment rates among single mothers in the last decade. Employment rates among single mothers, the group most affected by welfare reform, have been slowly increasing for over 15 years, but have jumped markedly since 1994 (figure 1). Employment rates rose from 60 percent in 1994 to 72 percent in 1999, a very large increase by historical standards. Among single mothers who have never been married (the group with the lowest levels of education and some of the highest rates of welfare receipt) employment rates rose even more, from 47 percent to 65 percent over the same period.

Not all of this increase can be attributed to welfare reform. Part of the increase has been the result of the robust economy and the longest and strongest peacetime expansion in the last 50 years. Until the recent economic slowdown, employers, desperate for workers, dipped deep into the pool of single mothers and other disadvantaged individuals.

Another factor encouraging employment is the expansion of the Earned Income Tax Credit (EITC), which provides major financial incentives to work. Given the boost in income the EITC provides (up to $4,000 per year for families with two children), many women have been encouraged to try and "make it" off welfare. Other supports for women leaving welfare, as well as for those never on welfare, include increased child care subsidies, food stamps, and health benefits through Medicaid and the State Children's Health Insurance programs. Nevertheless, despite these other factors, there is no question that welfare reform has played a significant role in increasing employment among single mothers. Even research studies that have attempted to parcel out the relative contributions of different forces on employment rates support this conclusion.

Most Women Leaving Welfare Find Work

These overall trends beg for more details on how individual families have fared in the wake of welfare reform. The largest body of evidence comes from data on women who were on welfare but have left, primarily those who left the Aid to Families with Dependent Children (AFDC) program before 1996 or those who left its successor, the Temporary Assistance for Needy Families (TANF) program, after 1996. Most states have conducted such studies. A recent review of these studies conducted by the U.S. Department of Health and Human Services indicates that the employment rate among welfare leavers is approximately 60 percent just after exiting welfare. Moreover, about three-quarters of welfare leavers worked at some point in the first year after leaving the rolls. When welfare leavers work, they generally work full-time. Their hourly wages range from $7–$8 per hour, somewhat above the minimum wage. Those who work earn about $3,000 per quarter, or $12,000 annually. However, the annual wage is an overestimate because most leavers do not work for four quarters in a row, only a little over one-third do, signaling a potential problem with employment retention and stability.

These employment rates are considerably higher than critics of the 1996 reforms feared; some predicted that families would be made destitute and homeless following the reforms, or that there would not be enough jobs for women leaving welfare. At least on average, this has not occurred. The fact that 60 to 75 percent of welfare leavers found employment is especially remarkable given that, over the decade prior to reform, the employment rate of mothers while they were on AFDC was never more than 9 percent. Equally notable in this light is the fact that almost 30 percent of women currently on the rolls are now employed.

The 60 percent employment rate of welfare leavers is not much different than that of women who left the AFDC program prior to welfare reform. Employment rates over the period 1984 to 1996 ranged from 48 percent to 65 percent, varying by the state of the economy and the area of the country. These rates are similar to the rates following reform. This is surprising because many more women have left the welfare rolls in this era of reform than in any prior period, and many of those who left recently are more disadvantaged than women who left the rolls in prior periods. The fact that employment rates of leavers have not been lower than those experienced by past leavers further supports the strong effect of welfare reform.

In addition, random assignment evaluations of pre-1996 reform programs which had time limits and work requirements and were reasonably close in character to the post-1996 programs put in place by the states also show positive effects on employment and earnings. The employment and earnings gains in these demonstration programs are the average gains for both women who have left welfare as well as women who stayed on the rolls, and they therefore represent a more comprehensive measure than studies of leavers alone.

Two of the most important reforms in the 1996 legislation were the imposition of federal time limits on the length of welfare receipt, and the use of more stringent sanctions for not complying with work requirements and other rules. A natural question is how women who hit a time limit or were sanctioned have fared relative to women who left welfare voluntarily or because of different inducements. Time limits have had relatively little effect so far because most states have retained the five-year federal maximum and, as a result large numbers of recipients did not begin to hit time limits until the late fall of 2001. Some states do have shorter time limits than five years, but they have exempted large numbers of families from those limits and have granted large numbers of extensions. These exemptions and extensions have typically been granted to the most disadvantaged families, so that it is primarily those with significant employment and earnings (while on TANF) who hit the time limit in these few states. As a consequence, in the one or two states where significant numbers of families have left welfare because they hit a time limit, post-welfare employment rates of those leavers are quite high (e.g., 80 percent). But in other states where fewer families have hit the limit, employment rates of time-limited leavers are no different than those of other leavers.

More is known about sanctions because they have been in force for most of the time since 1996 and in some cases even before then. Many more women have been sanctioned than have been hit by time limits. The studies of women who have left welfare because of sanctions show that such women are less likely to have jobs than other welfare leavers. This appears to be because sanctioned welfare recipients tend to be less educated, have lower job skills, and are in poorer health than other welfare recipients. Unfortunately, these findings suggest that sanctioning may often occur among women who are the most disadvantaged and have the greatest number of difficulties with work.

Women Leaving Welfare Have Low Incomes

Despite the high employment levels of women who have left welfare, their incomes increase only modestly after leaving the rolls. About half experience an increase in income immediately after leaving, with the other half experiencing a decline. After a year or two off the rolls, earnings gains slightly exceed the losses in TANF benefits. When EITC income is added in, the gains are slightly higher.

Despite the high employment levels of women who have left welfare, their incomes increase only modestly after leaving the rolls.

However, the major change in income after leaving welfare comes from increased income from other family members (very little from boyfriends and other unrelated persons, however). Such income is a larger component of total household income than either the earnings of the leaver herself or TANF and food stamp income. As a result of additional income from this source, total household income grows by about 20 percent after two years off the rolls. Income from other household members is thus a key ingredient to sustaining the incomes of women leaving welfare.

Random assignment demonstrations measuring the effects of several pre-1996 state welfare reform plans provide additional evidence of the impact of welfare reform on income. For states whose plans most resembled those implemented after 1996 (those with work requirements and time limits), income was essentially unchanged by the reforms three years after they began. However, neither the EITC nor the income of other family members was included in the income calculation, so it is probable that some income gains were in fact attained, possibly in the same 20 percent range found in other studies.

These demonstrations also show that, in the absence of earnings disregards, income is not likely to greatly increase for several reasons. One is that many women work part-time and thus have quite modest earnings, not enough to make up for lost benefits. Another is that many women are sanctioned off the rolls, when they have little or zero earnings, yet they still lose benefits. A third is that many states reduce TANF benefits dollar-for-dollar when earnings increase (at least if women stay on the welfare rolls), thereby canceling out any gain in income that might result from increased work.

The EITC has played a significant role in keeping household income from declining as much as it could. However, many women off welfare do not receive the EITC if they have not been able to achieve steady employment. Others who are working do not have enough earnings to achieve the maximum EITC payment, and others do not apply for it in their tax returns. Thus, the EITC has assisted some families but not all, and families with income declines tend to be those that have benefited from it the least.

Studies also show welfare leavers experience declines in their receipt of food stamps and Medicaid. It appears that this decline is not a result of loss of eligibility so much as it is a result of lower participation despite eligibility, possibly because access to offices that determine eligibility is difficult to sustain. For whatever reason, low rates of food stamp and Medicaid receipt are a significant problem among TANF leavers.

Women who have left welfare are not the only single mothers whose income has changed since the reform legislation of 1996. Low-income single mothers who choose to stay off welfare to try to make it in the labor market have had increases in income as well. The fact that the incomes of low-income single mothers as a whole have risen at the same time that incomes of welfare leavers have been relatively stagnant suggests that the incomes of such "non-entrants" have indeed risen, probably because they work more hours.

Some Leavers Are Not Doing Well

The flip side of the high employment rates of 60 to 75 percent of women who have left welfare is that 25 to 40 percent of those women are not working. Indeed, some studies have indicated that as many as 18 percent of leavers in some areas did not work at all for a full year after leaving the rolls.

This group is of some concern. Because they have lost their welfare benefits and do not have earnings, they have lower incomes than non-working women who are still on TANF. A fraction of these non-working leavers have a relative, spouse, or partner who brings some income to the household, and others supplement their income with benefits from other government programs.

One of the most common program benefits received by this group are disability benefits from either the Supplemental Security Income program or the Social Security Disability Insurance program for either the mother or her children. That many families leaving welfare receive disability benefits is a reflection of the high prevalence of health problems and disabilities that hinder work. Nevertheless, even with income from other family members and from government programs, non-working leavers have considerably lower income than they did when they were on welfare. Consequently, leaving welfare has been particularly disadvantageous for these women and their children.

The existence of such a group shows that there is great diversity in the experiences of welfare leavers, for while some have fared reasonably well, others have not. Not surprisingly, employment rates of less educated

---

There are two major problems that deserve attention. One is the broad issue of how to improve the income gains of women who have left welfare for work. The second is how to develop policies to assist families that have special difficulties in establishing employment.

---

leavers are considerably below those of more educated leavers, and poverty rates are higher, as are the employment and poverty rates of those leavers who are in relatively poor health.

Random assignment studies of time-limited pre-1996 welfare reforms show some evidence that welfare reform results in a larger fraction of families ending up with below average incomes. The presence of a group of women who have left welfare and are not doing well is consistent with broader trend studies indicating that the poorest single mother families have experienced declines in income in the post-reform period.

The Number of Women Going onto Welfare Has Declined

As noted previously, women who were once welfare recipients and have left welfare are not the only ones affected by welfare reform. Some women have chosen not to apply for welfare subsequent to reform, possibly discouraged by the work requirements and other new mandates that come with being on welfare, and possibly encouraged enough by the good economy to stay off welfare and work. Other women have applied for welfare but have been rejected.

Over twenty states have formal diversion programs, which encourage women through financial inducements and other means to not come onto the welfare rolls. More than thirty states have either diversion policies or have imposed work requirements that must be fulfilled prior to eligibility for benefits.

The decline in the number of women joining the TANF rolls has been very large in the post-reform era. In some states, the decline in entry onto welfare has been more important quantitatively than the increase in exit rates in accounting for the caseload decline. This finding casts a different light on the caseload decline and demonstrates that there is an important group of women other than leavers whose employment, earnings, and income should be of interest to policymakers.

Unfortunately, no studies have been conducted to date that examine this group, so their employment status and well-being remains unknown. However, the studies which have showed large post-reform increases in employment rates of single mothers as a whole, and which necessarily combine both those who have left welfare and those who have not come onto the rolls, strongly suggest that employment rates of women who choose not to enter the welfare system are high.

Issues for Reauthorization

The overall picture of employment among single mothers in the wake of welfare reform is a favorable one, indicating widespread work among former welfare recipients and among low-income single mothers as a whole. With this accomplishment a given, reauthorization should focus on policies that address the remaining problems.

There are two major problems that deserve attention. One is the broad issue of how to improve the income gains of women who have left welfare for work. Income gains are too modest for too many families, with earnings gains insufficient to counter reductions in benefits and with poverty rates—though lower than for families staying on welfare—remaining high. Aside from the need to increase the income of former welfare families for its own sake, income gains from leaving welfare will be necessary, in the long term, to provide financial incentives for women to leave welfare for work. While sanctions and work requirements can continue to be used to push women into the work force, they will operate much more successfully if the financial incentives operate in the same direction.

More supports for working families in the form of increased child care assistance, assistance with transportation, and other work-related services can substantially increase the incentive to work. Moving more women from part-time work to full-time work would be another direction to pursue, but this approach has limits if adequate child care and transportation are not available. Providing stronger financial incentives with state EITCs and enhanced TANF earnings disregards are also possible, although the latter policy will keep families on the TANF rolls longer. Major improvements beyond this are likely to come only from increased earnings. This calls for expanding policies aimed at job retention, skills enhancement, and job training. States are only now beginning to think about these types of policies and have a long way to go before such policies are widespread and have a major impact on incomes.

The second major issue is how to develop policies to assist families that have special difficulties in establishing employment. These families are sometimes called the "hard-to-serve," although that term begs the question of what types of services are needed. One important result of the studies reviewed here is that many of these families are found not to be on TANF or on any other major welfare program. Rather, they are already on their own, off welfare, and have very low incomes. Any set of services that is directed mainly to TANF recipients alone on the presumption that the most disadvantaged families are still on the rolls, will not reach these families. This fact requires a major expansion of assistance to the non-TANF population. Some states, notably Wisconsin, have made such an expansion a major goal, but most states are far from having penetrated this population deeply with services and programs.

Most observers already recognize that designing successful policies to move non-employed families into stable work will be very difficult, given the severity of the difficulties these families face. These difficulties include low levels of education and job skills, significant health problems (both physical and mental), substance abuse, and domestic violence. The multiple interlocking and overlapping sets of problems faced by these families should give pause to any optimistic view that easy solutions will lead to steady employment and significant earnings gains.

Given these difficulties, a more open discussion is needed of assistance policies for floundering families who are unlikely to achieve significant employment gains in the short-term or even medium-term. Long-term cash assistance accompanied by job training, health insurance, and better programs aimed at reducing substance abuse, mental health problems, and domestic violence need to be directed toward this population independent of employment considerations. While the strong work incentives that are currently in place should remain, thereby continuing to provide financial incentives to families to work at higher levels than they currently do, simply strengthening work supports and further increasing work incentives will not, by themselves, provide much help to these families.

Virtually all states have already taken steps to develop programs for these families. States have started to identify families with serious problems that are barriers to work, and then design an appropriate set of services for them. However, the states must further develop these programs before a successful set of identification procedures and an adequate service delivery structure is established. When coordinating treatment for these families with employment programs, states can use their ability to exercise exemptions from work requirements and time limits as a short-term strategy. But more active and aggressive policies should be implemented to address the needs of these floundering families, both on and off TANF.

Additional Reading

Acs, Gregory, and Pamela Loprest. 2001. *Initial Synthesis Report of the Findings from ASPE's "Leavers" Grants.* Washington, D.C.: Urban Institute.

Bavier, Richard. 2001. "Welfare Reform Data from the Survey of Income and Program Participation." *Monthly Labor Review* 124 (July): 13-24.

Bloom, Dan, and Charles Michalopoulos. 2001. *How Welfare and Work Policies Affect Employment and Income: A Synthesis of Research.* New York: Manpower Demonstration Research Corporation.

Brauner, Sarah, and Pamela Loprest. 1999. *Where Are They Now? What States' Studies of People Who Left Welfare Tell Us* (Paper Series A, No. A-32). Washington, D.C.: Urban Institute.

Loprest, Pamela. 1999. *Families Who Left Welfare: Who Are They and How Are They Doing?* (ANF Discussion Paper). Washington, D.C.: Urban Institute.

Pavetti, LaDonna, and Dan Bloom. 2001. "Sanctions and Time Limits: State Policies, Their Implementation, and Outcomes for Families." In *The New World of Welfare,* edited by Rebecca M. Blank and Ron Haskins. Washington, D.C.: Brookings.

PART IV

TANF FUNDING AND THE ECONOMY

10

R. KENT WEAVER

The Structure of the TANF Block Grant

Executive Summary
One of the major changes in the sweeping welfare reform legislation of 1996 was replacing the federal guarantee of cash welfare to all qualified families—the Aid to Families with Dependent Children (AFDC) program—with a block grant that provides a fixed and guaranteed level of funding to states. The new block grant, called Temporary Assistance for Needy Families (TANF), gives states great flexibility in spending their funds as long as they are pursuing one or more of the goals of the block grant. Several questions about the block grant need to be addressed during the debate on TANF reauthorization, which must be completed by October 1, 2002. These include the size of the block grant and the formula for allocating it among states, whether additional funds should be provided to states during recessions, and whether the TANF performance bonuses should be revised or dropped. This brief outlines several policy options for addressing these issues.

The 1996 welfare reform legislation replaced the Aid to Families with Dependent Children (AFDC) program with a new Temporary Assistance for Needy Families (TANF) block grant that is very different than its predecessor. In the old AFDC program, funds were used almost entirely to provide and administer cash assistance to low-income—usually single-parent—families. The federal government matched state expenditures, with poorer states' expenditures matched at a much higher rate than wealthier states. AFDC caseloads tended to go up during recessions and down during good economic times (although the linkage was not nearly as close as with the Food Stamp Program), so federal expenditures on TANF also showed some cyclical variation.

In the new TANF program, by contrast, federal expenditures are, with a few modest exceptions, fixed at $16.5 billion dollars a year for fiscal years 1997-2002. Thus they neither adjust for inflation nor rise and fall with economic cycles or the size of the caseload. Individual states' share of the total block grant is based on the amount they received from the AFDC program in the mid-1990s (states could choose the most advantageous from three alternative base periods). And unlike AFDC, in which federal expenditures matched state expenditures at a fixed rate, under TANF states are required to spend 75 percent of the amount they spent from state funds in 1994 (80 percent if they fail to meet federal work participation rate targets).

During the reauthorization debate, Congress and the administration will face six major issues concerning TANF block grants. First, how much money should the federal government spend on TANF? Second, should an inflation adjustment be built into the TANF block grant to keep its real value from being eroded over time? Third, should the current allocation of TANF funds across states—which gives much more money per low-income child to wealthier states than to poor ones—be revised? Fourth, should the TANF block grant include a counter-cyclical element so that states get more money during recessions, when need rises and state budgets are extremely tight? Fifth, should the "maintenance of effort" requirement that states spend at least 75 percent of the amount spent in 1994 be revised? Finally, should the structure of the performance bonuses associated with the TANF block grant be revised?

This debate will occur in an environment of tight fiscal constraints. The rosy budget forecasts of recent years have changed dramatically. Because of the recession, the tax cut of 2001, and increased spending on defense and homeland security, the federal government now faces a future of red ink. The states are facing large budget shortfalls themselves, and almost all of them have constitutional requirements to balance their budgets. They will be looking to Washington for fiscal relief, or at least to avoid cutbacks in the flow of funds from Washington.

The Size of the Block Grant

Perhaps the most fundamental question that Congress will face this year concerns the overall size of the block grant. Current annual funding of $16.5 billion expires at the end of fiscal year 2002. Congress must act—if only to pass a continuing resolution embodying current law and funding levels—to sustain the flow of funds to the states beyond September 30. But state governments would prefer more than a temporary extension of TANF: they want the stability of a multi-year funding stream to be able to make their own programmatic commitments for the new array of services being offered under TANF.

Some critics argue that funding levels in the block grant ought to be reduced. They note that current levels were set when TANF caseloads were more than twice the level they are today. Moreover, a number of states have not spent their full block grant allocations, especially in the early years of the TANF program. By 2001, however, most states were spending almost all of their current TANF allotments, and many had begun to draw on reserves from past years. Indeed, data from the U.S. Treasury Department show that for the first time in 2001, states actually spent more than the annual TANF allocation of $16.5 billion.

Defenders of current or even increased funding levels pose several counter-arguments. First, because the TANF block grant has no built-in inflation adjustment, it has been declining in real terms for six years—roughly 12 percent between 1997 and 2002. More importantly, they argue that the caseload number is no longer a meaningful indicator of states' funding commitments under TANF. States spend less than half of their TANF funds on cash benefits to those officially on the TANF caseload; the rest is spent primarily on child care, transportation, job search, and other work supports for the working poor and the hard-to-employ who may or may not be on the TANF caseload. Thus, states need the entire block grant amount because they are now running two programs—a cash welfare program and an

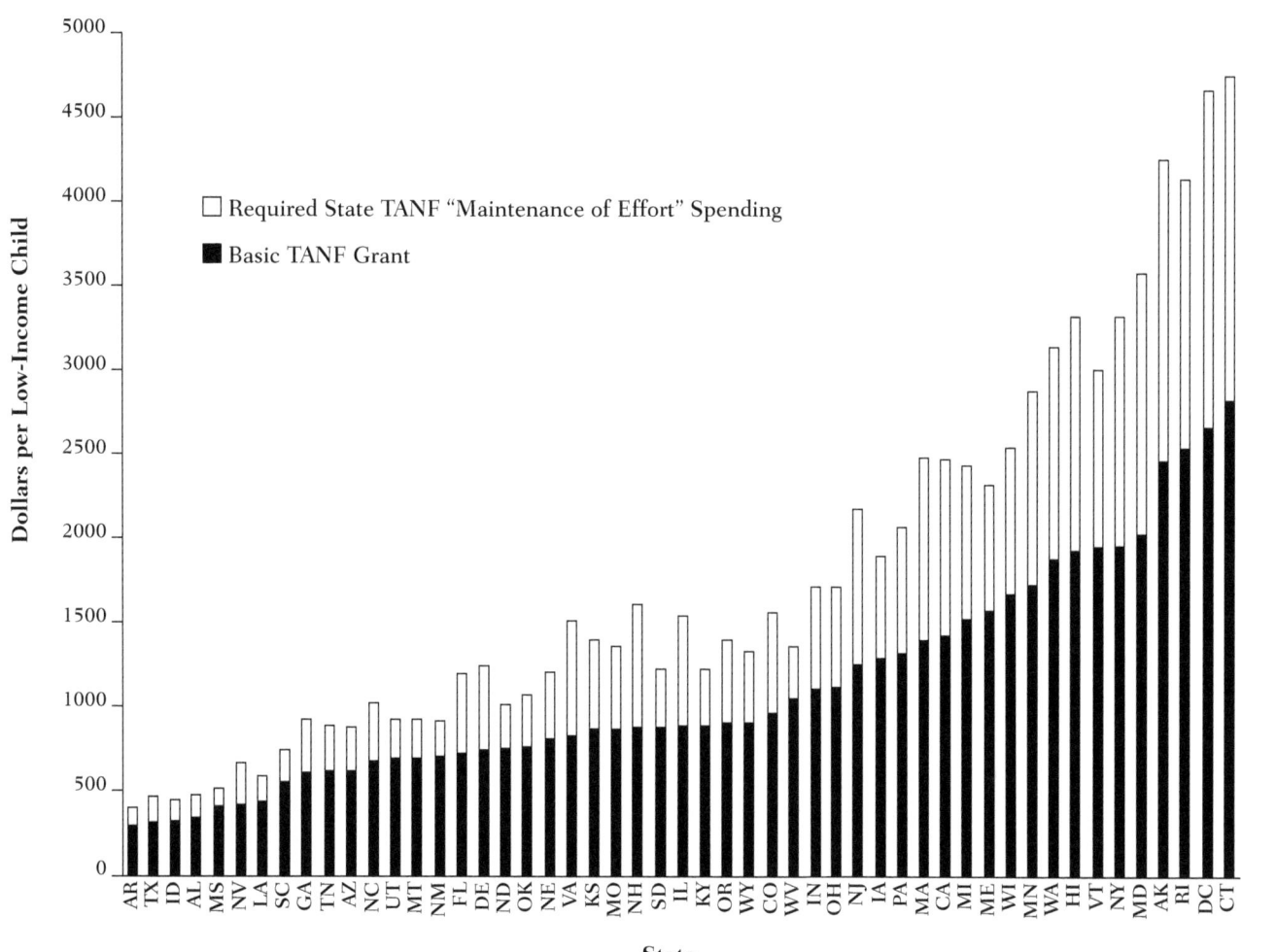

Figure 1
Federal TANF Grant Amount and State TANF Spending per Low-Income Child by State

Note: TANF = Temporary Assistance for Needy Families
Source: U.S. Department of Health and Human Services

employment program—with the same amount of money they had under AFDC.

Inflation Adjustment for the Block Grant

The decline in real purchasing power of the TANF block grant will continue, and is projected to be around 22 percent lower in 2007 than it was in 1997, if TANF funding remains at $16.5 billion. As a result of the decline in real dollars, states that have increased their spending on work supports in recent years will face difficult trade-offs between cutting cash benefits, cutting work supports, or increasing their own spending on TANF-financed programs. To avoid this financial squeeze on states, Congress can increase the TANF basic funding level to account for past inflation, build an inflation mechanism into TANF to take account of future inflation, or both. If Congress enacts a five-year extension of TANF, about $18 billion in extra funding over the 2003-2007 period would be required to account for inflation between 1996 and 2007; about $6.5 billion would be required over that period to account only for anticipated future inflation between 2002 and 2007.

Allocation of TANF Funds Across States

As noted above, TANF block grant allocations are based on states' historical spending levels under the AFDC program. Even though poor states enjoyed a much more advantageous match rate than wealthier states, their benefits were generally much lower, so the flow of federal funds per low-income child was much lower. This pattern carried over to the TANF block grant, as shown in figure 1. The lower part of each bar graph shows the TANF block grant dollars received per child living in a low-income family for each state in fiscal year 2002. As the figure clearly shows, there are immense disparities across states in the block grants received per low-income child. In the ten states receiving the least generous federal grant, the TANF block grant provides only $429 per low-income child, while in the ten states receiving the most federal dollars, TANF provides around five times as much. The disparities in TANF block grant funding are exacerbated by the fact that states that receive higher federal allocations also are required to spend more of their own money to meet federal "maintenance of effort" requirements. Thus, the actual funding disparities across states, shown by adding the upper and lower sections of the bars in figure 1, are actually much greater—more than a six-to-one disparity between the highest and lowest ten states.

There is little justification for the dramatically uneven levels of funding per low-income child, especially because the federal government provides fewer dollars to poorer states. However, it is much more difficult to come up with an acceptable resolution of the problem. Defenders of the status quo argue that reopening the allocation formula could destroy political consensus on TANF and lead to lower overall funding levels. Indeed, a formula fight helped to delay Senate consideration of welfare reform legislation in 1995. The reallocation fight would be particularly intense if it involved a zero-sum game in which richer states lost money so that poorer states could get more. The simplest change in allocation would be to gradually adjust the funding formula to give more money to states with low federal funding per low-income child. But even with a lengthy phase-in, such zero-sum funding changes would be opposed by large and powerful states that would lose money.

In short, changing the current allocation would be problematic unless all states are at least protected against a drop in the nominal value of their current allocation. But in a time of tight budgets, a major increase in funds is also difficult. The most likely candidate for increased funding is restoration of the TANF supplemental grant which gives increased funding to about one-third of the states with historically low AFDC grants per low-income person and/or fast-growing populations. The supplemental funding pot was only $319 million in 2001. Because the supplemental grant is not assumed to be included in the budget baseline, renewing it for 2003 and beyond will require offsetting savings or new revenues. The middle parts of the bars on figure 2 show the very modest

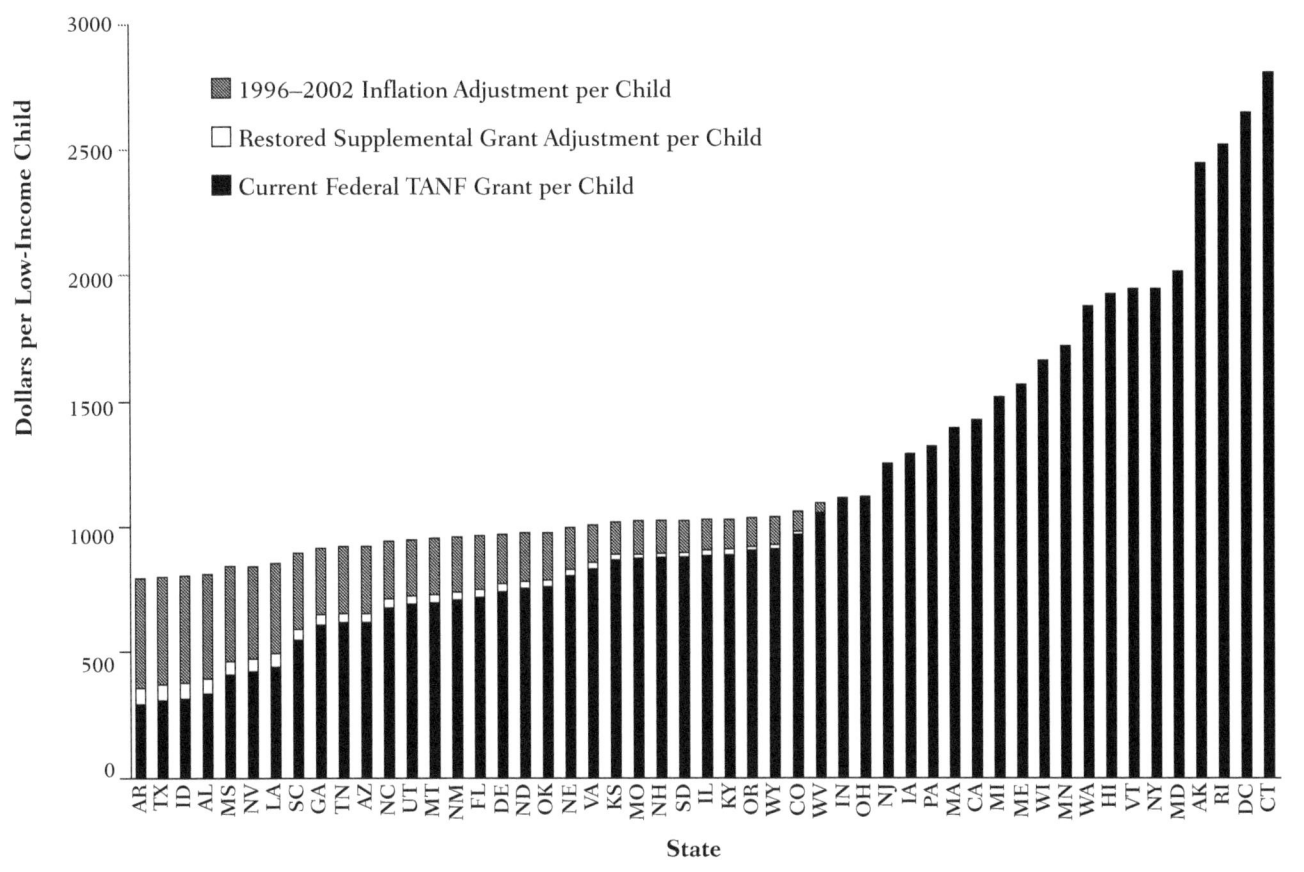

Figure 2
Effects of Adding New Funds to State TANF Allocations

Note: TANF = Temporary Assistance for Needy Families
Source: U.S. Department of Health and Human Services

impact on state grant levels of restoring the supplemental grant and reallocating it so that each state getting a grant below the national average of $1,114 per low-income child would have an equal percentage of the gap filled between its current level and the national average. Because the funding gap is so large—it would take $4.1 billion in 2002 to bring all states up to the current national average—the supplemental grant would make only a modest dent in achieving this goal, filling about eight percent of the gap.

Far more effective in filling the gap would be increasing the current TANF block grant for inflation since 1996, on top of restoring supplemental grant funding and devoting the entire amount to increasing benefits in low-grant states. These two steps together would permit filling 60 percent of the gap needed to bring below-average states up to the national average (top portion of bar graphs in figure 2), but would cost $2.5 billion in 2002 or $12.5 billion over five years.

A less expensive strategy for partially equalizing revenues across states would be to preserve nominal grant levels for richer states, while using future inflation adjustments to the TANF block grant (if Congress enacts them) primarily to bring grants for low-grant states closer to the national median or average. However, so long as inflation rates remain low, it would take many years for inflation adjustments alone to make a substantial impact on low-grant states. Moreover, it is unlikely that the entirety of an inflation adjustment could be used in this way for more than a few years.

Even if additional funding can be found for states with low TANF grants, additional problems exist. Two in particular are notable. First, any approach to filling the gap between low-grant and high-grant states will give almost one-third of the money to Texas, a very large state with a very low TANF grant. Concentrating such a high percentage of the gains on one state might be politically problematic.

Second, Congress would have to decide whether states receiving the funding boost would be required to increase their own spending levels to qualify for the money. Legislators from richer states would undoubtedly argue that it is not fair that they have to maintain their spending efforts at relatively high levels while poorer states get more money with no additional effort over their already very low spending levels. But it is not clear that low-grant states would be willing to spend more of their own money. After all, the reason that TANF grants are so low now in these states is that under the AFDC program, they were very reluctant to spend their own funds on poor families.

Politicians will be tempted to simply ignore the TANF allocation formula or reinstate the supplemental grant in its old form to avoid these political problems. Given the magnitude of the funding disparities, and the limitations they impose on the capacity of low-income states to provide adequate benefits and employment services to their citizens, retaining the current formula would be an unfortunate outcome.

Adjusting TANF for Recessions

Unlike the old AFDC program, the TANF block grant is a fixed funding stream to the states that does not respond to economic conditions. Nevertheless the law includes several provisions that are intended to help states that run into problems during recessions. First, states can carry over unspent TANF funds to future years. Second, states can borrow up to a total of $1.7 billion from the federal government, repayable at market rates of interest. Third, the 1996 law created a federal contingency fund of $2 billion that states could draw upon when they had substantial increases in unemployment or food stamp use; however, the increases necessary to trigger benefits from the fund were so stringent that states could not access these funds except in a very deep recession. Moreover, to qualify for contingency funds, states have to boost their own spending from 75 percent to 100 percent of the 1994 level, despite the fact that states often cannot find such additional funds during a recession.

Critics of these arrangements argue that states will have difficulty maintaining both increased cash assistance and needed work support commitments during a recession. While a number of states have carried over TANF funds from the good economic times of the late 1990s, they have been reluctant to carry over too much because of signals from Congress that they would lose the funds if they did not use them. Moreover, states are unlikely to borrow funds from the federal government when facing a budget squeeze. One option currently under discussion for dealing with a recession is improvement of the contingency fund, with changes in eligibility criteria and the state spending requirement to make it more accessible for states. Other options include giving states increased control of carry-over funds so that they do not fear the funds will be lost if they are not spent, and making the TANF block grant explicitly counter-cyclical by, for example, tying grant levels to the unemployment rate (see chapter 11 for an extended discussion of options for dealing with recessions).

Requirements for State Spending

The old AFDC program required states to contribute their own funds to finance cash benefits. About 45 percent of the total costs of AFDC were paid by states. The TANF program continued this tradition by requiring states to spend 75 percent of the amount they spent on AFDC and related programs in 1994 (80 percent if the state failed to meet required work participation rates). This provision was a subject of great controversy during the 1995-96 welfare reform debate. Some states lobbied to drop all requirements on state spending. Child advocates argued that if there was to be no individual entitlement, the TANF program should at least guarantee that a specific amount of money be available for a cash safety net program and for welfare-to-work activities.

There have been no prominent proposals during the debate on TANF reauthorization to reduce state maintenance of effort spending.

But the intense budget pressure faced by Congress could lead members of the congressional budget committees to look for cuts in the $16.5 billion TANF block grant. Cuts of this sort would lead, in turn, to a call from the states to allow them to reduce their own spending. The most likely outcome, however, is that both the federal block grant amount and the state 75 percent "maintenance of effort" requirement will be retained.

Changing Performance Bonuses

In addition to the basic TANF block grant, the federal government offers two sets of bonus grants to states that have achieved superior performance on goals defined by the federal government. One bonus offers a total of $100 million per year to up to five states that have achieved the highest reductions in the ratio of non-marital births to total births in the past year while reducing abortions. The second bonus offers $200 million per year to states that have met at least one of several performance criteria established by the Department of Health and Human Services. In its original form, the second bonus was awarded for job entry, job retention, and wage progression by TANF recipients. Starting in 2002, bonuses are scheduled to be added to reward states for success in enrolling eligible low-income families in food stamps and Medicaid or the State Children's Health Insurance Program, as well as for child care affordability, accessibility and quality, and for increases in the number of low-income children living in two-parent families.

In order for a bonus system to have the intended effect of boosting a state's effort to perform well, states must believe that their efforts can actually have a direct impact on the particular outcomes measured by the bonus system. But in the case of the illegitimacy bonus, high performance in reducing illegitimacy rates appears to have resulted largely from demographic factors that are not under state control rather than from any new state effort. Moreover, the underlying rationale of a bonus system is that it can encourage states to mount new programs to achieve the desired improvement in performance. New programs generally cost money. As we have seen, there is a wide discrepancy between states in the amount of money they receive from the basic TANF grant. Thus, wealthy states have an advantage in mounting new programs aimed at winning bonus payments simply because they have more money to invest.

The illegitimacy bonus appears to enjoy only weak support in Congress primarily because it is difficult to identify a clear relationship between states that have actually won the bonus and the efforts those states put forth to win the bonus. By contrast, there is considerable support for the performance bonus. To date, the performance bonuses have been awarded based on state success in placing and keeping recipients in jobs. Most observers believe that states can obtain reliable measures of job placements and job retention and that state programs seem to have an impact on state performance.

In a year in which money is tight, it might be expected that proposals to use bonus money for other purposes will be forthcoming. In fact, the Bush administration has already proposed to end the illegitimacy bonus and part of the performance bonus in order to use the money to provide funds for a marriage initiative. The bill introduced by Representative Benjamin Cardin, the ranking Democrat on the Ways and Means subcommittee responsible for welfare, would also eliminate the illegitimacy bonus. The illegitimacy bonus seems unlikely to survive; what happens to the performance bonus remains to be determined.

Additional Reading

General Accounting Office. 2001. *Challenges in Maintaining a Federal-State Partnership*, GAO-01-828.

Neuberger, Zoë, Sharon Parrott, and Wendell Primus. 2002. *Funding Issues in TANF Reauthorization*. Washington, D.C.: Center on Budget and Policy Priorities.

11

REBECCA M. BLANK

Welfare and the Economy

Executive Summary
Throughout the 1990s, the combination of economic expansion and major policy changes to the nation's public assistance programs resulted in rapidly declining welfare caseloads and rapidly increasing labor force participation. Program eligibility changed, with more applicants subject to sanctions, time limits, or diversion activities, and the robust economy fueled a strong labor market. It is difficult to forecast what will happen to caseloads and employment in a future recession. The 1996 welfare reform legislation contained three provisions to help states weather a recession: the ability to carry over block grant funds, a loan fund, and a contingency fund. These and other public assistance programs, however, need reworking to be entirely effective during a recession. Future policy options include making the welfare block grant funding cyclical, revising the trigger for contingency fund payments, authorizing state "rainy day" funds for welfare programs, increasing state flexibility on time limits, encouraging public employment programs, and reforming the current unemployment insurance system.

The 1990s produced a host of unexpected economic good news. Contrary to all economic predictions, unemployment fell to 4 percent by the end of the decade and inflation remained low and stable. Black and Hispanic Americans experienced record low unemployment rates, and women experienced unemployment rates nearly as low as in the 1960s, a time when far fewer women were in the labor force. At the same time, real wages for less-skilled workers began to rise steadily starting around 1995, following almost 20 years of decline or stagnation. Between 1994 and 1999, real wages rose 5 percent among male high school dropouts and 3.5 percent among female high school dropouts.

Even in the absence of any other changes, these exceptional labor market improvements should have increased employment and reduced welfare use among low-income families. But these economic changes coincided with a period of extensive policy change. The mid-1990s saw significant expansions in the Earned Income Tax Credit (EITC) and the minimum wage. The 1996 welfare reform legislation created the Temporary Assistance for Needy Families (TANF) block grant, replacing the old Aid to Families with Dependent Children (AFDC) cash welfare program. TANF gave states much greater discretion over the structure and operation of their public assistance programs, and states promptly began to implement programs designed to increase work and reduce cash assistance. These new work-oriented welfare programs were designed to move recipients (primarily single mothers) into employment as quickly as possible, and were surely helped by the strong labor market available to those newly seeking work.

The coincidence of a major economic expansion and a major shift in policy resulted in significant behavioral changes, with rapid declines in public assistance caseloads and rapid increases in labor force participation among single mothers. This policy brief investigates those changes, and explores what might happen in a future recession and how well prepared national and state public assistance programs are to deal with an economic slowdown.

What Happens in the Next Recession?

Since nobody knows what will happen in the next recession, the best way to predict the impact is to look at how past economic slowdowns have affected work behavior and public assistance caseloads. Notably, recent changes in programs and behavior have been so great and so fundamental that historical evidence may be quite unreliable.

Caseloads Public assistance caseloads have declined by more than half since the mid-1990s. Even the strongest proponents of welfare reform in 1996 would not have predicted such dramatic reductions in welfare usage. The key question is how much of the reduction is due to economic expansion versus policy change, and how much of it would be reversed in a recession. A growing body of research has tried to separate the impacts of policy and economy on welfare, with mixed success. The two are almost surely interacting with and reinforcing each other, so that a strong labor market has allowed states to put more energy into case management or move faster in placing recipients into welfare-to-work programs, without working as hard to help clients in these programs locate jobs. These interactions make it difficult to identify the separate effects of the economy and policy.

With this in mind, the existing research generally finds that a 1 percent increase in unemployment has historically increased welfare rolls by around 3 to 5 percent, although this effect occurs only over time and with a lag. These estimates are largely based on historical estimates from the AFDC program, when a smaller share of single mothers or welfare recipients were in the labor market and welfare had no time limit. Cyclical movements between the labor market and welfare were likely to be less common in this period than in the new world of TANF.

An alternative approach is to look at the historical response to changes in unemployment rates within the AFDC-Unemployed Parent (AFDC-UP) program. This program served married couples and was much more cyclical than the AFDC program for single mothers—more recipients left the program in good economic times and returned to seek assistance in times of high unemployment. Historically, a 1 percent increase in unemployment resulted in a 9 to 17 percent increase in the AFDC-UP rolls. This suggests that a serious recession that raises the unemployment rate from 4 percent to 7 percent could result in as much as a 30 to 50 percent increase in TANF caseloads.

This effect will be reduced if a share of these women is ineligible to return to welfare. For instance, sanction policies, time limits, or state diversion policies may keep some applicants off welfare, even when faced with serious economic need. Research based on recessionary effects within the AFDC program cannot take these TANF program changes into account.

Labor Force Participation As welfare usage declined, employment increased, particularly among single mothers with younger children. The rate of labor force participation among single mothers (age 20-65) with children under age 18 rose from 69 percent to 78 percent between 1990 and 2000. An important component of this change was a significant increase in the number of women who were both receiving welfare and working.

However, single mothers tend to have low levels of education, and jobs among less-skilled workers tend to be the least stable and most cyclical. Hence, a recession leading to a 1 percent increase in the aggregate unemployment rate would likely produce greater than 1 percent increases in unemployment among less-skilled workers.

How these newly employed single mothers respond to losing their jobs is important. Will they continue to search for work (thus remaining in the labor force and being counted among the unemployed), or will they leave the labor market entirely, either returning to public assistance (if they can, given sanctions and time limits) or relying on the income of boyfriends or other family members? One might assume that a loss of less-skilled jobs would reduce employment more than it will reduce labor force participation, if actively looking for work is a required component for receiving ongoing public assistance.

Poverty and Income Poverty fell in the 1990s, as one would have expected given the economic growth during this period. Poverty among female-headed households with children is now at an historical low (although it remains above 35 percent). However, as others have pointed out, many fewer people have left poverty than have moved off cash assistance. The result is an increase in the number of "working poor," that is, those in

> *Public assistance caseloads have declined by more than half since the mid-1990s. The key question is how much of the reduction is due to economic expansion versus policy change, and how much of it would be reversed in a recession.*

poverty who are also actively involved in the labor market. The share of working poor has typically increased in periods of economic expansion, as more low-wage jobs become available. Hence, a recession is likely to increase the overall number of poor people, as well as decrease the share of the poor who work.

There has long been a strong relationship between poverty and the overall economy. Estimates from the 1960s and 1970s suggested that a 1 percent decrease in unemployment rates decreased poverty by about 1 percent. However, despite a strong labor market and declining unemployment in the 1980s, poverty fell less over this period than historical data would have suggested. This effect appears to be related to the wage inequality of that decade, with wage declines among less-skilled workers offsetting the effects of the strong labor market. A stronger relationship between movements in unemployment rates and movements in poverty reemerged during the 1990s, although the declines in poverty in the 1990s are quite small relative to the dramatic declines in the 1960s.

Overall, the strong economy has clearly helped reduce caseloads and increase work opportunities. It has also helped reduce poverty and raise income (primarily through increases in earnings) in poor families. The economic expansion of the 1990s was surely not the only reason for declining welfare rolls and rising labor force participation, but it was an important component of those changes. Behavioral changes would likely be much smaller and less dramatic had we implemented welfare reform in a period of slower economic growth.

How Well Prepared are TANF Programs to Deal with a Recession?

Since TANF changed the funding for public assistance from a matching grant system to a fixed block grant, states now bear the residual financial risk of any changes in economic need. A key problem with fixed funding is that public assistance demand is countercyclical, that is, it rises in periods of economic need. Thus, states generally will need to put more money into public assistance programs during a recession. Of course, this creates serious problems for many states, most of which operate under a balanced budget requirement in their constitution and typically cut their spending in recessions.

TANF contains three provisions that are designed to help states prepare for or weather recessions that disrupt their ability to provide welfare benefits to all poor families. First, states are allowed to carry over TANF funds. The TANF block grant provides states with a fixed amount of federal funds, the level of which is based on spending in the old AFDC program in the early part of the 1990s. To receive these funds without penalty, states must meet a maintenance of effort (MOE) requirement which compels them to continue to provide state funding at 80 percent of the level provided to a core group of public assistance programs in the mid-1990s (75 percent if state work participation requirements are met). TANF explicitly authorized states to carry over any block grant money not spent in a given year into future years. A primary reason for this provision was to allow states to build up "rainy day" funds that they could tap if faced with rising economic need.

Many states have used this carryover provision. As of September 2000, states reported $9 billion in unspent TANF funds, which amounted to 14.5 percent of all TANF funds awarded since 1996. Some of these dollars have been obligated to state programs, but are still unspent, while others are unobligated. Determining exactly how many of these dollars might be available to meet extra spending needs in times of economic decline is difficult.

Unfortunately for states, the future of carryover funds is somewhat uncertain. Congress could pass legislation that would reallocate unspent state TANF funds to other budget uses. Some states have explicitly avoided carryovers because of the risk of losing this money. Logically, this risk makes it unlikely that states will fully utilize the carryover provisions to build up sufficient rainy day funds.

In addition, the carryover funds must be spent on cash welfare. This means that carryover dollars could not pay for increased costs in state work programs during a recession (such as increases in child care or wage subsidies), thereby further limiting the usefulness of TANF carryover funds as a recession-financing mechanism.

The second provision for dealing with recessions is a $1.7 billion Federal Loan Fund, authorizing states to borrow up to 10 percent of the value of their TANF block grant. A loan must be repaid within three years and states must pay interest at the market rate. To date, this provision has not been used by the states and is likely limited in its usefulness, as state borrowing for social welfare programs in recessions may not receive strong popular support.

The third and most important anti-recession provision within TANF is the contingency fund. This fund provides additional money to states in times of economic need, and thereby supplements the fixed TANF block grants. A $1.96 billion contingency fund was authorized, but the authority expires at the end of 2001 (and there is no request for reauthorization in current budget proposals). In order to draw down these funds, states must meet two criteria. First, state unemployment rates have to be above 6.5 percent and must have increased more than 10 percent over the past year; or their food stamp caseload must be 10 percent higher than in 1994 or 1995. Second, state TANF expenditures must be 100 percent or more of their 1994 expenditures on a group of core public assistance programs.

While perhaps reasonable in 1996, these criteria have become quite outdated. So far, the contingency fund has been used only once, and it is unlikely that many states will be able to draw upon the contingency fund in the near future. With unemployment rates well below 5 percent, the unemployment trigger in the first criterion will not be met until states have experienced large increases in unemployment. Since food stamp caseloads have fallen by 40 percent (along with welfare caseloads), the food stamp criterion will also be difficult to meet. Finally, since state MOE requirements are currently at 75 to 80 percent of their previous expenditures and few states are at 100 percent, state spending on TANF programs in a recession would have to be increased substantially before states would be eligible to draw down federal contingency dollars.

Given the serious limitations of the existing TANF provisions for recessions, many observers have suggested that a variety of changes are needed to "recession-proof" state TANF programs.

Even if the contingency fund did not have access problems, many claim that it would not provide an adequate backup to TANF funds for states in a serious recession. For instance, if the eight states with the largest block grants were to all qualify in one year for contingency fund dollars, it would exhaust the fund.

Finally, it is worth noting that TANF provides for special supplemental grants for poor states or states with rapidly growing populations. Although not an explicit anti-recession measure, these supplemental funds could be very helpful to states that receive them during a recession. This provision is due to expire at the end of 2001, and 17 states will lose funds if this occurs.

Policy Options

Given the serious limitations of the existing TANF provisions for recessions, many observers have suggested that a variety of changes are needed to "recession-proof" state TANF programs. These proposals include ways to solve the countercyclical financing problems faced by states in recession, as well as proposals to improve the states' ability to run effective work-oriented public assistance programs that can continue to operate in a more sluggish labor market.

The Contingency Fund In order to make this contingency fund usable to states, a new set of accessibility criteria is necessary. Keying access to the fund to large percent changes in unemployment or food stamp caseloads (without attention to the starting level) would enable states to obtain these funds in an economic downturn. Making access contingent only on the 75 percent or 80 percent MOE requirement (rather than the much more stringent 100 percent requirement in current law) is also necessary. If the current contingency fund is not renewed in 2001, it may be easier to create a new and more effective contingency fund, perhaps as part of the TANF reauthorization debate in 2002.

Strengthening TANF Given the current limitations of the contingency fund, an alternative would be to create cyclicality in the block grant funding amounts so that states with increased economic need would receive more federal dollars in their block grant. One idea for determining the formula by which this cyclicality occurs is to tie the additional money to changes in unemployment rates or other indicators of need. By itself, this approach would limit state access to increased dollars to a formula-based allocation of the block grant, which may not recognize specific high-need situations in states. Hence, it might make sense to also provide at least a small ongoing contingency fund program (accessed at state request under particular circumstances) even if block grant dollars are allowed to fluctuate.

State Rainy Day Funds for TANF Programs To address concerns about losing carryover funds, it may be important to explicitly give states authority to establish rainy day funds that allow a limited share of their TANF block grant allocations (maybe 10 percent) to be held without consequence should Congress decide to reallocate "excess" TANF funds. This policy would allow states some carryover ability, without encouraging them to build up large carryover balances. It might be useful to require that states justify their rainy day fund amounts through some sort of formal calculation of expected future need.

State Flexibility and Federal Time Limits In a recession, it will be harder for welfare recipients to find jobs and to earn enough to leave welfare. In this situation, welfare spells will lengthen and the five-year federal time limit may begin to bind on a larger share of families. Particularly in a time of limited job availability, removing people from public assistance due to rigid time limits is not an ideal option. States may need greater flexibility to issue more exemptions from time limits during recessions, or flexibility to extend eligibility for persons who meet certain criteria—such as actively participating in welfare-to-work activities—but are unable to find a job or earn enough to lose their welfare eligibility.

Encourage States to Create Public Employment Programs In a serious recession, it is unlikely that states can continue to run welfare-to-work programs that rely entirely on private sector job availability. If a state wants to enforce strong work requirements and assure that women on welfare who make every effort to meet the work requirements continue to receive assistance, then short-term paid public employment programs may be an attractive option. For instance, a woman might receive a six-month placement in a job provided in the public sector, after which she must spend a period of time seeking private sector work. Unfortunately, the expense and management challenges associated with public employment programs rise with the number of placements and the degree of state monitoring. However, a recent review of past U.S. employment programs by David Ellwood, a professor at Harvard University, offers lessons to help states design more effective programs. Federal funds to help design, initiate, and evaluate small-scale demonstration programs could help states begin to explore new options for building more effective employment programs.

Unemployment and Low-Wage Workers Very few low-wage workers currently collect unemployment insurance when they leave or lose their jobs. This unfortunate result is caused by a combination of factors. First, persons fired for cause—such as a mother whose child care arrangements have fallen through—are often not eligible for unemployment. Second, persons who voluntarily leave a job—such as a mother who cannot arrange transportation between a job and child care obligations—are often not eligible for unemployment. Third, many states will not pay unemployment to workers seeking part-time jobs. Finally, states have requirements about how long and how continuously an individual must work to qualify for unemployment insurance, which many low-wage workers do not meet. Changes that make unemployment more available to low-wage workers, such as shorter qualifying periods for benefits or payments to part-time job seekers, could help provide an alternative source of short-term support for low-wage workers who either do not want to or cannot return to the welfare rolls.

Conclusion

The strong economy has been very important to the success of welfare reform so far. A recession, particularly a deep recession which raises unemployment rates by 3 points or more, might substantially reduce the success states have achieved in reducing caseloads and increasing work among less-skilled workers. A variety of legislative changes might be useful to both provide financial support to states in times of rising economic need, and to assure that state welfare-to-work programs continue to function when private sector jobs are not as readily available.

Additional Reading

Blank, Rebecca M. 2001. *"Evaluating Welfare Reform in the United States."* Ann Arbor, MI: Ford School of Public Policy, University of Michigan.

Blank, Rebecca M., and Lucie Schmidt. 2001. "Work, Wages, and Welfare." In *The New World of Welfare,* edited by Rebecca M. Blank and Ron Haskins. Washington, D.C.: The Brookings Institution.

Danziger, Sheldon H. 1999. *Economic Conditions and Welfare Reform.* Kalamazoo, MI: W.E. Upjohn Institute.

Ellwood, David T. 2000. "Public Service Employment and Mandatory Work: A Policy Whose Time Has Come and Gone and Come Again?" In *Finding Jobs: Work and Welfare Reform,* edited by David Card and Rebecca M. Blank. New York: Russell Sage.

Falk, Gene. 2001. *Welfare Reform Financing Issues: Recession Funding.* Washington, D.C.: Congressional Research Service.

Hoynes, Hilary W. 2000. "The Employment, Earnings, and Income of Less-Skilled Workers Over the Business Cycle." In *Finding Jobs: Work and Welfare Reform,* edited by David Card and Rebecca M. Blank. New York: Russell Sage.

PART V

ENCOURAGING AND REWARDING WORK

ISABEL SAWHILL AND RON HASKINS

Welfare Reform and the Work Support System

Executive Summary
Although the sweeping welfare reform law of 1996 has received widespread attention in the media and among policymakers, the development of the nation's work support system, which is a vital complement to the 1996 reforms, has received far less attention. The work support system is a series of programs that provide benefits to poor and low-income working families. In popular parlance, they are programs that "make work pay." The most important of these programs are the minimum wage, the Earned Income Tax Credit, the child tax credit, income supplement programs conducted by states, food stamps, health insurance, child support enforcement, and child care. A recent study by the Congressional Budget Office showed that numerous expansions of these programs since the mid-1980s have increased by a factor of more than eight the value of federal work support benefits now being paid to working families. Given the important role these programs play in maintaining work incentives, supplementing earned income so working families can provide a minimum living standard for their children, and helping families when unemployment hits, the maintenance and even expansion of these programs will be a major part of this year's welfare reauthorization debate in Congress. In this brief, we provide an overview of work support programs and examine the pros and cons of proposals to expand them.

Overview of Work Support System

The 1996 welfare reform law represents a fundamental shift in how the federal government provides support to destitute families. Under pre-1996 law, low-income families were entitled to a package of welfare benefits that included cash, food stamps, and Medicaid. The American public came to believe that this system of entitlement benefits contributed to a decline in work by poor parents and an even more striking decline in the number of poor children being reared in two-parent families. Among other provisions, the 1996 reforms required work of almost every adult that joined the welfare rolls. In addition, with some exceptions, a limit of five years was placed on the receipt of cash welfare by individual families.

Far less visible than the widely debated welfare reform revolution was a second set of reforms in public policy that may be even more important in the long run. Beginning roughly in the mid-1970s with the enactment of the Earned Income Tax Credit (EITC), the federal government originated or expanded a series of programs that provide benefits to working families. Unlike welfare benefits, which are intended primarily for the destitute, these work support benefits are designed to provide cash and other benefits to working adults and their families. In addition to the EITC, the major benefits in the system include the child tax credit, the minimum wage, state income supplement programs, food stamps, health insurance, and child care. In 1999, low- and moderate-income families were eligible for $52 billion in assistance from these programs, compared to the $6 billion they would have been eligible for if these programs had not been expanded by Congress after the mid-1980s. As a result, the typical one-parent family with children was far better off working than on welfare, and employment rates among this group increased dramatically, due to the strong economy of the 1990s, welfare reform, and the availability of these expanded work supports.

This evolution toward a work-based system of support progressed further as a result of state responses to the 1996 welfare law. The sharp drop in caseloads after 1994 freed up funds that states have devoted primarily to supporting work. By fiscal year 2000, only half of total federal and state spending under Temporary Assistance to Needy Families (TANF) was devoted to cash assistance, compared to 70 percent in fiscal 1995, according to Gene Falk of the Congressional Research Service. However, if a recession-induced increase in caseloads requires states to reallocate these funds to pay basic benefits, these investments will almost certainly decline.

The value of these new work support programs at both the federal and state level cannot be overemphasized. The EITC alone provides roughly $4,000 a year in extra benefits to a low-wage worker with two or more children, and the children remain eligible for Medicaid. The average woman leaving welfare earns about $7 an hour, or $13,000 in after-tax income. The combined value of food stamps and the EITC, then, brings her total income up to about $19,000–enough to boost a single parent family with three or fewer children above the federal poverty line (the poverty threshold for a family of four was about $18,000 in 2001).

Notwithstanding the expansion of work supports in recent years, advocates for the poor point to the low wages earned by many adults and believe that the next phase of welfare reform should be devoted to ensuring that jobs are available and work more adequately rewarded. Polls show that the public is willing to do more for those who work. Two-thirds of the electorate, including 71 percent of Democrats and 63 percent of Republicans, say it is very important for President Bush and the Congress to do more to help those trying to work their way off welfare, according to a poll conducted last spring by Peter D. Hart Associates. Voters rank this goal just below other major concerns such as providing prescription drug coverage for seniors and improving education.

The ability to make ends meet is especially serious for low-income families who must pay for child care and other work-related expenses, and who have no access to subsidized health insurance through an employer. Child care costs average $2,000 a year for the 40 percent of working poor families that pay for care, according to a Brookings analysis of Census Bureau data. Because health insurance can easily cost $6,000 a year or more, most adults in low-income families without employer-based health coverage remain uninsured, although most of the children are covered by federal programs. Current measures of poverty fail to incorporate these realities. Thus, many are advocating for an expanded definition of poverty and a more generous set of supports for low-income working Americans. These supports could include a higher minimum wage, additional income supplements, greater access to subsidized child care, more health care and job training, and a stronger safety net of community service jobs for those unable to find work in the private sector.

The purpose of this policy brief is to provide basic information about the current work support system and to discuss ways in which it might be expanded. A commonly advanced set of policy proposals that would help low-income working families, along with their advantages and disadvantages, is summarized in Table 1 in the last pages of this brief. Many of these policies respond to complaints that the 1996 welfare law placed too much emphasis on reducing caseloads and not enough on reducing poverty.

Goals of Work Support System

The work support system serves three primary goals. First, it provides incentives for work. Under the pre-1996 welfare system, able-bodied adults who did not work were given benefits, but these benefits were often reduced dollar-for-dollar as earnings increased, leaving adults no better off financially after they went to work. Research now shows that increasing the incentive to work through programs such as the EITC contributes to large increases in employment among less skilled workers. Still other research shows that programs that combine work requirements with financial incentives can improve educational and other outcomes for children because these incentives raise income beyond what is available from either welfare or work alone.

A second goal of the work support system is to help ensure that parents working at low-wage jobs have enough total income to provide an adequate standard of living. In the past, many low-skilled workers, especially men, were able to find reasonably well-paid jobs in manufacturing. However, in the post-industrial economy, many jobs require high levels of education and far fewer jobs provide good wages for workers with limited education and training. In the long run, the solution to this problem is to improve the nation's education system to equip young people with the job skills needed in the new economy. Another long-run strategy is to increase the proportion of children growing up in families where there are two parents who can share bread-winning and child care responsibilities. But in the short run, and especially for those single parents who have already completed their education and need to support a family, supplementing the low earnings of the least skilled may be the only feasible response—and is a better and more popular approach than expanding welfare.

The third goal of the work support system is to insure that those who lose their jobs or cannot find work will not be destitute. Although this was not a major issue in the late 1990s when the demand for workers was high, it could be a bigger problem during a recession or a prolonged slowdown in the economy. A number of current programs address one or more of these three objectives.

Reforming Work Support Programs

Minimum Wage The current minimum wage of $5.15 an hour has not been raised since 1997 and leaves a family of three with one full-time worker below the poverty line. This has led to proposals in Congress to raise the minimum wage by $1.00 or $1.50 and to index it for inflation. These proposals spark heated debate, with liberals generally arguing that a higher minimum would put a floor under the incomes of low-wage workers and conservatives often arguing that it would be too costly for business and might reduce employment opportunities for the least skilled.

The minimum wage is not very well-targeted. Only one quarter of minimum-wage earners live in poor families. Many teenagers or others in higher income families earn the minimum. At the same time, as shown in research by Isabel Sawhill and Adam Thomas of the Brookings Institution, over 60 percent of wage earners in poor families would benefit from a $1.00 increase in the minimum wage because they are currently earning less than $6.15 an hour. The same study also suggests that, even if one makes a relatively strong assumption about the number of jobs that would be lost as a result of a minimum-wage increase, a $1.00 boost would still lift almost one million people out of poverty.

Earned Income Tax Credit (EITC) Enacted in 1975 primarily as a way to offset the payroll taxes paid by low-wage workers, the EITC now provides a 40 percent cash supplement for every dollar of earnings up to about $10,000 for families with two or more children. Unlike some other tax credits, the EITC is refundable—meaning that families with little or no income tax liability get a check from the Treasury. The maximum benefit of $4,000 remains flat up to earnings of a little more than $13,000 and then phases out at the rate of around 20 cents for every dollar of earnings above $13,000. The supplement is completely gone when earnings reach about $32,000. By 2000, the federal EITC was providing over $30 billion in cash supplements to working families, making it the biggest program other than Medicaid and Supplemental Security Income that provides benefits to low-income families. And unlike nearly every other program for low-income families, it provides benefits only to families that work. It is, in short, the quintessential work support program.

Child Tax Credit Prior to 2001, the child tax credit provided few benefits to lower-income families because it was not refundable. But the 2001 tax bill not only expanded the credit from $500 to $1,000 per child but also made it partially refundable for families with modest amounts of earned income and little or no income tax liability.

The credit provides important assistance to low-income working families but is also very complicated. It could be both simplified and better integrated with the EITC. One option would be to eliminate the child tax credit and create instead a second, and more generous, benefit tier in the EITC available to families that work full-time (as proxied by their having earnings above $10,000 a year). A two-child family with full-time earnings of less than $20,000 a year might qualify for a $6,000 EITC, phasing down to a flat $1,200 ($600 per child) at an income of $44,000 a year. Research done at the Manpower Demonstration Research Corporation suggests that conditioning benefits on full-time work creates a potent incentive for families to work and earn more with few net costs to the government. Moreover, this type of two-tiered working family tax credit has operated quite successfully in Great Britain. However, unless offset by savings from the expansion of the child tax credit to higher income families (not yet phased in), this proposal would be very expensive.

State Income Supplements Not all the improvements in the work system have come at the federal level. States have taken two major approaches to improving work incentives. First, since enactment of the 1996 reforms, nearly every state has allowed parents who find jobs to retain more of their welfare benefit. This policy enables many families to work and continue receiving earnings supplements from welfare. These "earned income disregards" vary in duration and generosity. In California, for example, families that go to work can keep $225 per month plus 50 percent of earnings over $225 before their welfare benefit is reduced. The disadvantage of generous rules like this is that they discriminate against low-income families that have never been on welfare. Also, under current federal rules, working families can exhaust their five-year limit on welfare while receiving just a small supplement to their earnings. For this reason, time limits may actually discourage work, and have led to proposals to "stop the clock" on the five-year time limit for those who are working a certain number of hours but still receiving some welfare.

A second approach states have followed is to create their own EITC programs. These programs, now available in sixteen states, typically supplement the federal EITC by adding a fixed percentage to whatever is due the family under federal rules. The amount of state supplementation varies from 4 to 25 percent of the federal benefit. However, not all of the state EITCs are refundable, and nineteen states still tax the incomes of families below the poverty line. One way to provide more assistance to low-income working families would be to provide a federal incentive for states to expand their EITCs. The incentive would be a federal matching rate for state EITC payments similar to that in the Medicaid program; states that have high per capita incomes (and hence a bigger tax base) would get a smaller match than states with lower per capita incomes.

Still another approach the federal government could take to encourage work would be to replace the current caseload reduction credit with an employment credit. Under the caseload reduction credit, states are allowed to fulfill their TANF mandatory work requirement by reducing their TANF caseload rather than by placing adults on welfare in actual jobs or in work programs. The employment credit would be designed to encourage states to move people into jobs and not just off the rolls. Such a credit, however, would be administratively complex.

Food Stamps Although not a program well targeted to the working poor, the rules governing food stamp eligibility ensure that families of three earning up to around $19,000 remain eligible for some benefits. Thus, nearly all the families leaving welfare are eligible for food stamps. In a typical situation, with a mother of two earning $14,000 per year, the family would be eligible for about $1,000 in food stamps, a major income boost.

Unfortunately, the food stamps program has a number of serious deficiencies in the way it is administered. Research conducted by Sheila Zedlewski and her colleagues at the Urban Institute in Washington, D.C. shows that less than half the families leaving welfare receive the food stamp benefits to which they are entitled. If the administrative problems that contribute to such low participation rates can be reduced, food stamps could take their place alongside the EITC as a benefit of considerable value to working families. Possible reforms include less emphasis on error rates, less frequent redeterminations of eligibility for working families, and presumptive eligibility for some period of time for those leaving welfare for work.

Medicaid and State Child Health Insurance Program (SCHIP) A major flaw in the original Medicaid program, enacted in 1965, was that the only way families could qualify for coverage was to join either the Aid to Families with Dependent Children program or the Supplemental Security Income program. Confining Medicaid coverage to welfare beneficiaries was a classic case of building perverse incentives into the nation's welfare system. Thus in 1984 Congress embarked on a series of reforms that broadened Medicaid coverage for children, including those not on welfare. Health insurance for children was expanded still further through enactment of the SCHIP program in 1997. States are now required to cover all poor children under the age of 19, and most states are providing coverage to children in families with incomes under 200 percent of poverty ($29,000 for a family of three in 2001). Even so, according to the Urban Institute, 23 percent of children in families below 200 percent of poverty remained uninsured in 1999. In addition, state laws vary enormously and families, faced with major hurdles in establishing and maintaining eligibility, often drop out of the system. Although mothers are covered for up to a year after leaving welfare in most states, government health insurance coverage for adults is much narrower than that for children. And only about one quarter of those leaving welfare for work have health coverage through an employer.

There are several ways in which this system could be improved. One would be to cover the parents of eligible children. An Urban Institute study reports that 37 percent of low-income children with public coverage in 1999 had a parent who was uninsured. Another option would be to extend coverage to still more children through either Medicaid or SCHIP. Most low-income working families with incomes above the poverty line but below, say, 200 percent of poverty, find it difficult to afford health insurance. The result is that unless they have coverage through an employer, too many become part of the uninsured population. Reluctance to extend health insurance to this group has foundered on the high cost and disagreements about the best way to do so.

Child Care Especially for mothers with young children, child care is a vital work support. As a result, the federal government has a long history of enacting legislation to support child care. The basic outlines of current federal child care policy are as follows. First, the federal government provides states with major funding (almost $4.6 billion) in the form of a block grant to help low- and moderate-income working families pay for child care. States also use around $4 billion in TANF dollars to subsidize child care. Although they must ensure that parents have choices in their selection of child care types and facilities, states have tremendous flexibility in the use of federal child care dollars. Second, the federal government does not regulate child care. Rather, responsibility for the quality of care is left to parents and to state and local government. Third, the federal government provides child care subsidies to low-income working and middle-class families through the tax code. However, because these child care tax credits are not refundable, families with no or little income tax liability lose all or part of the credit and most of the benefits accrue to relatively well-off families. Fourth, Head Start and a few other programs provide early education and developmental services to many of the children whose mothers are likely to be on welfare. However, because these programs are not usually full-day or full-year, they do not fully meet these mothers' need for child care while they work.

The 1996 welfare reform legislation boosted funding for the child care block grant by around $4.5 billion over 6 years. In addition, states were given authority to spend an unlimited amount of money for child care from their annual share of the $16.5 billion TANF block grant. Largely as a result of these provisions, total federal spending on child care, Head Start, and other child development programs has increased from $9 billion in 1993 to over $20 billion in 2001. State spending on child care has probably increased as well.

Nonetheless, a widely cited Department of Health and Human Services study shows that only 12 percent of children potentially eligible under federal guidelines are receiving subsidies through the child care block grant. These guidelines permit families with incomes of up to 85 percent of a state's median (median family income in the United States was $51,000 in 2000) to receive state child care subsidies. However, it was not Congress' intent to make all of these families eligible and most states have established somewhat lower income eligibility limits.

Other studies suggest that current funding is adequate to provide subsidized care for all families leaving welfare who need it, but many families have difficulty accessing the benefits for which they are eligible and only about a third of mothers leaving welfare receive subsidized care. Equally important, research suggests that there is not enough funding to serve all of the working poor, especially those who have never been on welfare. Some states, such as Illinois, have sought to extend child care assistance to this group. Waiting lists exist in some states and child development experts are concerned about the quality of available care. If every state were to provide as much assistance to the working poor as Illinois now does, funding for child care would need to increase by about 50 percent, according to a study by Jean Layzer and Ann Collins conducted at Abt Associates in Cambridge. But even this level of funding would provide little room for quality improvements. For these and other reasons, proposals to expand funding for the child care block grant are likely to be considered during the reauthorization debate.

Child Support Enforcement Child support enforcement is a federal-state program that attempts to collect money from parents who do not live with their children. There are now over 50,000 child support caseworkers in the U.S. who, thanks to sweeping reforms enacted as part of the 1996 welfare reform law, have numerous collection mechanisms and information systems at their finger tips. In the last decade, child support collections nationwide have nearly doubled to about $18 billion.

Child support payments are potentially a major support for struggling single mothers and their children. If a mother of two earning $10,000 received even the modest sum of $2,000 in child support, her total income including EITC, food stamps, and child support would be $18,000. Unfortunately, data from the Census Bureau show that only about one quarter of single mothers with total incomes below $23,000 received child support in 2000 and the average amount they received was only $620. On the other hand, the mothers who actually received child support in 2000 got almost $2,600, a considerable sum to these families. It does appear that both the percentage of families receiving child support and the amount of money they receive are creeping up, although the pace of improvement is slow.

Even so, a realistic assessment of the role of child support in supporting low-income single mothers requires us to have modest expectations. The program is improving and the help provided to mothers who actually receive payments is substantial. But future improvement is constrained by the fact that many of the fathers of poor mothers have limited income, especially when they are young. Even so, the nation should continue its current course of aggressive improvement in the child support program. The frequency of paternity establishment, which more than doubled between 1994 and 2000, is one of the great successes of social policy in recent decades and implies that the program can expect to continue its current path of modest improvement. One policy that would lead to instant improvement in the financial status of single mothers is reversing the current practice of government retention of some child support payments to mothers who spent time on welfare. Approximately half the money collected on overdue child support owed to mothers who have left welfare is retained by states as an offset for welfare payments. If Congress provided financial incentives for states to give all this money to mothers, the income of these mothers could be increased by as much as $1 billion per year.

Education and Training Greater access to education and training would seem to be an obvious solution to the low wages earned by less skilled workers. For this reason, the pre-1996 welfare system stressed the importance of helping recipients acquire skills before taking a job. In contrast, the new law stresses "work first" and limits access to skill-building programs among those still on welfare.

This new emphasis is based on research, such as a recent comprehensive study by the Manpower Demonstration Research Corporation, suggesting that "work first" is a more cost effective approach to increasing employment and earnings. In addition, welfare leavers have the same opportunities to access community colleges, tuition assistance through Pell grants, and other forms of training as the rest of the low-income population. However, some liberalization of the amount of education and training that can be counted toward a state's work participation requirement might enable more mothers on welfare to gain the skills they need to get better jobs with higher pay. This approach might be especially appropriate for mothers returning to the welfare rolls because they have been laid off from their jobs during a recession. This group is likely to have a better understanding of the world of work, to be highly motivated to find work in another sector of the economy, and to have "earned" the right to upgrade their skills.

Not all education and training programs are effective. But programs that are closely aligned to the needs of employers, that use existing institutions such as community colleges, and that train for jobs in high growth sectors such as health care could probably help families move up the occupational ladder. Calls for more state flexibility in the use of TANF funds for such purposes, and especially for demonstration programs, are likely to be an important part of the reauthorization debate.

Streamlining the Process There are a variety of other support programs that low-income working families can access, including housing assistance, transportation assistance, and several child nutrition programs. Indeed, one problem for families is that there are a multitude of programs, all with somewhat different eligibility rules and administrative systems. Finding the time to apply, or reapply, for all of these different forms of assistance can be an exercise in frustration for an employed parent trying to balance work and care of children, especially if the benefits are uncertain or small. The result is that many families simply give up and fail to receive benefits for which they are eligible.

A possible solution is to establish a single application process for as many of these benefits as possible, to allow families to apply at times and places consistent with their work obligations, and to extend eligibility certification periods for those in regular jobs. If a single application for the EITC, the child tax credit, food stamps, Medicaid, and a child care voucher or tax credit could be established, it would go a long way toward solving the problems these families experience with bureaucratic hurdles. It would also make more visible a troubling feature of the entire system: as earnings increase these benefits disappear at a rapid rate, thereby undermining one of the goals of a system that is supposed to reward work. Unfortunately, there are no easy solutions to this problem, since making benefit reduction rates less steep would be very costly to the federal budget.

When Work Disappears: Unemployment Insurance, a Contingency Fund, and Community Service Jobs

Before welfare was reformed in 1996, the prevailing assumption was that low rates of employment among less educated mothers reflected, to a large degree, a dearth of jobs for which they qualified. But the experience of the late 1990s proved that even low-skilled individuals can, if pushed by the welfare system, pulled by the work support system, and buoyed by a strong economy, find work and increase their earnings. Employment rates among women with less than a high school degree, for example, increased from 33 percent to 53 percent between 1994 and 2001, according to the Urban Institute.

But there will always be some adults for whom finding a private-sector job is difficult and the number of such people invariably increases substantially during an economic downturn. Adults with an adequate work history who have been laid off (rather than quit their job) and who want to work full-time qualify for unemployment insurance. Research by Harry Holzer of Georgetown University suggests that 30 to 40 percent of welfare leavers qualify and might be eligible for benefits of around $400 a month. Proposals have been made to broaden coverage by including the most recent quarter of work in the base period earnings calculation; to include those seeking part-time as well as full-time work; to make the weekly benefit more generous; and to extend benefits from the normal 26 weeks to 39 weeks. If enacted, these reforms would increase the proportion of newly employed welfare mothers eligible for unemployment insurance. Even so, many mothers would remain ineligible, mainly because they often voluntarily leave rather than lose their jobs. In addition, the vast majority of adults who have left welfare since 1996 have not exhausted their five-year time limit and thus would be eligible to return to the welfare rolls.

Also worrisome is the possibility that fiscally-strapped states will not have sufficient funds during a recession to pay for both rising caseloads and continued work supports. Without some encouragement and assistance from the federal government, states are likely to cut back on existing work support services, such as child care, and channel the funds into paying for cash assistance. The progress that has been made over the past five years in linking many of the welfare poor to jobs could be threatened. To avoid this outcome, the federal government needs, at a minimum, to maintain existing TANF funding and may want to provide a cyclically based contingency fund to the states. A contingency fund was provided in the 1996 law but it expired at the end of fiscal 2001. Some states have been able to save a portion of their TANF block grant and can draw down these rainy day funds to pay for rising caseloads. But others have exhausted these surpluses, responding in part to congressional prompting that they should use them or lose them.

Still another possibility is that the economy will remain somewhat depressed for a lengthy period and fail to replicate the very low unemployment conditions of the late 1990s. In this case, states may want to provide community service jobs for those unable to find work in the private sector. In the absence of such programs, it will be hard for states to enforce existing work requirements and time limits on welfare. The availability of community service jobs is not only the ultimate safety net but helps to discriminate between those who really want to work and those who use the perceived lack of jobs as a reason to stay home. So far only a few states and communities have felt the need to provide jobs of last resort for those unable to find jobs in the private sector.

Summing Up The reform of the welfare system in 1996 has tended to overshadow equally important reforms in the work support system over the past decade and a half. Not only has the federal government expanded its support—especially for the EITC, Medicaid, and child care—but the states have used the funds freed up by the decline in their welfare caseloads to invest heavily in these same supports. When Congress takes up welfare reform reauthorization in 2002, policies to maintain and improve the work support system should be an important part of the debate.

Table 1
Pros and Cons of Proposals to Expand the Work Support System

Pros	Cons
Raise the Minimum Wage and Index it for Inflation	
• A $1.00 increase would remove roughly one million people from poverty	• Business might hire fewer low-wage workers, especially youth
• Indexation would protect low-wage workers' standard of living and ensure that Congress does not have to continually adjust the minimum	• Costs would be a burden to the private sector, especially as it struggles to recover from recession
• Benefits would ripple up the wage scale, producing additional benefits for low-wage workers	• Most people who receive the minimum wage are not poor
Add a Second Tier to EITC and Integrate with Child Tax Credit	
• Encourages work, especially full time work, and improves living standards	• Depending on generosity of second tier, and phase out rates, could be expensive
• Simplifies the tax system	• Uses the tax system to achieve social objectives (a back-door spending program)
• Better targets existing tax credits on low and moderate-income families	• Does not help those unable to earn $10,000 a year
• Helps mothers stay off welfare	• Does not get funds to people on a weekly or monthly basis (tax payments are usually annual)

Table 1, continued

Pros	Cons
Stop Clock for Recipients Working More than Twenty Hours a Week While on Welfare	
• Encourages mixing of welfare and work among low-wage workers which research shows to be a more cost-effective strategy for reducing poverty and improving child outcomes than welfare or work requirements alone • Simplifies state funds accounting	• May lead to long-term dependency on government benefits • May not send strong signal to frontline workers or recipients about temporary nature of assistance
Provide Federal Incentive for States to Expand their EITCs	
• Makes work pay • Unlike work disregards, not limited to welfare recipients • Promotes federal-state sharing of financial responsibility for working poor • Two-parent families might have one parent spend more time with their children	• Potentially very expensive • Bigger EITC benefit would cause some adults to work fewer hours
Encourage States to Strengthen Work Supports by Increasing TANF Funding	
• Maintains momentum of existing state efforts to help the working poor and thereby reduces dependency • Recognizes that cash assistance caseload is no longer an adequate measure of need • Allows for local choice and experimentation	• No assurance states will use TANF funds to expand work supports • Expensive
Replace TANF Caseload Credit with Credit Linked to Employment	
• Provides greater incentive for states to meet their participation requirements by moving people into jobs and not just off welfare • Encourages states to develop work programs so more TANF recipients can be productively engaged	• Difficult to administer; must define what counts as employment and how long it needs to last • Does not recognize marriage as important route off welfare
Improve Application Process for Food Stamps and Other Noncash Benefits	
• Addresses the problem that low participation rates are caused in part by difficulty of applying for benefits • Rewards working families for responsible behavior • Increases the well-being of working families	• Political and bureaucratic hurdles • Increased error rates • Increased costs

Table 1, continued

Pros	Cons
Expand Medicaid Coverage to Parents	
• Improves access to health care for low-income adults who are working but uninsured • May increase participation among eligible children	• Imposes new costs on both federal and state governments • May substitute for employer-provided coverage
Increase Funding for Child Care	
• Allows states to serve more low-income families, increase provider reimbursement rates, or lower co-payments by families • Promotes equity between welfare leavers and other low-income families • Allows states to make additional investments in quality child care	• Possible substitution of paid for unpaid care • Federal Government is already spending a lot • Does not sufficiently reward other reasons for reduced dependency (e.g., marriage) • Expensive
Allow More Education and Training to Count Toward Work Participation Rates	
• Encourages states to design programs to upgrade skills • May lead to increased earnings and reduce welfare use, especially over longer run	• Evidence that education and training for adults on welfare increases employment or wages is weak • Might undermine effort to change culture and expectations in welfare offices to focus on work
Give All Child Support Payments to Mothers and Children	
• Will increase the financial security of female-headed low-income families • May allow mothers to work less and spend more time with their children • May provide incentives for low-income fathers to pay child support • May improve relations between fathers and their children and the children's mother	• May reduce work effort by mothers • Expensive for both federal and state governments
Provide a Contingency Fund to Pay for Increase in Caseloads During Recessions	
• Provides safety net for laid-off low-income workers • State balanced budget requirements limit state spending during recessions • Provides federal stimulus to offset state spending decline	• Work support a lower priority than welfare and may have to be sacrificed during a downturn • Expensive

Table 1, continued

Pros	Cons
Reform Unemployment Insurance	
• By making more low-wage workers eligible, reduces likelihood of return to welfare	• Most proposals would not reach many adults who have left welfare
	• Part-time workers and those with limited experience have not earned benefits
Encourage States to Provide Community Service Jobs	
• Helps the hardest to employ and those unemployed in a slack economy	• Hard to administer
• Makes a work requirement more reasonable	• Could displace low-paid workers who are already employed
• Identifies those already working or unwilling to work	• Expensive

Additional Reading

Congressional Budget Office. 1998. *Policy Changes Affecting Mandatory Spending for Low-Income Families not Receiving Cash Welfare.* Washington, D.C..

Falk, Gene. August 6, 2001. *Welfare Reform: FY2000 TANF Spending and Recent Spending Trends.* Washington, D.C.: Congressional Research Service.

Hart, Peter D. 2001. *Poll on Tax Policies and the Needs of Poor and Low-Income Americans* (Memorandum). See: http://www.makingwageswork.org/hartmemo.htm.

Holzer, Harry J., and Douglas Wissoker. 2001. *How Can We Encourage Job Retention and Advancement for Welfare Recipients?* (Series A, No. A-49). Washington, D.C.: Urban Institute.

Manpower Demonstration Research Corporation. 2001. *National Evaluation of Welfare-to-Work Strategies.* New York.

Robins, Philip K., Charles Michalopoulos, and Elsie Pan. 2001. "Financial Incentives and Welfare Reform in the United States." *Journal of Policy Analysis and Management*, 20(1): 129-149.

Sawhill, Isabel, and Adam Thomas. 2001. *A Hand Up for the Bottom Third: Toward a New Agenda for Low-Income Working Families* (Children's Roundtable Working Paper). Washington, D.C.: Brookings.

Zedlewski, Sheila R., Sara H. Brauner. 1999. *Are the Steep Declines in Food Stamp Participation Linked to Falling Welfare Caseloads?* (Series B, No. B-3). Washington, D.C.: Urban Institute.

13

JUDITH M. GUERON AND GAYLE HAMILTON

The Role of Education and Training in Welfare Reform

Executive Summary

To what extent should welfare-to-work programs emphasize education and training versus immediate job placement? This controversial question will be important in the 2002 debate on welfare reform. Findings from rigorous studies show that there is a clear role for skills-building activities. The key lesson is balance. Rigid job-search-first and rigid education-or-training-first programs increase employment, but the former get people jobs sooner and at lower cost and the latter do not ultimately get people better jobs. The most successful programs use a mixed strategy—where some people are urged to get a job quickly and others are offered work-focused, short-term education or training. While encouraging overall, the findings provide no basis for complacency. The failure of mandatory basic education to help high school dropouts, the lack of clear guidance on what makes training effective, and the low earnings and persistent poverty of most welfare leavers point to the continued need to identify pre- and post-employment strategies that are more successful in getting people higher-wage jobs. The implication for welfare reform is that participation standards should retain their focus on work but avoid restrictions that discourage a mixed strategy.

In recent years, single mothers on welfare have gone to work in unprecedented numbers. But with limited skills and work histories, they usually get low-paying jobs and remain in poverty. The situation is especially acute for the half of the caseload that does not graduate from high school. Since recipients with higher skills tend to get better jobs, it seems logical that education and training should play a central role in welfare reform. But what kind of role?

Alternative Strategies in Welfare-to-Work Programs

Welfare policy reflects an ongoing effort to balance two objectives—reducing poverty and ending dependency. Reformers on all sides favor these goals, but disagree on which should receive priority and on the most effective strategy for achieving them. As a result, states have used variants of three broad approaches to structure the welfare-to-work component of welfare reform.

Education or Training First Adherents of putting adults on welfare into education or training programs before requiring them to find work stress antipoverty goals and view reforms that substitute work for welfare as insufficient if there is no increase in income. Before looking for work, they argue, welfare recipients need to improve their skills so they can get a job—especially one that is relatively stable, pays enough to support their children, and leaves them less vulnerable during an economic downturn. For those who lack a high school diploma or GED (high school equivalency) certificate, this view translates programmatically into referral to basic education courses, including remedial instruction in reading and math, English as a Second Language classes, or preparation for the GED test (much less common are programs that mix adult education and vocational training). For those with a high school diploma or GED, the education-or-training-first approach usually means assignment to vocational training, rather than to degree-producing, post-secondary academic courses.

Job Search First Others place greater emphasis on reducing the welfare rolls and saving money. They advocate strategies that move people quickly into jobs, even if the jobs pay low wages. Some, focused on welfare reduction, see work as the most direct route to ending what they view as the negative effects of welfare on families and children. Some focus on the savings to be attained by both diminished caseloads and the relatively low cost of job search services themselves, reasoning that, given fixed budgets, they can serve more people using this strategy. A job-search-first strategy can also reflect anti-poverty goals. Some hold that getting a job, even a low-paying one, is the best way to build skills that can eventually lead to better jobs. Others believe that, in any labor market, most welfare recipients will inevitably get low-wage jobs and that the best, most realistic way to reduce poverty is through more generous subsidies and services to working families. In job-search-first programs, virtually everyone must start by looking for a job independently or through a job club, which teaches such skills as résumé-writing and interviewing. After several weeks, participants typically get aided in their search by program staff. Job search first is usually not, however, job search only. People who fail to find work may be referred to education or training.

Mixed Strategy Some reformers favor a more flexible approach, allowing staff and participants more choice in the initial and subsequent activities. Some participants, usually those lacking a high school diploma or GED, are assigned initially to basic education or training, while others are most often assigned first to job search. Subsequent activities vary for those still on welfare. Some mixed programs strongly emphasize employment: staff urge participants to find work and permit only short-term education or training activities. Others emphasize skill-building: participants may enter long-term education or training programs, and getting a job quickly is not paramount.

Education and Training in the Context of Welfare Reform

Since 1971, federal welfare legislation has required that an increasing share of welfare recipients participate in some form of work-directed activities as a condition of receiving full (or, more recently, any) welfare benefits. Even without any special welfare-to-work program, however, many low-income people enroll in school, training, community college, or some other program to help them gain skills and find work. This voluntary activity may have a big payoff, but it is not due to welfare reform and cannot reliably be captured in studies of reform programs.

Thus, asking about the value of education and training as part of welfare reform has a special meaning: does requiring education or training for people who may or may not want to participate have the intended positive results relative to what people would have achieved on their own or to other approaches such as job search? This question is particularly relevant to mandatory basic education, since few welfare recipients (only 8 percent in some studies) state that they want to go back to school to study reading and math; they have had poor experiences in school in the past and prefer to get specific skills training (around 60 percent) or help looking for a job (about 30 percent).

The Studies

The research on these three strategies, based on programs that operated between 1985 and 1999, is unusually reliable because it:

- covers programs representing a variety of specific approaches and conditions;
- includes results from almost 100,000 single parents, a sufficient number for reliably assessing the programs' effects;
- follows people for five years, long enough to determine whether an up-front investment in education or training pays off;
- measures what the three strategies produce when implemented under real-world conditions; and
- uses random assignment, the most powerful research design, in which welfare recipients are placed through a lottery-like process in a mandatory welfare-to-work program or in a control group. Control group members are not required to participate in any activities but can (and very often do) seek out such services in the community.

The last factor is the most fundamental. By assigning people randomly to either a welfare-to-work program or a control group, the studies can safely attribute any subsequent difference in their or their children's behavior to the particular program strategy. These differences are called the program's "impacts." Throughout this brief, saying that a program increased some outcome—for example, earnings—does not refer to how people's behavior changed over time, but to how people subject to a particular welfare-to-work strategy performed relative to the study's control group.

The findings come primarily from comparing results across twenty programs in five of the largest welfare-to-work studies—the National Evaluation of Welfare-to-Work Strategies (NEWWS; 11 programs), the evaluations of California's Greater Avenues for Independence Program (GAIN; 6 programs), Los Angeles's Jobs-First GAIN, Florida's Project Independence, and San Diego's Saturation Work Initiative Model (SWIM)—and from a head-to-head test in NEWWS of the first two approaches. Thus, this brief builds on the work of many people, especially researchers at the Manpower Demonstration Research Corporation in New York City who conducted these studies and analyzed the results.

The studies were launched prior to the 1996 welfare reforms (some of the programs continue today with modifications) and thus assessed the impact of different pre-employment strategies before there were time limits on welfare receipt, more generous limits on what people can earn and still receive welfare, and larger penalties (sanctions) for noncompliance with the program. The implementation of the 1996 welfare reforms might change somewhat the magnitude of the impacts, but would be unlikely to affect the relative success of the three strategies.

The Findings

Summary All three strategies increased single parents' work and reduced welfare

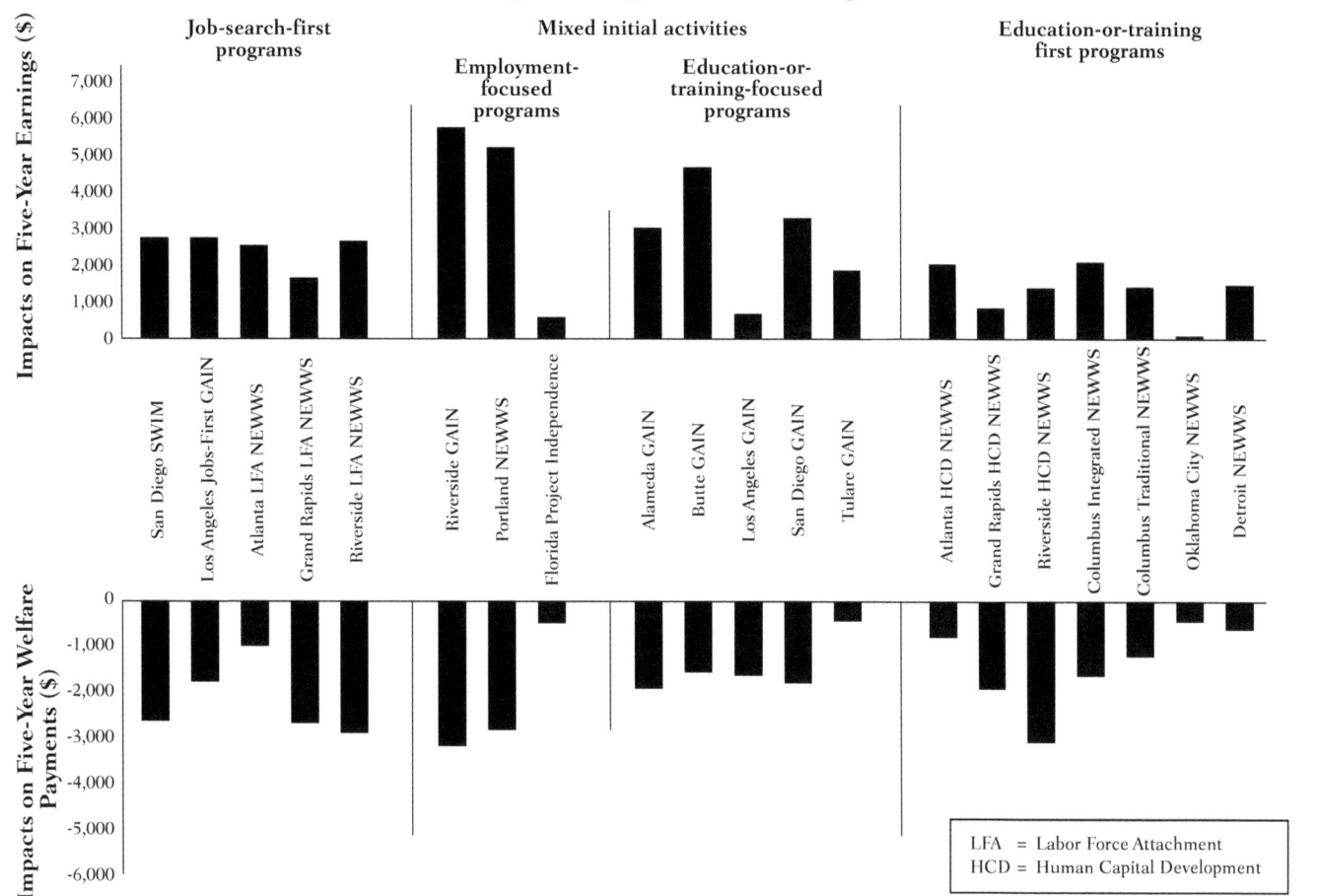

Figure 1
Work-Focused Mixed Programs Were Most Successful in Both Increasing Earnings and Reducing Welfare

Source: Published reports from Manpower Demonstration Research Corporation (MDRC) program evaluations and new MDRC analyses.

Notes: Results are in 1997 dollars. For Los Angeles Jobs-First GAIN, Florida Project Independence, and Oklahoma City NEWWS (welfare payments only), five-year impacts were estimated from two- or three-year data. Impacts were statistically significant at the 10 percent level or below except for earnings in Los Angeles GAIN, Grand Rapids HCD NEWWS, and Oklahoma City NEWWS; and for welfare payments in Butte GAIN and Tulare GAIN.

receipt compared to what would have happened in the absence of the programs, but they did not increase people's income or have many or consistently positive or negative effects on children, except for adolescents.

People in job-search-first programs took jobs sooner. Those in education-or-training-first programs eventually caught up, but the larger up-front investment had no clear payoff in higher wages or income, or in improved outcomes for children, relative to job-search-first programs.

The best results came from programs that used a mix of initial activities, where some people started with job search and others with short-term, work-focused education or training. These findings hold true for high school graduates and nongraduates alike.

Twenty-Program Comparison Figure 1 shows the impact, over the five years after a person enrolled, of programs that used different variants of the three strategies. Each bar represents one program and shows the difference between the average total earnings (top panel) or welfare payments (bottom panel) of all single parents required to participate in the program and all those in the study's control group. The top panel shows that all the programs increased earnings, with almost all differences reaching statistical significance, but those that used a mixed strategy tended to have the largest impacts. The bottom panel shows that welfare savings were largest in job-search-first and mixed programs that focused on employment.

The mixed-strategy programs that were employment-focused (Portland and Riverside GAIN) emerged as clear winners, producing unusually large earnings gains and taxpayer savings and, for Portland (not shown), more stable employment and higher wages. The Florida results in figure 1 show, however, that this approach does not guarantee success. Other features of the Florida program—limited child care funding, weak job search activities, and a rigid method for determining who received education or training—probably compromised its success.

Although most programs increased earnings, they reduced welfare and food stamp payments by a similar amount. Over five years, people derived more of their income from earnings but were generally not better off financially as a result of the program compared to control group members. These findings hold even when estimates of Earned Income Tax Credits, state and federal taxes, and Medicaid are included in the calculations.

Figure 1 is persuasive because it shows patterns replicated over a number of locations. But there is always a question as to whether such cross-site comparisons reflect differences in the value added by the welfare-to-work strategy itself, the characteristics of the people studied, the local economy, or the welfare and community context.

Three-Site Test of Two Approaches To eliminate this uncertainty, NEWWS fielded a highly unusual study in Atlanta, Georgia; Grand Rapids, Michigan; and Riverside, California. In each of these sites, welfare recipients were assigned at random to one of three groups: a job-search-first program that allowed short-term education or training only for those who did not initially get work through job clubs (an approach labeled "Labor Force Attachment," or LFA, in this evaluation); an education-or-training-first program that assigned most people to education or training before requiring job search (called "Human Capital Development," or HCD); or a control group. A comparison of results for the LFA and HCD groups, presented in figure 1, reveals few differences: the HCD approach did not produce the expected added benefits. Any differences for particular years or measures or subgroups that did occur favored the LFA programs.

The five-year results shown in figure 1 mask a strong difference in the pattern of impacts over time. People in the LFA programs found jobs and got off welfare sooner, a clear advantage when welfare is time limited. People in the HCD programs caught up with those in the LFA programs some time after leaving education or training, but did not end up in higher-paying, more stable jobs, even though the HCD programs ultimately cost 40 to 90 percent more to operate. Finally, there was no difference in the effects of the two approaches on the well-being of children, despite some hope that the HCD parents' greater attendance in education or training might lead their children to do better in school. In NEWWS, both types of programs had few effects or, in the case of adolescents, some negative effects on a few outcomes such as grade repetition.

Looking at different subgroups within the welfare caseload, this basic pattern held true for most groups, including those with different skills, work history, and race/

ethnicity. The findings were particularly disappointing for those without a high school diploma (or GED) and for other highly disadvantaged groups who were expected to benefit most from the initial investment in basic education. Whether because of the quality of the services or the short time that most people stayed in them, people without a high school diploma in the HCD programs did not measurably improve their reading or math literacy or end up with better jobs than those in the LFA programs. Quite the contrary: where differences showed up, it was the LFA programs that led to higher earnings and income. In a nonexperimental analysis, however, Johannes Bos of the Manpower Demonstration Research Corporation finds some evidence that the small number of women in the HCD programs who obtained a general equivalency degree may ultimately have had higher earnings, particularly if they went on to vocational skills training. But he also found that staying longer in general equivalency degree test preparation classes would not have appreciably increased the proportion of women who obtained this credential.

The findings on training for welfare recipients with a high school diploma or GED are somewhat more mixed. The most relevant data, again from the HCD/LFA comparison, show no added impact from the HCD strategy. Two major evaluations of voluntary programs suggest some reasons why the training-focused programs did not perform better. The National Job Training Partnership Act Study (JTPA), led by Larry Orr of Abt Associates, found that, on average, classroom skills training did not increase the earnings of welfare recipients, although other JTPA activities that included a combination of on-the-job training and job search did. In the Minority Female Single Parent Demonstration, John Burghardt at Mathematica Policy Research studied four remedial education and skills training programs for single mothers, most of whom were on welfare. One program, the Center for Employment Training in San Jose, increased earnings and wages. Researchers attributed this success to the program's strong connection to the job market, its integration of education and training curricula, the absence of entry tests, and easily accessible child care. These findings suggest that the unimpressive results from past training programs may derive, in part, from the inflexible structure of the courses (education preceding skills training), the people enrolled, the support services, or the types of training women are placed in. However, the evidence is thin and, importantly, does not encompass rigorous studies of training provided by community colleges or of degree-granting, post-secondary academic programs.

Characteristics of the Most Successful Programs

The welfare-to-work programs that were the most successful overall for both high school graduates and nongraduates—Portland and Riverside GAIN—were flexible about initial activities. Both programs strongly enforced participation requirements, had experience operating job search programs, stressed the importance of finding jobs (a message that permeated all aspects of Riverside's operations), and used job developers. In Portland, however, job search participants were counseled to wait for jobs that paid well above the minimum wage and that offered the best chance for long-lasting, stable employment, whereas Riverside participants were advised to take the first job offered, since any job was viewed as a good job.

Regarding education and training, staff in both programs communicated that improving people's employability was the goal—assignments were limited in duration (usually six months or less), and people were not allowed to "languish" in these activities without making progress. Most people not ready to enter the labor market—based on such factors as work history, education, and literacy test scores—were first assigned, in both programs, to basic education or, in Portland, to three- to five-week life skills classes or occupational training. The others—usually those who had a high school diploma or GED—were most commonly assigned first to job search or, in Portland, to life skills, vocational training, or work experience. Finally, the small number already enrolled in degree-granting, post-secondary academic programs when they entered the program were allowed to continue, provided they could obtain their degree in a short time.

The two programs differed, however, in how they provided education and training. In Portland, program administrators took the unusual step of partnering with the community college system to design and implement the courses and provide comprehensive case management. In contrast, the Riverside welfare department solely administered its program and, while using some community colleges to provide education and training, relied primarily on adult education schools, offering payments based on measures of student performance to several of the schools.

Lessons and Implications for TANF Reauthorization

These findings point to several lessons about the role of education and training in welfare reform. First, whether the goal is reducing poverty, reducing dependency, saving money, or helping children, there is no evidence to support a rigid education-or-training-first policy. The findings are particularly discouraging for mandatory basic education.

Second, there is a clear role for skills-enhancing activities in welfare reform. The unusually successful Portland and Riverside GAIN programs suggest a balanced approach, which emphasizes employment but uses some work-focused, short-term education and training.

Third, the solution to low earnings is not more of the same kind of training used in the past. Historically, training programs have often had no direct link to jobs in demand in the local economy or to local employers. They have also often shut out the most disadvantaged. Remedial education and GED test preparation programs could not retain people or, conversely, kept them for years without clear progress. All this suggests that program operators need to identify and systematically evaluate alternative pre- and post-employment approaches. The approaches should include training that fosters career advancement, integrates basic education and skills training, and engages local employers. Welfare recipients should also have access to support services that will increase program retention.

Finally, the findings reported here show that while well-designed welfare-to-work programs can substantially increase earnings and reduce dependency, there are limits to this approach. In the typical NEWWS program, after five years, working women's annual earnings were about $12,500, 25 percent were still on welfare, and children were doing worse in their school performance and social behavior than children nationally. Recent research showing that children do better in school when work leads to higher income points to the importance of services and policies, like the Earned Income Tax Credit, that augment the efforts of the working poor to support themselves and their families.

The welfare-to-work pendulum has swung from quick employment in the early 1980s, to skills enhancement in the late 1980s, and then back to quick employment in the mid-1990s—when the federal welfare reform legislation gave states great flexibility but sent a clear pro-work, anti-education message through its detailed language on what activities would "count" in federal participation rates. The Temporary Assistance for Needy Families (TANF) shift was prompted in part by the demonstrated success of Riverside's GAIN program, but reflected Riverside's strong pro-work message while ignoring its more balanced service mix.

This brief suggests that the pendulum has swung too far. TANF's focus on employment is well placed, but does not encourage states to maximize the payoff that education and training can have. The frustration for policymakers is that, while the potential payoff to the flexible use of work-focused, short-term training and GED preparation is clear, the research leaves many questions unanswered. We still know little about the success of more innovative pre- and post-employment training and community college programs, yet innovation is clearly called for if welfare reform is to deliver on its potential not only to save money but also to help families increase their income.

Additional Reading

Bloom, Dan, and Charles Michalopoulos. 2001. *How Welfare and Work Policies Affect Employment and Income: A Synthesis of Research.* New York: Manpower Demonstration Research Corporation.

Burghardt, John, and others. 1992. *Evaluation of the Minority Female Single Parent Demonstration: Volume 1, Summary Report.* New York: Rockefeller Foundation.

Freedman, Stephen, and others. 1996. "Five-Year Impacts on Employment, Earnings, and AFDC Receipt." GAIN Evaluation Working Paper 96.1. New York: Manpower Demonstration Research Corporation.

Hamilton, Gayle, and others. 2001. *How Effective Are Different Welfare-to-Work Approaches? Five-Year Adult and Child Impacts for Eleven Programs.* Washington, D.C.: U.S. Department of Health and Human Services and U.S. Department of Education.

Orr, Larry L., and others. 1996. *Does Training for the Disadvantaged Work? Evidence from the National JTPA Study.* Washington, D.C.: Urban Institute.

Riccio, James, and others. 1994. *GAIN: Benefits, Costs, and Three-Year Impacts of a Welfare-to-Work Program.* New York: Manpower Demonstration Research Corporation.

NANCYE CAMPBELL, JOHN K. MANIHA, AND HOWARD ROLSTON

Job Retention and Advancement in Welfare Reform

Executive Summary
Building on their success in moving welfare recipients into work, some state and local governments are implementing programs to help low-income parents retain jobs, quickly find new jobs after job loss, and advance to better jobs. Although quite a bit is known about what circumstances are associated with job retention and advancement, much less is known about what government or private programs can do to encourage them. Several studies suggest that wage subsidies or better initial placements can lead to greater job stability, but that broad, non-targeted post-employment services are likely to be ineffective. However there are not enough of these studies to provide states with definitive, reliable information. Congress will need to continue to support flexibility and funding in its welfare programs if state governments and the research community are to develop accurate information about how to promote retention and advancement.

With implementation of welfare waivers and the subsequent enactment of federal welfare reform legislation in 1996, state and local governments began to transform the welfare system through systematic implementation of mandatory programs to help welfare recipients get jobs. These efforts built on fifteen years of innovative efforts and rigorous evaluations at the state and local level. The resulting growth in employment for low-income mothers has surpassed all expectations. Analysis of Census Bureau data by Richard Bavier of the Federal Office of Management and Budget (OMB), for example, shows that real annual earnings (in 2000 dollars) of females heading families with children who were in the next-to-bottom fifth of the income distribution (with family incomes between $13,000 and $21,000 in 2000) increased from $2,254 in 1993 to $9,555 in 2000, a more than four-fold increase over this seven-year period.

Programs that help low-income mothers get jobs are now being augmented by programs that help them keep jobs and move up the employment ladder. Typically the term "retention" means not necessarily keeping a particular job (since changing jobs could be a step up the job ladder) but rather staying steadily employed in any job. Although "advancement" can encompass many things, including increased benefits or the quality of work itself, this brief will focus on wage or earnings growth. The major purposes of this policy brief are to examine why government has an interest in job retention and advancement, to analyze the policies that may promote retention and advancement among current and former welfare recipients, and to describe the current state and local programs aimed at promoting retention and advancement.

Research Findings on Patterns of Retention and Advancement

Research shows that the employment pattern for many welfare recipients has been getting a job, losing or quitting the job, and then experiencing long periods between jobs. Anu Rangarajan and her colleagues at Mathematica Policy Research in Princeton, New Jersey used information from a national survey to study the employment experiences of welfare recipients who found jobs. The survey showed that a substantial majority of adults leaving welfare lost their jobs fairly quickly. Few became steadily employed over five years: only 30 percent were employed for more than three-fourths of the weeks over the five-year period. Clearly, sporadic employment contributes to the low average earnings of these mothers. But it is also likely that it has contributed to poor job advancement, since working intermittently at low-wage jobs is unlikely to lead to better jobs over time.

Not only are welfare leavers likely to lose their jobs, but even when they stay employed, their wages grow slowly if at all. Rangarajan found little wage rate growth over time, around 10 percent over five years on average. However, Rangarajan found substantial increases in earnings due to increased hours of work. Based on data from a national survey, Gary Burtless of the Brookings Institution found that young women who received cash welfare between 1979 and 1981, but then left welfare for employment, experienced annual hourly wage gains of less than one percent through 1990. Despite this lack of wage growth, these young women nearly tripled their earnings over the period because they greatly increased their hours of work. Still, even after this substantial increase, average annual earnings were less than $7,000. Thus, even when wage growth is positive, it is on base earnings that are so small that the wage increases still result in extended periods of low

---

Even when wage growth is positive, it is on base earnings that are so small that the wage increases still result in extended periods of low earnings.

---

earnings. Of course, these estimates constitute averages, made up both of individuals whose wages and earnings progress well, and of others whose wages are stagnant.

Although these descriptive statistics provide good evidence for why states should be paying attention to job retention and advancement issues, they may be somewhat outdated. This is especially the case because there were positive changes in the economic and policy environments during the 1980s and the 1990s as well as a substantial increase in the level of work among welfare recipients during the 1990s. These changes could have altered prior patterns of wages and earnings for the better. Certainly, both the rewards for working and the costs of not working are greater now.

Despite these improvements in the

economy and in employment rates, Pamela Holcomb of the Urban Institute in Washington, D.C., using data from the National Survey of American Families conducted by the Urban Institute, finds that although welfare leavers in 1999 had greater stability in a particular job than did leavers in 1997, there were still substantial levels of job instability. Richard Bavier of OMB, using data from the Survey of Income and Program Participation for a somewhat different period, finds that individuals who left welfare for employment in recent years were more likely to lose their jobs than those who left earlier.

In sum, research strongly supports governments' continued interest in enhancing the ability of low-income mothers to work steadily and advance in the workforce. If the goal of welfare reform is to substitute a system of work supports for a system of welfare supports, then investments to help low-income parents work steadily and move into jobs that can more fully support their families is integral to that agenda.

Circumstances Associated with Retention and Advancement

Anu Rangarajan and her colleagues found that the characteristics of both the individual and the job were important factors in sustained employment. Welfare recipients who became parents in their teens, had no high school diploma or GED, or had low skills worked less than those without these characteristics. Job characteristics, such as wage level and health insurance availability, were also strongly associated with employment stability. Other research has found that low-skilled workers in some industries and occupations keep their jobs longer and make higher wages than low-skilled workers in other industries and occupations. For example,

Research strongly supports governments' continued interest in enhancing the ability of low-income mothers to work steadily and advance in the workforce.

those who work in health and professional/educational services are relatively better off on these measures than those who work in other occupations.

Other research has found no link between having a high school diploma and wage growth, other things equal. Post-high school education or training, however, is strongly linked to subsequently higher wages. Some studies have found that changing jobs can be associated with higher wages, but not involuntary changes or too many changes.

Evidence on What Causes Better Retention and Advancement

While these analyses provide useful insights, their causal implications are limited because they do not account for certain intangible factors, such as motivation, that may lead to greater job retention and higher wages. In addition, the findings are often inconsistent. Better evidence comes from evaluations that randomly assign individuals to different treatments. These random-assignment evaluations almost always show that welfare-to-work programs have only small effects on employment stability and little or no impact on wage rates, even in programs that substantially increase earnings as people work more hours. These findings hold true both for programs that emphasize job search and those that emphasize education and skill training (see chapter 13). One exception to this pattern is a government program in Portland, Oregon that led to large gains in stable employment and earnings growth. Unlike other programs, the Portland program, while maintaining a strong emphasis on the goal of rapid employment, allowed initial participation in short-term training programs and encouraged participants to seek not just any job, but good jobs with salaries above minimum wage and with benefits. This result is consistent with the studies described above, but provides stronger evidence that the quality of the first job may play a causal role in subsequent job stability and advancement.

The findings discussed thus far are from programs providing pre-employment services such as job clubs, job search assistance, education, and training. There is a more limited amount of research on post-employment programs. A study by Rangarajan and Tim Novak of Mathematica evaluated case management-based retention programs in four states. This study found that only one program produced even small effects on employment stability. Consistent with earlier research, the evaluations found that many recipients lost their jobs within the first few months, with only about 40 percent continuously employed in the same job for 12 months. Although the impact findings were disappointing, there are some lessons that can be drawn from this evaluation. Case managers focused their efforts on helping remove employment barriers, but the evaluation suggests that this by itself did not affect employment outcomes. Also, the programs attempted to provide services to all experimental group members. Perhaps more intensive services targeted to those most at risk of poor outcomes would provide for more efficient use of resources and produce larger impacts. Finally, there is evidence from several experimental evaluations that providing wage subsidies increases job stability, especially for more disadvantaged workers.

Perhaps more intensive services targeted to those most at risk of poor outcomes would provide for more efficient use of resources and produce larger impacts.

State and Local Efforts to Increase Retention and Advancement

Current research does not provide strong evidence for specific programs and policies that could be adopted to help mothers leaving welfare increase their wages. Nonetheless, state and local policymakers and program administrators need to make informed decisions about how to invest resources to boost wages and income. The Administration for Children and Families (ACF) of the U.S. Department of Health and Human Services is currently working with fourteen intervention programs in nine states to test several interventions that may help parents acquire the skills they need to get better jobs with higher wages. The Manpower Demonstration Research Corporation is evaluating the effectiveness of these programs.

A primary assumption of the state programs is that a strong employment focus will continue to characterize welfare-to-work efforts and that enhancements to improve retention and advancement should not result in lengthy absences of individuals from the workforce. Thus, states have attempted to enhance the work first approach, which emphasizes rapid placement in a job, with additional services that may help mothers get better jobs. Within this general context, a program's design can be examined along five dimensions:

- Is the primary focus of the program retention or advancement?
- Are services embedded in work, or do they occur outside it?
- Are services embedded in pre-employment or post-employment activities?
- What are the incentives to participate, including whether the program is mandatory or voluntary?
- Are parents on welfare, former welfare recipients, or all low-income parents eligible for services?

Keeping these five dimensions in mind, we turn to a description of program models that illustrates the range of choices states in the current ACF study are making to promote better jobs and more permanent employment. In Texas, the program's centerpiece is an individual plan for each parent that specifies both work supports and a career plan for how the parent can move ahead. Intensive case management is provided to assist individuals in complying with the plan. The focus is on both elements related to retention, such as planning for back-up child care, and elements related to advancement, such as options for further training. Recipients in work preparation activities are required to develop a plan and are subject to sanction for noncompliance. Because of fairly low benefit levels in Texas, however, individuals quickly lose eligibility for cash assistance when they become employed. To improve continued engagement and compliance, the state provides a $200 per month expense allowance for one year to working individuals who continue to comply with their plan. Thus, the Texas program addresses both retention and advancement, contains both pre- and post-employment services, and includes incentives—both mandatory requirements with potential sanctions and financial incentives—to participate.

The program in California faces different issues than the program in Texas in that, due to California's high welfare benefit, a family of three remains eligible for cash assistance even if a parent is working full-time at over $8 an hour. As a result, much of the program's focus is on job advancement in order to help families achieve a high enough level of earnings so they will no longer depend on welfare. One program being tested in Riverside involves the modification of a 32-hour work requirement to allow individuals established in the workforce to replace some hours of work with education or training. The relaxation of the work requirement allows individuals more time to obtain additional education and training primarily through post-employment, non-worksite training and education programs such as community college classes.

Illinois faces a similar challenge to California in that a substantial earnings disregard has created a very large pool of working recipients on the TANF caseload. Since Illinois does not count months of cash assistance receipt against the federal time limit for working parents, state officials are concerned about the significant number of individuals who appear to have "settled into" low-paying jobs. Illinois is now targeting working recipients who have remained on TANF after six months of employment (suggesting at best low earnings growth) and requiring them to participate in job advancement activities. These activities include substituting training and education for work (as long as a minimum 20 hours per week are worked), establishing a job advancement plan with their employer, and learning how to use past and current work experience to move into better jobs. Part of the underlying assumption in Illinois is that who have serious barriers to employment. Although goals may change in a weaker economy, most welfare agencies have come to believe that almost all individuals are capable of some kind of employment, and that retention is the primary employment problem for more disadvantaged recipients. The Portland model is targeting "recyclers," individuals who come back on assistance after working for some period of time. New York is using vocational rehabilitation services, work-based education, and specialized work

---

The federal government should continue to provide funds and flexibility to states so that better methods for increasing job retention and advancement can be created.

---

inexperienced workers may not know how to parlay their work experience into promotions or better jobs.

While the programs in Texas, California, and Illinois target current cash assistance recipients, other state programs target former recipients. South Carolina's program involves aggressive outreach to individuals who have been off cash assistance for at least nine months. Through this outreach and a variety of small financial incentives that reward achievements, the program aims to help individuals who are not working get a job, and help current workers move up the job ladder. The South Carolina study is important not only because it will measure the effectiveness of job services, but also because it will test the ability of state agencies to locate and work with individuals who have been off cash assistance for some time.

Programs in New York, Minnesota, and Oregon are focused almost exclusively on retention for hard-to-employ individuals

experience programs to improve employment performance by those with medical problems. And Minnesota is developing a program to provide work supports for those with mental health disorders.

Los Angeles is building on the Portland program that helped individuals locate better jobs with higher wage rates and better benefits. The Los Angeles model includes enhanced job clubs which initially assist recipients in looking for better jobs with higher wages and benefits, then reduce job quality expectations in stages over a two-week period for those who are not successful. This approach will be compared with the county's regular job clubs, which have been shown in a rigorous evaluation to have substantial and broad positive effects on employment and earnings.

Policy Implications

State and local officials have developed and are now implementing a range of strategies for employment retention and advancement. As Congress considers the reauthorization of TANF, lawmakers should keep in mind that flexibility within the current system has allowed state and local officials to design and test programs to address the retention and advancement needs of current or former TANF recipients. The evaluation partnerships that have been formed among local, state, and federal governments, businesses, evaluation companies, and local education and training entities have also supported this effort. States will need resources to continue to test these new approaches to job retention and advancement. The history of research and state demonstration programs shows the need for multiple efforts over time in order to ensure reliable information upon which successful policies can be constructed. As we have shown, the current research on job retention and advancement is not sufficient to recommend sweeping policy changes. Rather, the federal government should continue to provide funds and flexibility to states so that better methods for increasing job retention and advancement can be created.

Additional Reading

Bloom, Dan, and others. 2002. *New Strategies to Promote Stable Employment and Career Progression.* New York: Manpower Demonstration Research Corporation.

Burtless, Gary. 1995. "Employment Prospects of Welfare Recipients." In *The Work Alternative: Welfare Reform and the Realities of the Job Market,* edited by Demetra S. Nightengale and Robert H. Haveman. Washington, D.C.: Urban Institute.

Cancian, Maria, and others. 1999. *Work, Earnings and Well-Being after Welfare: What Do We Know?* Madison: Institute for Poverty Research.

Martinson, Karin. 2000. *The Experiences of Welfare Recipients Who Find Jobs.* New York: Manpower Demonstration Research Corporation.

Rangarajan, Anu, and others. 1998. *Employment Experiences of Welfare Recipients Who Find Jobs: Is Targeting Possible?* Princeton: Mathematica.

Rangarajan, Anu, and Tim Novak. 1999. *The Struggle to Sustain Employment: The Effectiveness of the Postemployment Services Demonstration.* Princeton: Mathematica.

Strawn, Julie, and Karin Martinson. 2000. *Steady Work and Better Jobs.* New York: Manpower Demonstration Research Corporation.

15

LADONNA PAVETTI
Helping the Hard-to-Employ

Executive Summary
Although the number of families receiving cash assistance has declined by 50 percent, and employment of never-married mothers has increased by an unprecedented amount since welfare reform legislation was enacted in 1996, the goals welfare reform set out to accomplish have not yet been fully achieved. A group of families deemed "the hard-to-employ" remain out of the labor force. These families face a broad range of potential barriers to employment including: personal and family challenges, such as mental health issues; human capital deficits, including limited work experience; and logistical obstacles, including transportation and child care. Welfare recipients facing these barriers—especially recipients facing more than one—are less likely to work than other welfare recipients. To help mothers facing barriers, states have implemented screenings and assessments, interventions such as mental health treatment programs, intensive case management, and enhanced transitional employment programs, including subsidized employment and unsubsidized supported employment programs. Congress should consider expanding the range of activities that count toward the work requirement, redesigning the time limit, assessing the design of sanction policies, and funding the implementation and evaluation of innovative strategies that address the needs of hard-to-employ families.

In the last five years, the nation has witnessed unprecedented changes in the circumstances of single-parent families and in the structure of the safety net available to assist them. These changes are due, at least in part, to the passage of the 1996 welfare reform law. Under the new Temporary Assistance for Needy Families (TANF) block grant, the cash welfare rolls have fallen more than 50 percent. Even more impressive is the fact that the number of never-married mothers who are working increased by 50 percent between 1993 and 1998.

These changes occurred during a time when welfare offices have undergone a major transformation (see chapter 5). Instead of focusing almost exclusively on determining eligibility for cash assistance, welfare offices have expanded their role to promote employment as the primary means of income support for low-income families. To this end, many states have adopted more generous earned income disregards and expanded the child care and transportation assistance available to parents working or looking for work. In addition, they have put in place a variety of job search and job readiness activities to help recipients find employment, and case management services to provide support to families as they make the transition from welfare to work. To enforce their work mandates, many states have adopted stringent sanction policies.

The early results of comparable welfare employment programs implemented as demonstration projects suggest that these programs increase earnings and lower welfare payments for both more and less disadvantaged groups. While these results are encouraging, there is growing concern that traditional welfare employment programs do not work for all families. A substantial number of poor parents remain unemployed, making it important to reassess what it will take to help them keep their jobs and whether there may be a subset of families that may need ongoing income support.

Who Are the Hard-to-Employ?

The first challenge in assessing the options for addressing the needs of the hard-to-employ is to define which families fall into this category. The group that is most often referenced in discussions of the hard-to-employ is parents who have been receiving assistance for many years. In the short-term, these families are at the greatest risk of being affected by time limits. Although there is a general perception that the current caseload is harder to employ than the caseload prior to reform, the available evidence does not support this claim. As was true prior to reform, the current caseload appears to include a mix of families that are new to the welfare rolls, some that have received assistance for modest periods, and some that have received assistance for an extended period. This means that some, but not all, of the current caseload is likely to be having some difficulty finding or maintaining paid employment. The available evidence does indicate that families who remain on the caseload face more obstacles to employment than those who have already left.

As more information has become available on the characteristics and needs of families that have left the TANF rolls and on poor families in general, it has become evident that not all hard-to-employ families are currently on the TANF caseload. For example, families that have left because of a sanction have low rates of employment and higher than average barriers to employment. In addition, nearly every study of families that have left TANF finds a substantial fraction of former recipients who are not employed or only marginally employed. An analysis of Census Bureau data shows that as many as 700,000 families with children had less income in 1999 than in 1995.

What Obstacles Do Hard-to-Employ Parents Face?

It is difficult to identify the specific factors that prevent some low-income parents from succeeding in the paid labor market. The available research examines the prevalence of a broad range of potential obstacles and then tries to determine which of them have a significant influence on whether a TANF recipient is employed, taking into account a parent's demographic characteristics and previous welfare experience. The potential obstacles vary, but generally fall into three broad categories: personal and family challenges (including substance abuse, mental or physical health problems, domestic violence, and learning disabilities); human capital deficits (including limited work experience and low levels of education); and logistical obstacles (including transportation and child care).

Table 1 shows the prevalence of many of these barriers in an urban community in Michigan and in Kern and Stanislaus counties in California. In each of these studies, the most common potential barriers to work are human capital deficits and transportation issues, which affected between one-third and one-half of the recipients. Personal and family challenges were also common, affecting as

Table 1
Percentage of Potential Barriers to Employment from Two Studies

Barrier	Michigan Women's Employment Study	The CalWORKS Project	
		Kern County	Stanislaus County
Personal and Family Challenges:			
Mental Health:	NA	44	34
Major Depression	25	36	22
Anxiety	7	25	23
Post-Traumatic Stress Disorder (PTSD)	15	13	13
Alcohol/Drug Dependence	NA	9.5	12.6
Alcohol Dependence	3	NA	NA
Drug Dependence	3	NA	NA
Domestic Violence (Severe or Physical Abuse in Last Year)	15	16	25
Poor Physical Health	19	24	22
Learning Problems, Special Ed, Disability	NA	21	22
Caring for a Child with Special Learning, Health, or Emotional Needs	22	22	13
Human Capital:			
Less than High School Degree	31	52	36
Less than 4 of 9 Occupational Skills	21	42	26
Limited Work Experience			
No Work in Last 3 Years	NA	37	15
Worked <20% of Years Since Age 18	15	NA	NA
Logistical:			
Child Care Hard to Arrange	NA	22	13
No Driver's License/No Access to a Car	47	51	45

Note: NA = Not Available.
Source: Sandra Danziger, "Barriers to the Employment of Welfare Recipients," 2000. CalWORKS Project, California Institute for Mental Health.

many as four out of ten recipients. Major depression affected between 22 and 36 percent of recipients. Between one-fifth and one-quarter were in poor physical health, and between 13 and 22 percent were caring for a child with special learning, health, or emotional needs. Between 15 and 25 percent experienced physical abuse from a partner in the last year. Alcohol and drug dependence was the least common obstacle, affecting no more than 13 percent of recipients.

Several studies have used the Michigan data to identify which of these factors have the strongest influence on employment. A number of key results emerge from these studies. Drug dependence has the strongest negative effect on employment, although the number of recipients who fit this classification is quite small. Other barriers that show strong relationships to employment include human capital deficits; transportation problems; major depression; and poor health. These studies also show that the presence of multiple barriers to employment further reduces the likelihood that a parent will work 20 or more hours per week.

How Are TANF Agencies Addressing the Needs of the Hard-to-Employ?

Unlike job search programs that are well established in almost every welfare office, services for the hard-to-employ are still in their infancy and remain the exception rather than the norm. Still, there are far more programs in place today than in 1996. These programs fall into four general categories: specialized screening and assessment; specialized interventions; enhanced transitional employment programs; and intensive case management.

Specialized Screening and Assessment Numerous welfare offices are conducting screenings to identify which clients require more extensive assessment or specialized service in areas such as substance abuse, mental health conditions, domestic violence, and learning disabilities. Because the purpose of conducting these screens is to identify clients who may need more help to make the transition from welfare to work, welfare offices generally implement them only when resources exist for addressing the potential barrier. Information from specialized screens may also be used to exempt clients from participation in work activities or to modify their work requirements.

Specialized assessments are less common, but a few states have implemented them. In contrast to specialized screenings, which are conducted simply to identify which clients should be referred for additional assessment, specialized assessments are conducted to provide a clinical diagnosis that can be used to develop a treatment and employment plan with the client.

Specialized Interventions Interventions are designed to eliminate or reduce potential barriers to employment. Strategies that fit into this category include alcohol, drug, and mental health treatment; accommodations for recipients with learning disabilities; and development of safety and treatment plans for victims of domestic violence. While these strategies are implemented in order to facilitate the transition to employment, the initial emphasis often is on reducing or eliminating the barrier rather than on placing recipients immediately into a job. Since implementation often requires professional expertise that extends beyond the capabilities of welfare office staff, interventions usually are carried out in partnership with other agencies that specialize in addressing these issues. In some cases, TANF agencies are paying for these more specialized services; in other cases they are implementing procedures to improve access to existing services.

Enhanced Transitional Employment Programs Programs of this type assume that some families need to make a more gradual transition to work. These programs attempt to develop supervised volunteer or work opportunities for recipients that allow them to gradually assume more and more responsibility.

Included in this category is unpaid community work experience, subsidized employment, and supported unsubsidized employment programs. While these programs take many different forms, most of them provide intensive personal support and emphasize rapid job placement. However, they often are expensive to operate, with costs between $5,000 and $10,000 per participant.

Intensive Case Management This is perhaps the most common strategy being used to help hard-to-employ recipients make the transition to employment. Welfare offices attempt to link welfare recipients with a broad range of services and provide more individualized attention to ease the transition to employment. Since welfare offices that use this approach often link recipients with community resources, the offices are able to respond to a broad range of needs. Consequently, successful implementation requires the availability of a broad range of services in the local community or a willingness to expand services to respond to unmet needs. In addition, the welfare workers responsible for providing intensive case management need to have strong assessment, relationship building, and case planning skills.

Are These Strategies Effective?

States began their efforts to reform welfare with a wealth of knowledge about the effectiveness of job search programs. In contrast, the knowledge base on what works best for recipients who do not succeed in traditional welfare employment programs is extremely thin. Only a few relevant studies have been conducted and none of them have been conducted with welfare recipients facing the same set of incentives and mandates that welfare recipients currently face. Some non-experimental studies of the cost effectiveness

Unless new and more effective programs are developed, or existing approaches are successfully modified, we should have modest expectations about helping welfare recipients with serious employment barriers enter the labor force.

of substance abuse treatment programs indicate that clients who participate in treatment programs fare better than those who do not participate. Experimental evidence of supported employment programs suggests that these programs may produce an increase in employment that is statistically significant but modest, and that intensive case management may not increase employment among hard-to-employ welfare recipients. Thus, unless new and more effective programs are developed, or existing approaches are successfully modified, we should have modest expectations about helping welfare recipients with serious employment barriers enter the labor force.

What Congress Can Do

The 1996 reforms provide states with considerable flexibility to decide how to use their TANF block grant funds, making it possible for them to implement a variety of approaches to help hard-to-employ families make the transition to employment. Despite this flexibility, several problems remain in addressing the needs of these families.

First, many welfare offices perform inadequate assessments of barriers to employment and/or wait until recipients are close to hitting time limits before performing in-depth assessments. These problems reflect high caseloads per worker, inadequate skills and training of caseworkers, and the absence of adequate assessment procedures and tools in many states.

Second, there is an inadequate knowledge base about what kinds of services are likely to be most helpful to parents with particular barriers or combinations of barriers. Third, many of the service options for the hard-to-serve, as well as options like subsidized transitional employment, are very expensive.

Fourth, a work-first TANF culture and the structure of federal work requirements may also discourage states from implementing innovative strategies for the hard to employ. Fifth, the current structure of federal time limits may be inappropriate for addressing the needs of recipients with severe barriers to employment. There are several things that Congress can do to address these problems during the reauthorization debate.

Expand Activities that Count Toward Work Participation In order to promote the development of a work-based assistance system, TANF explicitly defines the participation rate that a state must achieve and the activities that can count toward that rate. With the exception of enhanced transitional employment programs, none of the strategies states are currently implementing for the hard-to-employ can count fully towards participation rates. Many states have had their work participation requirement significantly reduced because they receive credit for reducing their TANF caseload. This outcome makes it feasible for states to place recipients in activities that do not count toward the work requirement—such as those described above to help the hard-to-employ. However, many states seem reluctant to do so, owing in part to the structure of federal law.

Expanding the activities that can count toward a state's work participation rate to include those designed to assist the hard-to-employ may send a signal that these activities are consistent with the goals of TANF, thereby encouraging more states to implement them. In addition, easing the restriction on the length of time clients can spend in job search may encourage states to invest in longer job readiness programs, which may help to better prepare clients with limited labor market experience. In order to respond to concerns that this expansion of countable activities might weaken the emphasis on work, additional activities could be added with constraints. For example, services designed to alleviate barriers to employment could be allowed for a restricted period of time or in conjunction with work activities for a minimum number of hours.

Redesign the Time Limit Time limits were designed to remedy what many viewed as a major flaw of the AFDC program: at any point in time, the welfare caseload was comprised of families that had received cash assistance for an average of 12 years. But the current caseload is very different than the pre-welfare reform caseload. Some families with long spells on welfare have already left the caseload for work or for other reasons. Other families have left welfare because the mother was sanctioned for not meeting work requirements. In fact, in a state that has implemented full-family sanctions, the only families that will reach time limits are those that have looked for employment and not found it or those that have found employment but are not earning enough to be self-sufficient. Moreover, some families on the rolls are working 20 to 25 hours per week but still receive welfare benefits because their state has generous disregard rules that allow the family to continue receiving welfare after the mother begins working. States may wish to continue subsidizing these families even after they reach the five-year time limit.

Given the new environment in which families are currently receiving cash assistance, there are several alternatives for modifying the time limit to make it more consistent with the structure of most state TANF programs. First, the time limit could be suspended for any family that is actively participating in a plan to find employment or is currently working. Second, states that impose full-family sanctions could be exempted from having to impose time limits, as long as they demonstrate that families are actually sanctioned for failure to comply with work requirements. Third, states could be allowed to replace the 20 percent exemption with a more flexible provision that requires each state to define specific criteria that would determine who is exempted from the time limit. Basing exemptions on set criteria rather than on an arbitrary percentage of the caseload would allow states to define criteria that are consistent with their work expectations and the message they want to send to clients. It would also allow states to implement a consistent policy as caseloads rise and fall during good and bad economic times.

Reconsider Sanction Requirements and Protections Sanctions for noncompliance with work requirements are an important component of most states's efforts to promote work. Except for the requirement that states impose a pro-rata reduction for families that fail to comply with work requirements, the federal welfare reform legislation is silent on the design of sanction policies for TANF recipients. Moreover, a recent U.S. General Accounting Office report suggests the procedures followed in some states to notify recipients of sanctions may not be adequate for recipients with serious employability barriers. Congress should consider requiring states to provide assistance to any family that demonstrates its willingness to comply with program requirements after they have been sanctioned. Currently, several states permanently ban recipients from receiving assistance after they have been sanctioned repeatedly. Due to the nature of their personal or family challenges, some hard-to-employ parents may make several failed attempts to comply with program requirements before they eventually succeed. Other states require that a sanction be imposed for a minimum period of time before it can be lifted. This policy makes it impossible for families to comply with requirements when the family begins to feel the sanction's impact—a time when some hard-to-employ families may be most ready to address their personal and family challenges.

Earmark Funds for Innovation and Evaluation Given the limited evidence available on the effectiveness of strategies to help the hard-to-employ keep their jobs or quickly find new ones, there is growing support in Congress for providing additional funding to states that are interested in implementing and evaluating innovative strategies. Providing a targeted pool of money for specialized programs could provide the impetus states need to invest in these programs. Testing innovative programs would provide invaluable information on the relative effectiveness of various approaches and the costs and benefits associated with them. The federal government should also play a more active role in fostering evaluation and dissemination of "best practices" in assessing TANF recipients for employment barriers.

In the five years since the passage of the 1996 reforms, welfare offices across the country have made significant progress in transforming the welfare system into a system that promotes and rewards work. However, until strategies to assist the hard-to-employ become an integral part of that system, the full promise of welfare reform will remain unrealized. Targeted financial resources, acknowledgment that some families require more assistance than others to become employed, and support for innovation are key to achieving the full potential of welfare reform.

Additional Reading

CalWORKS Project. 2000. *The Prevalence of Mental Health, Alcohol and Other Drugs, and Domestic Violence Issues among CalWORKS Participants in Kern and Stanislaus Counties.* Sacramento: California Institute for Mental Health.

Danziger, Sandra, and others. 2000. "Barriers to the Employment of Welfare Recipients." In *Prosperity for All? The Economic Boom and African Americans,* edited by R. Cherry and W.M. Rogers III. New York: Russell Sage.

Derr, Michelle, and others. 2001. *Providing Mental Health Services to TANF Recipients: Program Design Choices and Implementation Challenges in Four States.* Washington, D.C.: Mathematica.

Pavetti, LaDonna, and Debra Strong. 2001. *Work-Based Strategies for Hard-to-Employ TANF Recipients: A Preliminary Assessment of Program Models and Dimensions.* Washington, D.C.: Mathematica.

U.S. General Accounting Office. 2001. *Welfare Reform: More Coordinated Federal Effort Could Help States and Localities Move TANF Recipients with Impairments Toward Employment* (GAO-02-37).

Wagner, Suzanne L., and Daria Zvetina. 2001. "Welfare Reform: The Next Phase." *Applied Research in Child Development.* Chicago: Erikson Institute, Herr Research Center.

Zedlewski, Sheila, and Pamela Loprest. 2001. "How Well Does TANF Fit the Needs of the Most Disadvantaged Families?" In *The New World of Welfare,* edited by Rebecca M. Blank and Ron Haskins. Washington, D.C.: Brookings.

PART VI

FAMILY FORMATION

PAUL OFFNER

Reducing Non-Marital Births

Executive Summary
When Congress passed welfare reform legislation in 1996, it had two main objectives: cut welfare dependency and reduce non-marital childbearing. The first of these objectives has been amply realized over the last five years as millions of welfare recipients have gone to work and welfare caseloads have dropped by over 50 percent. The second goal, however, has received less attention. From the standpoint of children, this is puzzling. After all, there is strong evidence that children are better off in two-parent families, whereas there is much less evidence that putting single parents to work improves things for children. Still, it is easier to get people to work than to live together, so perhaps it is not surprising that states have concentrated their efforts on the first objective. Reducing non-marital births remains the unfinished part of the 1996 welfare reform law. This brief examines why non-marital births happen, the effort states have made to address the problem, and what additional steps could be taken to reduce non-marital births when Congress reauthorizes welfare reform legislation next year.

The Problem

Thirty-five years ago in "The Negro Family: A Call to Action," Daniel Patrick Moynihan, who was then assistant secretary of labor, called the nation's attention to the growing problem of non-marital births within the African American community. At the time, his views were attacked as racist, although just about everyone now agrees that Moynihan was right in his diagnosis. Today, the non-marital ratio (non-marital births as a proportion of all births) is one of our most carefully watched social indicators, and is seen by many as a measure of our society's sexual permissiveness, as well as its less than total commitment to the needs of children.

It would be a mistake, though, to think of this statistic as simply a gauge of the nation's sexual mores, for it is much more than that. Between 1960 and 1999, the non-marital ratio went from 5.3 percent (low enough to please even the most committed conservative) to 33 percent, a more than six-fold increase (see figure 1). But most of this rise was due to demographic changes only indirectly related to sexual behavior. As table 1 shows, if the marriage rate (marriages per 1,000 women) and the birth rate of unmarried women (births per 1,000 unmarried women) had remained frozen at their 1960 levels, the non-marital ratio would still have doubled (11.5 percent) by 1999 simply because married women were having fewer babies. If the birth rate of unmarried women had stayed at its 1960 level, and we allowed for other demographic changes to occur during this period, the non-marital ratio would have risen to 19.2 percent, almost four times the 1960 ratio.

The same pattern holds for African Americans, who are disproportionately represented on the welfare rolls, and whose non-marital ratio went from 23.3 percent in 1960 to an alarming 69.1 percent in 1999. Yet the birth rate of unmarried black women actually dropped by one quarter during this period. The non-marital ratio rose because the birth rate of married black women dropped by almost two thirds, and the marriage rate declined by over 40 percent.

Three things could be done to bring down the non-marital ratio: convince married women to have more children; convince people to marry earlier; or convince unmarried couples to defer childbearing until they are married. No one is advocating the first of these, and the second is problematic because early first marriages often end in divorce and shorten the educational careers of both partners at a time when increased knowledge is essential for success in the new economy. That leaves us with the task of convincing unmarried women to defer childbearing. While almost everyone is in favor of this policy, it is worth noting that among blacks, the rate of non-marital births has been falling for 40 years (both marital and non-marital birth rates have been falling, but marital birth rates have been falling faster, which has caused the proportion of non-marital black births to rise). And in any event, simply reducing the non-marital birth rate solves only part of the problem. If we were able to roll it back to its 1960 level, we would still have a non-marital ratio today of almost 20 percent, which, while an enormous improvement over the current situation, would still be a far cry from the low 5.3 percent of the 1960s.

How Did We Get Here?

Although there is a consensus on the need to reduce non-marital births, there is little

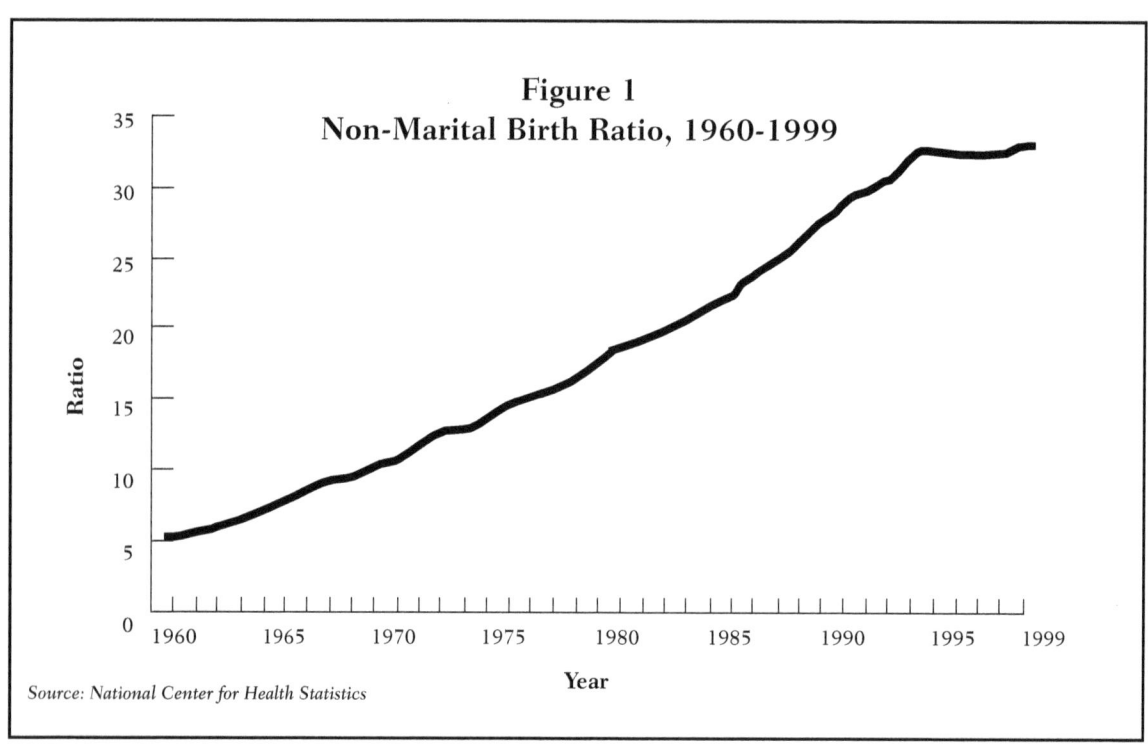

Figure 1
Non-Marital Birth Ratio, 1960-1999

Source: National Center for Health Statistics

Table 1
Non-Marital Ratio in 1999 (Percent)

If nothing had changed from 1960	5.3
If nothing had changed except the fertility of married women	11.5
If nothing had changed except the fertility of married women and the marriage rate	19.2
Actual	33.0

agreement on the causes of our current predicament. Some argue that as more women entered the work force over the last 50 years, they were better able to support themselves and thus had less reason to marry. The evidence on this theory is mixed. Some researchers have found that greater economic independence has contributed to higher divorce rates and more non-marital births. Others report that trends in female employment and earnings have had little effect on marriage rates for either blacks or whites.

A second thesis is that the marriage rate is down because work opportunities have deteriorated for males, making them less attractive as marriage partners. This position was popularized by William Julius Wilson, now at Harvard University, based on his work in the inner city of Chicago. Part of the problem is disentangling cause and effect—is it that economically attractive men are more likely to get married, or that married men tend to be more productive in the workplace? Another problem is that researchers have found that marriage rates fell almost as much among well-educated black men as they did among poorly educated black men. Marriage rates among those with jobs fell as much as among those who were unemployed. On balance, the decline in earnings or employment cannot explain more than about 20 percent of the change in black family structure since 1960.

A third hypothesis is that non-marital births rose because of welfare, which allegedly provided an alternative, more stable means of support for women who wanted to have children but were not ready for marriage. While researchers in the 1970s and early 1980s generally found little support for this thesis, Robert Moffitt of Johns Hopkins University reports that now "a slight majority" of researchers find "a significant negative effect on marriage or positive effect on fertility." Even so, the effect is uncertain and modest.

Another theory is that sexual mores have changed. Many observers believe that beginning roughly in the 1960s, Americans began to feel less strongly that all adults should be married and that sex outside marriage was wrong. By the 1980s and 1990s, television shows, for example, regularly featured characters who were single and who acted as if sex outside marriage should not be proscribed.

A fifth explanation points to the so-called

marriage penalties. Under all means-tested programs (those providing benefits to people with incomes below a certain level), benefits decline as income increases, and combining the incomes of two people increases family income, thus reducing benefits. This is a characteristic of welfare, food stamps, and Medicaid, as well as of state and federal tax systems (the Earned Income Tax Credit is a particular culprit). Taken together, these provisions reduce benefits by as much as 85 cents for each extra dollar of income, and those benefit reduction rates extend well up into the middle-income range. But there is little research evidence to support the claim that these provisions discourage marriage, perhaps because the complexities of the law make it difficult for most people to know how marriage will affect them, or because such penalties do not loom large in the marriage decision. So we are in a fix: everyone wants to reduce non-marital births and promote marriage, but there is no consensus on how we got to where we are today or what we should do about it.

What Have States Done?

The authors of the welfare reform legislation were deeply committed to promoting marriage and reducing non-marital births, and the legislation contains 17 provisions designed to advance these objectives. Yet the focus of state efforts has been on moving people from welfare to work. According to the Washington, D.C.-based child advocacy group Child Trends, 23 states provided contraceptive education in public schools statewide in 1999, while 26 states had school-based abstinence education programs (15 provided both). General media campaigns discouraging non-marital pregnancies were conducted in 17 states, and three—Georgia, North Dakota, and Tennessee—had programs to encourage couples expecting a child to marry. Still, the total resources spent on these activities were small. According to state data compiled by the Center on Budget and Policy Priorities in Washington, D.C., approximately one half of one percent of funds from the Temporary Assistance to Needy Families (TANF) program is being spent on reducing non-marital births and promoting marriage. Research from the Rockefeller Institute at the State University of New York, which is monitoring state implementation of the 1996 reforms, comes to a similar conclusion.

One of the most popular initiatives to reduce non-marital births has been the family cap, which reduces or eliminates any benefit increase for mothers who have additional children while on welfare. Twenty-three states have such programs. Unfortunately, the few good evaluations that exist have produced inconclusive results (the best of these comes from New Jersey, and shows some reduction in birth rates, but also some increase in abortions). One problem is that the family cap programs were implemented at the same time as a broad set of other changes, any number of which could impact on fertility behavior. Disentangling the effects of these initiatives is a big challenge, and current evaluations are generally not up to the job.

The welfare reform legislation also includes a bonus to be awarded each year to the five states that are most successful in lowering their non-marital ratios while decreasing abortions. When the first year's results were announced in 1999, the winners were the District of Columbia, California, Michigan, Alabama, and Massachusetts—all jurisdictions with large African American and Hispanic populations (D.C., Michigan, and Alabama also won bonuses in the second round). Between 1994–95 and 1996–97, black and Hispanic non-marital birth rates dropped twice as fast as white non-marital birth rates. This suggests that demographic factors may have been as important as any actions taken by the states in determining the bonus winners.

One state that has had some success in increasing marriage within its low-income population is Minnesota. Its welfare reform plan allows recipients to keep more of the money they earn (the welfare grant declines more slowly than in other states as earnings rise), and recipients remain eligible for cash benefits until income equals 140 percent of the poverty level. An evaluation by the Manpower Demonstration Research Corporation (MDRC) found a 3.6 percent increase in marriage by the end of the third year, and a 19 point increase in marital stability (67 percent of couples who were married at the program's beginning were still married three years later, compared with 48 percent in the control group). The typical pattern in this study was for the second earner in a two-parent family to cut back her work effort, suggesting that allowing welfare families to keep more of their earnings reduced the stress on couples. Still, this is just one state, and we should be cautious in drawing conclusions.

In general, while there has been some improvement in reducing non-marital births in the 1990s, little of it can be attributed to welfare reform. Among African Americans, for instance, non-marital births dropped from 90.5 per thousand in 1990 to 73.3 per thousand in 1998, a decline of 19 percent. Almost all of the improvement, however, predated the 1996 legislation.

What Do We Do Now?

The good news is that non-marital birth rates have been declining in recent years. Most of the improvement has been among teens—there has been little change in the rate for older women. There is also clear evidence that a more conservative attitude toward premarital sex is taking hold, whether as a result of the AIDS epidemic, or for other reasons. Among African Americans, over 70 percent say that it would be unacceptable for a daughter to have a child out of wedlock. In order for the trends to continue, the 2002 welfare reform reauthorization legislation should aim to make several improvements.

Testing New Approaches First, Congress and the states should promote wide-ranging experimentation on non-marital birth policy, with the goal of identifying approaches that will work. One could argue that states should use some of their TANF surpluses for this purpose, but they have done that only modestly to date, and there is no reason to expect them to do much more of it in the future. Accordingly, Congress should allocate roughly $200 million a year to fund such efforts. Applications could be submitted by state or local governments, or by private organizations like universities or research organizations. The Secretary of Health and Human Services should convene a group of experts representing all parts of the political spectrum to develop guidelines for the initiative. Proposals would be rigorously evaluated, with control group experiments given preference in the selection process.

One area that particularly deserves to be tested is employment initiatives for men. Consider the current situation of young African American males. Over the last seven years, the employment rate of black men between the ages of 20 and 24 increased only modestly, and the percentage of this group that was either working or looking for work actually dropped, even though the economy was experiencing strong growth. The employment rates for these men are now 20 points below those of white and Hispanic men of the same age. Meanwhile, the employment rates of young black women increased by 18 points, a truly remarkable change in such a short period of time. So young black women are doing relatively well in the job market, while their male counterparts are floundering, which does not augur well for the future of marriage within this population. While the evidence linking employment and marriage is not strong, the work of such researchers as William Julius Wilson and Kathryn Edin of Northwestern University suggests that such a link exists. Most low-income women are not going to marry unemployed men who cannot help support them and their children. So demonstration programs aimed at examining the link between employment and marriage should be encouraged.

Eliminating Marriage Penalties Second, Congress should reduce the fiscal disincentives to marriage. A single mother working full-time at the minimum wage and a single man earning $8 an hour who is not the father of her children can lose as much as $8,060, primarily in cash from the Earned Income Tax Credit, if they get married. Wendell Primus and Jennifer Beeson of the Center on Budget and Policy Priorities point out that this is less of a problem in cases where the prospective husband is the children's father, because in the absence of marriage, the father would still owe child support. Those instances aside, many other cases are still subject to significant disincentives.

While little evidence has been found linking marriage penalties and the drop in marriage over the last 40 years, there are at least three reasons for addressing this problem. First, the fact that no relationship has been found does not mean that none exists. It may take a long time for such factors to influence behavior, and the lags may have been specified incorrectly in past research. Moreover, many factors have contributed to

---

We cannot afford to give up. Public attitudes evolve, as may already be happening, and behaviors change, as in the case of smoking.

---

the drop in marriage; financial disincentives were not the primary variable. Eliminating financial disincentives will not reverse the trend as long as other factors are present. If those factors are removed, however, then disincentives will likely reduce progress on the marriage front. In other words, reducing the penalties is a necessary, although not a sufficient, condition for increasing marriage.

Finally, marriage penalties send an unmistakable signal that society is not serious about this problem. At a time when there is growing support for a broad range of initiatives that promote marriage and fatherhood—with some conservatives even proposing to give cash bonuses to young women who defer childbearing until they are married—surely the first priority should be to eliminate the financial disincentives to getting married.

Conclusion

Above all, Congress must be realistic in its approach. The non-marital ratio is largely determined by variables over which it has little control, such as the marriage rate and the birth rate of married women, so large changes are not likely. The other important variable is the birth rate of unmarried women, which rose steadily from 1960 to 1990, but has changed little since then. Everyone would like to see this rate come down, but no one knows how to make that happen, especially for the adult population (we have more leverage over teenage behavior). Because of that, expectations should remain low. Senator Moynihan, now retired, has cited sociologist Peter Rossi's law, which states that the expected value for any measured effect of a social program is zero.

Still, we cannot afford to give up. Public attitudes evolve, as may already be happening in this area, and behaviors change, as in the case of smoking.

Congress should remove the impediments to marriage and create a broad-scale demonstration and evaluation program, out of which may come promising initiatives that can be replicated elsewhere. There has already been some success in reducing teenage pregnancy, and it is likely that Congress would support efforts to build on these successes.

Additional Reading

Bos, Johannes, et al. 1999. *New Hope for People with Low Incomes: Two-Year Results of a Program to Reduce Poverty and Reform Welfare*. New York: Manpower Demonstration Research Corporation.

Gennetian, Lisa and Cynthia Miller. 2000. *Reforming Welfare and Rewarding Work: Final Report on the Minnesota Family Investment Program, Volume 2: Effects on Children*. New York: Manpower Demonstration Research Corporation.

Moffitt, Robert. 1988. "The Effect of Welfare on Marriage and Fertility." *Welfare, the Family, and Reproductive Behavior: Research Perspectives*. Washington, D.C.: National Academy Press.

Morris, Pamela and Charles Michalopoulos. 2000. *The Self-Sufficiency Project at 36 Months: Effects on Children of a Program That Increased Parental Employment and Income*. Ottawa: Social Research and Demonstration Corporation.

Moynihan, Daniel Patrick. 1965. *The Negro Family: The Case for National Action*. U.S. Department of Labor.

Nathan, Richard P., and Gais, Thomas L. 1999. *Implementing the Personal Responsibility Act of 1996: A First Look*. Albany: Rockefeller Institute of Government.

Wilson, William Julius. 1996. *When Work Disappears: The World of the New Urban Poor*. New York: Knopf.

17

SARA MCLANAHAN, IRWIN GARFINKEL, AND RONALD B. MINCY

Fragile Families, Welfare Reform, and Marriage

Executive Summary
Marriage will be an important issue in the upcoming debate over the reauthorization of welfare reform. According to recent studies, both children and adults benefit from marriage. Still, one of three children in the U.S. is born to unmarried parents. At the time of birth, most unmarried parents are committed to each other and to their child and have high hopes of marriage and a future together. But these parents face numerous barriers to creating and maintaining a stable family life, including low education and job skills, lack of jobs, and poor relationship skills. Helping these parents achieve their goal of stability will require new ideas and new policies such as providing services that start at birth; treating the parents as a couple rather than as individuals; offering services that promote communication and increase employability; reducing marriage penalties; and making child support enforcement more reasonable for low-income fathers. While some of these ideas have been tried in the past, others have never been fully implemented, and none has been offered as a single, comprehensive package. Because Congress is unlikely to enact a full package of services, the federal government should consider funding state-run demonstrations to ascertain the benefits and costs of the proposed reforms.

Promoting marriage and two-parent families is of great importance to policymakers. The benefits of marriage for adults (better health, greater longevity, and higher earnings) have been well documented, and the benefits of growing up with two biological parents (more education, greater marital stability, and better mental health) are widely acknowledged. Moreover, Congress and the Bush administration seem determined to make marriage a major issue in the welfare reform reauthorization debate.

Welfare rolls have dropped dramatically since 1996, and large proportions of welfare recipients have moved from dependency to work. At the same time, the proportion of births to unmarried mothers, after several decades of relentless increases, has remained constant at around 33 percent. In response, some policymakers have argued that more dollars from the Temporary Assistance for Needy Families (TANF) should be spent on programs for poor parents who marry. Others have argued that, rather than promoting marriage, TANF money should go towards making poor parents, especially fathers, more "marriageable" or better able to support themselves and their families.

This policy brief will assess "marriage" and "marriageability" strategies and discuss policies to promote both. Strategies for increasing father involvement and improving communication among parents who live apart will also be considered. Most of the analysis is based on data from the Fragile Families and Child Wellbeing Study being conducted at the Center for Research on Child Wellbeing at Princeton University and the Social Indicators Survey Center at Columbia University. The study is following a birth cohort of approximately 5,000 children born to unwed parents in large cities (populations of 200,000 or more) at the turn of the 21st century. Based on interviews with mothers and fathers, the four-year study provides extensive information about parents' relationships, views on marriage, intentions to marry, and expectations about the role of unmarried fathers.

Unwed Parents: What We Know

One of the most striking findings from the Fragile Families Study thus far is the high rate of cohabitation among unmarried parents. At the time of birth, half of unmarried mothers are living with the fathers of their children. Another third are romantically involved with the fathers, but living apart in what are called "visiting relationships." Eight percent of parents are "just friends" and 9 percent have "little or no contact."

The majority of unwed parents are optimistic about their future together. Nearly three quarters of the mothers believe their chances of marrying the father of their child are "50-50" or better. Almost two thirds "agree" or "strongly agree" with the statement, "it is better for children if their parents are married." There is also strong consensus among unmarried parents about what qualities are necessary for successful marriage. Roughly 90 percent of mothers rate "husband having a steady job" and "emotional maturity" as very important qualities for a successful marriage. In addition, 69 percent of mothers rate "wife having a steady job" as very important.

Most fathers are highly involved during the pregnancy and around the time of birth. According to the mothers surveyed, four out of five fathers provided some financial support during the pregnancy, 84 percent will have their name on the birth certificate, and 79 percent of the children will take the father's surname. Most fathers say they want to help raise their child, and the overwhelming majority of mothers say they want the fathers to be involved.

At the time their child is born, the vast majority of unmarried parents are committed to each other and to their child. Most mothers and fathers have high hopes about their future together and most view marriage as a positive institution that benefits children. Clearly, these parents are likely to respond positively to programs and policies that promote marriage, which is good news for policymakers who favor this strategy.

Unfortunately, many unmarried parents are poorly equipped to support themselves and their children. Table 1 shows that although nearly all the fathers in the Fragile Families Study worked in the past year, almost three out of ten were out of work in the week before their baby was born. In addition, the human capital of both parents is low: 37 percent of mothers and 34 percent of fathers lack a high school degree, and less than a third of parents have any education beyond high school. These findings are consistent with those in the 1995 *Report to Congress on Non-Marital Childbearing* by the U.S. Department of Health and Human Services, and with

Table 1
Parents' Ability to Support a Family

	Mothers	Fathers
Worked in past year	84	98
Worked in past week	NA	72
Education		
Less than high school	37	34
High school only	32	40
Some college	27	22
College or higher	4	4
Age		
Under 20	21	10
20–24	43	34
25–29	19	26
30 and older	17	30
First birth	43	46
Very good or excellent health	65	69
Drugs or alcohol problems	3	5
Incarceration (interim data)	NA	38
Partner hit or slapped	4	14
Partner unfair	11	7

Note: Figures are percentages. NA = Not Available.
Source: Sara McLanahan and others, "The Fragile Families and Child Well Being National Baseline Report," Princeton University, 2001.

other research on unwed parents and non-custodial fathers. Elaine Sorensen of the Urban Institute in Washington, D.C., for example, finds that poverty rates among non-custodial fathers may be as high as 25 percent, and Irwin Garfinkel and his colleagues at Columbia University report that 20 percent of non-custodial fathers earn less than $6,000 annually. Studies of teen parents and mothers on welfare paint an even bleaker picture of the capabilities of unwed parents.

The Fragile Families Study also shows that although a majority of unmarried parents are in fairly good health, some engage in "unhealthy" behaviors. Three percent of mothers and 5 percent of fathers report that a drug or alcohol problem interfered with their work or personal relationships in the past year. Drug and alcohol problems are likely to be underreported, so we should assume that the true prevalence of substance abuse is higher. Approximately 38 percent of unwed fathers have been incarcerated, which suggests that a substantial proportion of these men have had lifestyles that are potentially harmful to their children. As shown by Cynthia Miller and Virginia Knox in their recent review, evaluations of the Parents' Fair Share program, a large scale demonstration program that provided services to unwed fathers, found that noncustodial fathers who were delinquent in their child support payments faced severe employment barriers, including criminal records and poor health.

Many policymakers and advocates worry that promoting marriage will increase domestic violence. The Fragile Families Study data suggest that violence is rare among new unwed parents. Only 4 percent of mothers and 14 percent of fathers report being hit or slapped by their partner during the past year. While these figures are reassuring, they should be viewed with caution. Mothers are likely to underreport the incidence of violence, especially if they are still romantically involved with the fathers. Indeed, reported rates of violence are much higher among mothers who are no longer in contact with the father of their child.

Finally, 11 percent of mothers and 7 percent of fathers report that the other parent is "never fair or willing to compromise." At worst, such behavior may be a precursor to physical violence. At best, it signals a relationship in trouble.

Estimates based on preliminary data from twenty cities in the Fragile Families Study indicate that less than 20 percent of the new parents had married by the time their child was 12-18 months old. Table 2 shows that of the parents who were living together at birth, 12 percent had married and an additional 63 percent were still cohabiting. Thus, 75 percent of the children who were living with both biological parents at birth were still living with both parents nearly a year and a half later. Research based on the National Longitudinal Survey of Youth suggests that about half of unmarried parents who are cohabiting at birth are still living together after six years.

The findings discussed above underscore the precarious socioeconomic circumstances of unwed parents and the barriers to marriage that many of them face. They also support the argument that a substantial proportion of unwed parents are not ready for marriage because of low employment skills, risky behavior such as drug use, and poor relationship skills (defined as the ability to maintain a nonviolent, mutually supportive relationship).

Table 2
Durability of Parents' Relationship

Relationship at Birth	Married	Cohabiting	Romantic	Friends	No contact
Married	99	0	0	0	0
Cohabiting	12	63	8	10	7
Not cohabiting-romantic	4	15	34	25	21
Not cohabiting-friends	0	5	5	62	27
Not cohabiting-no contact	1	4	5	17	73

Note: Figures are percentages. "Romantic" indicates that parents have a romantic relationship with each other; "friends" indicates that they are not romantically involved but are friends, and "no contact" indicates that they see each other rarely or never.
Source: Sara McLanahan and others, "The Fragile Families and Well Being National Baseline Report," Princeton University, 2001.

Policy Implications

Marriage and cohabitation among fragile families can be encouraged by increasing the capabilities of parents, reducing marriage and cohabitation penalties in current spending programs and tax policies, and making child support enforcement more suitable to the circumstances of unmarried parents who live together. No matter how successful such policies are, however, a substantial proportion of unwed parents will live apart. The dilemma for policymakers is how to address the needs of these parents and their children without undermining marriage. Based on the findings in the Fragile Families Study and broader research on the effects of public policy on families, a reform agenda for promoting marriage, marriageability, father involvement, and the security of single-parent families should be considered as part of the welfare reform reauthorization debate.

Services Services to strengthen fragile families should begin before or at birth when the overwhelming majority of unwed parents are still romantically involved and should offer services to mothers and fathers. The "magic moment" of birth may be particularly important for motivating fathers. The Parents' Fair Share program, which had limited success with fathers, provided help too late—long after the romantic relationship between the mother and father had ended.

A promising model to build on is the home visiting nurse program pioneered in Elmira, New York, and Memphis, Tennessee, by David Olds and his colleagues at the University of Colorado in Denver. In the Olds program, now being implemented statewide in Oklahoma and at over 200 sites in 23 other states, nurses visit first-time mothers during pregnancy and for two years following birth. This program could be extended to include fathers as well as mothers and assessment of both parents on education, employment status, health and mental health issues (including substance abuse problems), and relationship problems (including domestic violence). When a problem is indicated, one or both parents would be offered appropriate help. In addition, the visiting nurses would inform parents of the other supports and services for which they are eligible, including health care, welfare, child support enforcement, the Earned Income Tax Credit, and child care programs.

TANF Reforms Services alone are unlikely to substantially strengthen fragile families. To the extent that welfare policies or practices favor one-parent families over two-parent families, they discourage marriage and cohabitation and push biological fathers out of the picture. Although many state TANF programs appear to have reduced or eliminated restrictions for two-parent families, others still retain such restrictions. Similarly, many states and localities give preference to one-parent families in allocating scarce child care and housing subsidies. If the goal is to promote marriage and family stability, states should eliminate this kind of unfavorable treatment of two-parent families.

The absence of categorical restrictions, however, is still not sufficient to make welfare policy neutral with respect to family formation. Because welfare is income tested, it creates an incentive for fathers with earnings and mothers without earnings to live apart (or feign living apart). To reduce this disincentive, only a portion of a resident father's earnings—say 50 percent—should be counted when determining a family's eligibility and benefits for TANF. Although doing so will increase welfare costs and caseloads in the short run, the time limits and work requirements of the new TANF program would limit these extra costs, and the long-term gains in strengthening two-parent families will be considerable for families as well as society.

Child Support Reforms Strict child support enforcement also reduces the disincentives to marriage and cohabitation in welfare policy by increasing the costs (for fathers) of living separately. However, if child support obligations are imposed on cohabiting fathers or are grossly inconsistent with their ability to pay, they may drive fathers away and discourage their involvement. If the parents reside together, they should be treated as a family by TANF, only a portion of the income of each parent should be counted in determining eligibility and benefits, and services should be provided to fathers as well as mothers.

Services for fathers, like those for mothers in TANF, should be geared primarily towards obtaining employment. In cases in which either the mother or father demonstrates the potential to benefit from further education and training, however, TANF should provide such support. Services for both mothers and fathers should also be directed at educating the parents about their mutual rights and responsibilities, including establishing the paternity of the father.

All unwed fathers, including those who live with the mother and child, should be required to establish paternity. Those who live with the mother, however, should not be required to pay child support. Both parents should be fully informed of the nonresident parent's potential child support obligation in the event of a separation.

If the parents live apart, fathers should be required to pay child support, and enforcement should be strict. But the amount of the obligation should be proportional to fathers' ability to pay. Poor fathers are routinely required to pay much higher proportions of their income than middle- and upper-income fathers, and many are required to pay unreasonable amounts of arrearages (past-due child support). These unrealistic arrearages arise because child support agencies and courts base these payments not on fathers' actual earnings, but on their "presumptive" earnings; e.g., the minimum wage multiplied by full-time, full-year work or, if he is unemployed, how much he earned at some point in the past. Fathers are even required to pay back the mother's welfare costs and, in some states, her Medicaid costs. Many fathers who become unemployed or incarcerated build up huge arrearages during these periods of unemployment. Such onerous child support obligations are rarely paid in full, and they can prompt fathers to avoid legitimate work where their wages are easily intercepted. Ultimately, they breed resentment among fathers and mothers toward the system and perhaps toward each other. Imprisonment for non-payment of support exacerbates this negative dynamic. Given what we know about the low earnings capacity of most unwed fathers, these practices are not likely to be effective and may even have unintended negative consequences.

If child support obligations were expressed as a flat percentage of the father's income in every state, many of these problems would be reduced. Obligations would automatically decline when the father is unemployed or in jail and would automatically go up when his earnings rise.

Judi Bartfeld and Irwin Garfinkel of Columbia University find that support orders expressed as a percentage of income lead to substantially higher, not lower payments. States should reconsider their guidelines so that the child support obligations imposed on low-income, nonresident fathers can be no higher in percentage terms than those imposed on middle-income, nonresident fathers. Finally, through TANF or other workforce programs, unemployed fathers should be offered a job at the minimum wage and be required to pay a portion of their earnings in child support.

Most states now reduce TANF benefits by one dollar for each dollar of child support paid. This policy reduces the incentive for mothers to cooperate with the child support program and for fathers to pay child support. Counting only a portion of support in determining eligibility and benefits would increase cooperation and payments as well as the child's standard of living. Congress should require or encourage states to ignore a substantial portion—say 50 percent—of child support payments in determining TANF eligibility and payments.

Finally, creating a publicly-financed child support benefit that is conditional on the prior establishment of a child support order and tied to fathers' payments would have positive effects on both mothers and fathers. Although a public child support benefit would also increase government expenditures and parents' incentives for living apart, it would nonetheless reduce the poverty, insecurity, and welfare dependence of single mothers and their children.

Policy Experiments Congress is not likely to enact all of the changes discussed in this brief, but could provide federal funding for state-run experiments to help ascertain the full costs and benefits of these and similar reforms. Such experiments will have to be carefully designed and monitored, and they will be costly if they are to yield useful information. Participants would be randomly assigned to a control group or to experimental groups that receive one or more of the new policies outlined above. Multiple treatments would be necessary to disentangle the effects of different components of the reform package, and the experiment should last at least five years or it will fail to mimic permanent changes in policy. Both mothers and fathers would have to be interviewed periodically in order to assess the effects.

Based on the costs of previous large-scale social science experiments, we estimate that the costs of the experiment would be at least several hundred million dollars. While such an experiment is costly, it is cheap compared to the full fiscal costs of implementing all of the recommendations and will allow policymakers and social scientists to determine whether the benefits it produces warrant an expanded slate of reforms.

Creating a publicly-financed child support benefit that is conditional on the prior establishment of a child support order and tied to fathers' payments would have positive effects on both mothers and fathers.

Additional Reading

Bartfeld, Judi, and Irwin Garfinkel. 1996. "The Impact of Percentage-Expressed Child-Support Orders on Payments." *Journal of Human Resources,* 31(4): 794-815.

Garfinkel, Irwin, and others. 1998. *Fathers Under Fire: The Revolution in Child Support Enforcement.* New York: Russell Sage.

Lerman, Robert, and Elaine Sorensen. 2000. "Father Involvement with their Nonmarital Children: Patterns, Determinants, and Effects on their Earnings." *Marriage and Family Review,* 29(2): 137-158.

McLanahan, Sara, and Gary Sandefur. 1994. "Growing Up with a Single Parent: What Hurts, What Helps." Cambridge: Harvard.

Miller, Cynthia, and Virginia Knox. 2001. "The Challenge of Helping Low-Income Fathers Support their Children: Final Lessons from Parents' Fair Share." New York: Manpower Demonstration Research Corporation.

Olds, David L., and others. 1997. "Long-term Effects of Home Visitation on Maternal Life Course and Child Abuse and Neglect." *Journal of the American Medical Association,* 278(8): 637-643.

Sorensen, Elaine, and Chava Zibman. 2001. "Poor Dads Who Don't Pay Child Support: Deadbeats or Disadvantaged?" Washington, D.C.: Urban Institute.

U.S. Department of Health and Human Services. 1995. "Report to Congress on Out-of-Wedlock Childbearing." Hyattsville: National Center for Health Statistics.

Waite, Linda J. 1995. "Does Marriage Matter?" *Demography* 32(4): 483-507.

18

ISABEL SAWHILL

What Can Be Done to Reduce Teen Pregnancy and Out-of-Wedlock Births?

Executive Summary
When welfare reform was enacted in 1996, Congress placed high priority on reducing out-of-wedlock births and encouraging the formation of two-parent families. These goals remain somewhat controversial, but there is an emerging consensus that if we knew how to achieve them, children's lives would be improved. This brief argues that one of the least controversial and most effective ways of achieving these goals is to focus on preventing teen pregnancy. Almost everyone is in favor of reducing teen pregnancy and new evidence suggests that a variety of programs have achieved this objective. For this and other reasons, teen pregnancy and birthrates have declined during the 1990s, which in turn has contributed to the leveling off of the proportion of all children born to unwed mothers. When Congress reauthorizes the Personal Responsibility and Work Opportunity Reform Act in 2002, it should build on this success by providing additional funds for teen pregnancy prevention efforts while maintaining the emphasis on work and child support enforcement. The evidence suggests that this emphasis, rather than any of the more specific provisions of the law, is the reason for recent progress in reducing unwed childbearing.

Why Focus on Teen Pregnancy?

Virtually all of the growth of single-parent families in recent decades has been driven by an increase in births outside marriage. Divorce rates have leveled off or declined modestly since the early 1980s and thus have not contributed to the rising proportion of children being raised by only one parent nor to the increase in child poverty and welfare dependence associated with the rise in single-parent families.

Not all non-marital births are to teen-agers. In fact, 70 percent of all births outside marriage are to women over age 20. For this reason, some argue that a focus on teens fails to address the real problem and that much more attention needs to be given to preventing childbearing, or raising marriage rates, among single women who have already entered their adult years.

But there are at least four reasons to focus on teens:

First, although a large proportion of non-marital births is to adult women, half of first non-marital births are to teens. Thus, the pattern tends to start in the teenage years, and, once teens have had a first child

> *Only one out of every five teen mothers receives any support from their child's father, and about 80 percent end up on welfare. Once on welfare, they are likely to remain there for a long time. In fact, half of all current welfare recipients had their first child as a teenager.*

outside marriage, many go on to have additional children out of wedlock at an older age. A number of programs aimed at preventing subsequent births to teen mothers have been launched but few have had much success. So, if we want to prevent out-of-wedlock childbearing and the growth of single-parent families, the teenage years are a good place to start.

Second, teen childbearing is very costly. A 1997 study by Rebecca Maynard of Mathematica Policy Research in Princeton, New Jersey, found that, after controlling for differences between teen mothers and mothers aged 20 or 21 when they had their first child, teen childbearing costs taxpayers more than $7 billion a year or $3,200 a year for each teenage birth, conservatively estimated.

Third, although almost all single mothers face major challenges in raising their children alone, teen mothers are especially disadvantaged. They are more likely to have dropped out of school and are less likely to be able to support themselves. Only one out of every five teen mothers receives any support from their child's father, and about 80 percent end up on welfare. Once on welfare, they are likely to remain there for a long time. In fact, half of all current welfare recipients had their first child as a teenager.

Some research suggests that women who have children at an early age are no worse off than comparable women who delay childbearing. According to this research, many of the disadvantages accruing to early childbearers are related to their own disadvantaged backgrounds. This research suggests that it would be unwise to attribute all of the problems faced by teen mothers to the timing of the birth per se. But even after taking background characteristics into account, other research documents that teen mothers are less likely to finish high school, less likely to ever marry, and more likely to have additional children outside marriage. Thus, an early birth is not just a marker of preexisting problems but a barrier to subsequent upward mobility. As Daniel Lichter of Ohio State University has shown, even those unwed mothers who eventually marry end up with less successful partners than those who delay childbearing. As a result, even if married, these women face much higher rates of poverty and dependence on government assistance than those who avoid an early birth. And early marriages are much more likely to end in divorce. So marriage, while helpful, is no panacea.

Fourth, the children of teen mothers face far greater problems than those born to older mothers. If the reason we care about stemming the growth of single-parent families is the consequences for children, and if the age of the mother is as important as her marital status, then focusing solely on marital status would be unwise. Not only are mothers who defer childbearing more likely to marry, but with or without marriage, their children will be better off. The children of teen mothers are more likely than the children of older mothers to be born prematurely at low birth weight and to suffer a variety of health problems as a consequence. They are more likely to do poorly in school, to suffer higher rates of abuse and neglect, and to end up in foster care with all its attendant costs.

How Does Current Welfare Law Address Teen Pregnancy and Non-Marital Births?

The welfare law enacted in 1996 contained numerous provisions designed to reduce teen or out-of-wedlock childbearing including:

- A $50 million a year federal investment in abstinence education;
- A requirement that teen mothers complete high school or the equivalent and live at home or in another supervised setting;
- New measures to ensure that paternity is established and child support paid;
- A $20 million bonus for each of the 5 states with the greatest success in reducing out-of-wedlock births and abortions;
- A $1 billion performance bonus tied to the law's goals, which include reducing out-of-wedlock pregnancies and encouraging the formation and maintenance of two-parent families;
- The flexibility for states to deny benefits to teen mothers or to mothers who have additional children while on welfare (no state has adopted the first but 23 states have adopted the second); and
- A requirement that states set goals and take actions to reduce out-of-wedlock pregnancies, with special emphasis on teen pregnancies.

Research attempting to establish a link between one or more of these provisions and teen out-of-wedlock childbearing has, for the most part, failed to find a clear relationship. One exception is child support enforcement, which appears to have had a significant effect in deterring unwed childbearing.

Are Teen Pregnancies and Births Declining?

Teen pregnancy and birthrates have both declined sharply in the 1990s (figure 1). The fact that these declines predated the enactment of federal welfare reform suggests that they were caused by other factors. However, it is worth noting that many states began to reform their welfare systems earlier in the decade under waivers from the federal government, so we cannot be sure. In addition, the declines appear to have accelerated in the second half of the decade after welfare reform was enacted. And finally, most of the decline in the early 1990s was the result of a decrease in second or higher order births to women who were already teen mothers. This decrease was related in part to the popularity of new and more effective methods of birth control among this group. It was not until the second half of the decade that a significant drop in first births to teens occurred.

Teen birthrates had also declined in the 1970s and early 1980s but in this earlier period all of the decline was due to increased abortion. Significantly, all of the teen birthrate decreases in the 1990s were due to fewer pregnancies, not more abortions.

Equally significant is the fact that teens are now having less sex. Up until the 1990s, despite some progress in convincing teens to use contraception, teen pregnancy rates continued to rise because an increasing number of teens were becoming sexually active at an early age, thereby putting themselves at risk of pregnancy. More recently, both better contraceptive use and less sex have contributed to the lowering of rates.

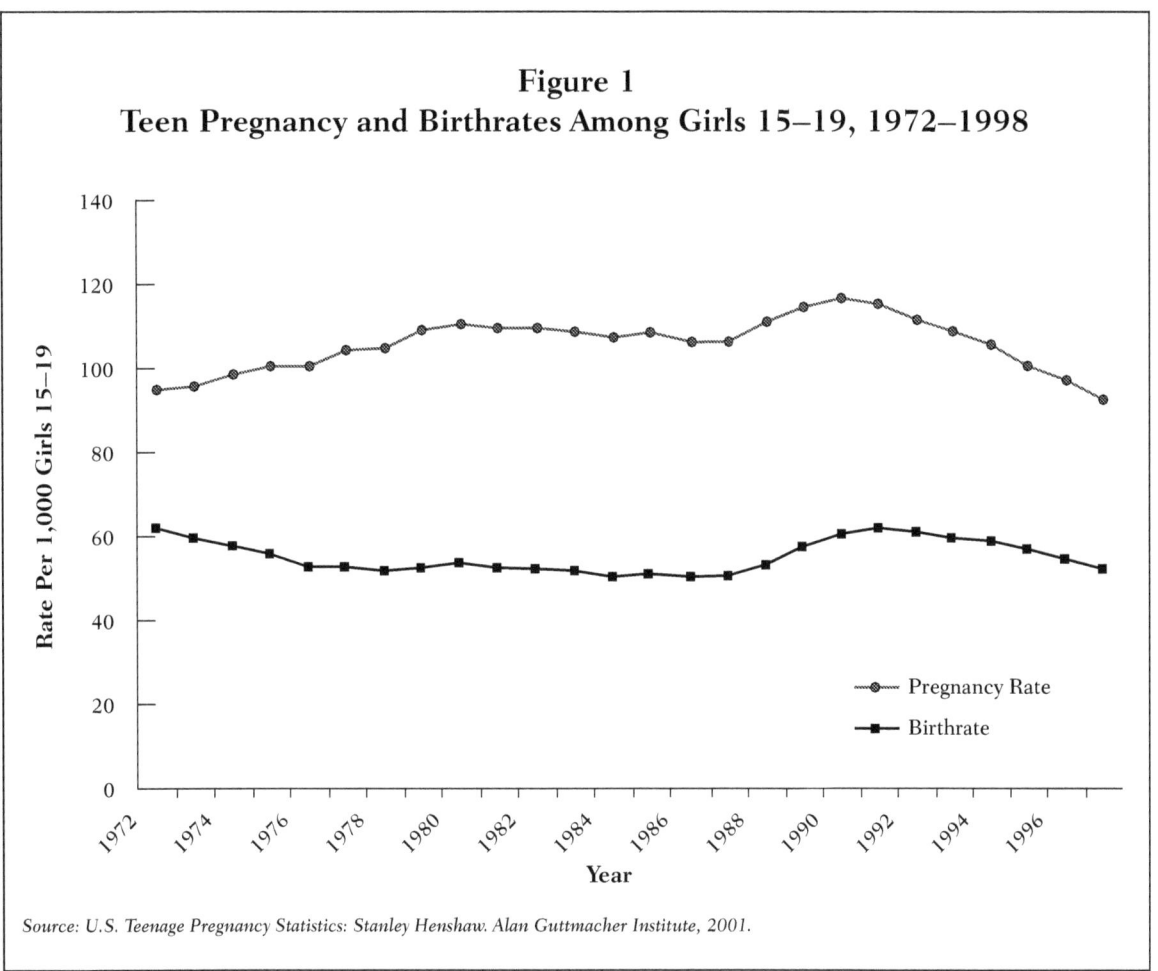

Figure 1
Teen Pregnancy and Birthrates Among Girls 15–19, 1972–1998

Source: U.S. Teenage Pregnancy Statistics: Stanley Henshaw. Alan Guttmacher Institute, 2001.

Given that four out of five teen births are to an unwed mother, this drop in the teen birthrate contributed to the leveling off of the proportion of children born outside marriage after 1994 (figure 2). More specifically, if teen birthrates had held at the levels reached in the early 1990s, by 1999 this proportion would have been more than a full percentage point higher. Thus, a focus on teenagers has a major role to play in future reductions of both out-of-wedlock childbearing and the growth of single-parent families.

What Caused the Decline in Teen Pregnancies and Births?

Although the immediate causes of the decline—less sex and more contraception—are relatively well established, it is less clear what might have motivated teens to choose either one. However, many experts believe it was some combination of greater public and private efforts to prevent teen pregnancy, the new messages about work and child support embedded in welfare reform, more conservative attitudes among the young, fear of AIDS and other sexually transmitted diseases, the availability of more effective forms of contraception, and perhaps the strong economy.

Some of these factors have undoubtedly interacted, making it difficult to ever sort out their separate effects. For example, fear of AIDS may have made teenagers—males in particular, for whom pregnancy has

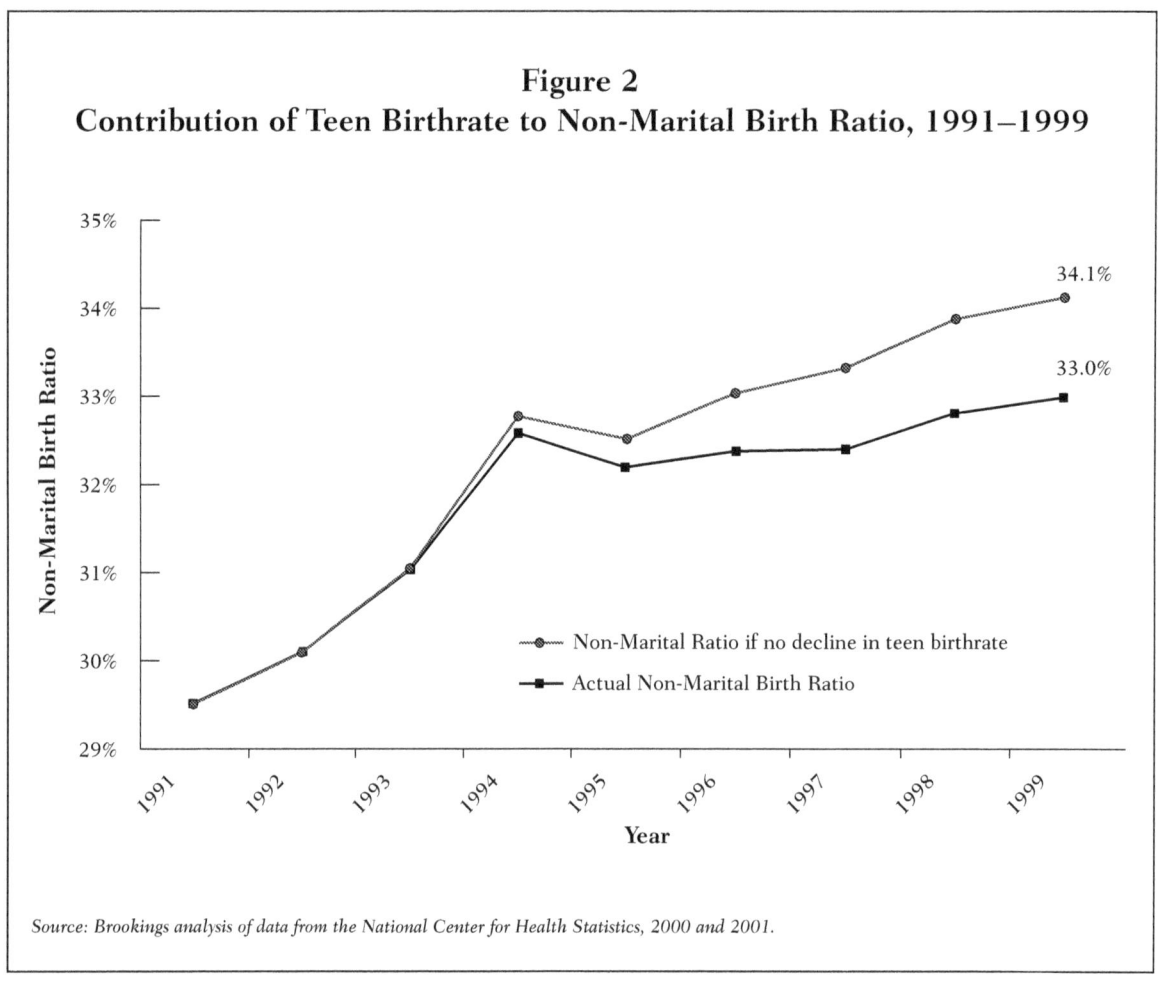

Figure 2
Contribution of Teen Birthrate to Non-Marital Birth Ratio, 1991–1999

Source: Brookings analysis of data from the National Center for Health Statistics, 2000 and 2001.

traditionally been of less concern—more cautious and willing to listen to new messages. Indeed, as shown by Leighton Ku and his colleagues at the Urban Institute in Washington, D.C., the proportion of adolescent males approving of premarital sex decreased from 80 percent in 1988 to 71 percent in 1995. The Ku study also linked this shift in adolescent male attitudes to a change in their behavior.

The growth of public and private efforts to combat teen pregnancy may have also played a role, as suggested by surveys conducted by the National Governors' Association, the General Accounting Office, the American Public Human Services Association, and most recently and comprehensively, by Child Trends. The Child Trends study, conducted by Richard Wertheimer and his associates at the Urban Institute, surveyed all 50 states in both 1997 and 1999. The survey shows that states have dramatically increased their efforts to reduce teen pregnancy (figure 3). These efforts include everything from the formation of statewide task forces to more emphasis on sex education in the public schools and statewide media campaigns. Although such efforts have been greatly expanded in recent years, they are still relatively small. State spending on teen pregnancy prevention averages only about $8 a year per teenaged girl. In addition to being small, such efforts may or may not be effective in preventing

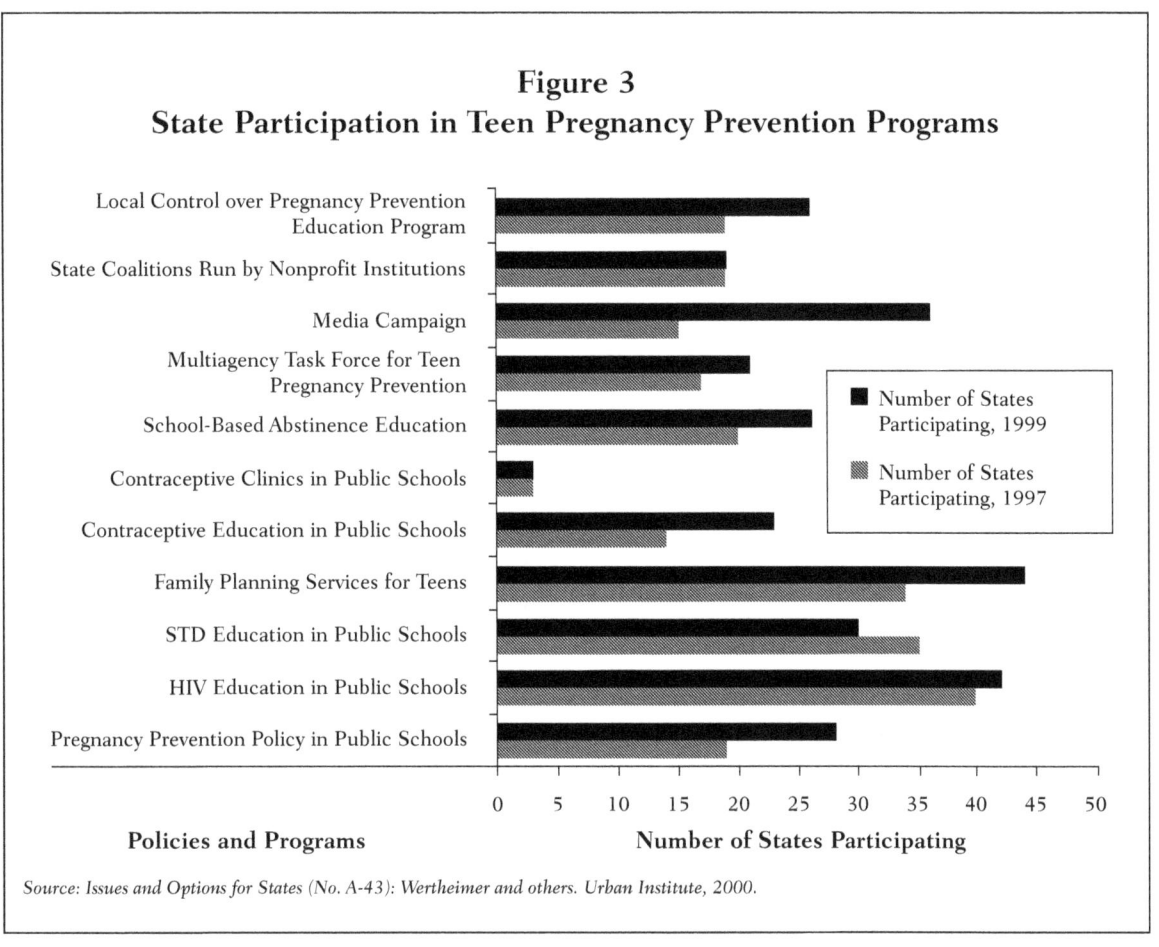

pregnancy. Fortunately, we know more about this topic now than we did even a few years ago.

Do Teen Pregnancy Prevention Programs Work?

The short answer is "yes, some do." Based on a careful review of the scholarly literature completed by Douglas Kirby of ETR Associates in Santa Cruz, California, a number of rigorously evaluated programs have been found to reduce pregnancy rates. Two of these programs have reduced rates by as much as one-half. One is a program that involves teens in community service with adult supervision and counseling. The other includes a range of services such as tutoring and career counseling along with sex education and reproductive health services. Both have been replicated in diverse communities and evaluated by randomly assigning teens to a program and control group. In addition, a number of less intensive and less costly sex education programs have also been found to be effective in persuading teens to delay sex and/or use contraception. Such programs typically provide clear messages about the importance of abstaining from sex and/or using contraception, teach teens how to deal with peer pressure to have sex, and provide practice in communicating and negotiating with partners.

"Abstinence only" programs are relatively new and have not yet been subject to careful evaluation, although what research exists has not been encouraging. More importantly, the

> *A strong abstinence message is totally consistent with public values, but the idea that the federal government can, or should, rigidly prescribe what goes on in the classroom through detailed curricular guidelines makes little sense. Family and community values, not a federal mandate, should prevail, especially in an area as sensitive as this one.*

line between abstinence only and more comprehensive sex education that advocates abstinence but also teaches about contraception is increasingly blurred. What matters is not so much the label but rather what a particular program includes, what the teacher believes, and how that plays out in the classroom. A strong abstinence message is totally consistent with public values, but the idea that the federal government can, or should, rigidly prescribe what goes on in the classroom through detailed curricular guidelines makes little sense. Family and community values, not a federal mandate, should prevail, especially in an area as sensitive as this one.

Do Media Campaigns Work?

Community-based programs are only part of the solution to teen pregnancy. Indeed, only 10 percent of teens report they have participated in such a program (outside of school), while on average teens spend more than 38 hours a week exposed to various forms of entertainment media. By themselves, teen pregnancy prevention programs cannot change prevailing social norms or attitudes that influence teen sexual behavior. The increase in teen pregnancy rates between the early 1970s and 1990 was largely the result of a change in attitudes about the appropriateness of early premarital sex, especially for young women. As more and more teen girls put themselves at risk of an early pregnancy, pregnancy rates rose. More recently, efforts to encourage teens to take a pledge not to have sex before marriage have had some success in delaying the onset of sex.

In an attempt to influence these attitudes and behaviors, several national organizations as well as numerous states have turned to the media for assistance. Between 1997 and 1999 alone, the number of states conducting media campaigns increased from 15 to 36. Typically, such campaigns use both print and electronic media to reach large numbers of young people with messages designed to change their behavior. Such messages can be delivered via public service announcements (PSAs) or by working with the media to incorporate more responsible content into their ongoing programming. Most state efforts rely on PSA campaigns but several national organizations are working with the entertainment industry to affect content.

Research assessing the effectiveness of media campaigns is less extensive and less widely known than research evaluating community-based programs, but it shows that they, too, can be effective. A meta-analysis of 48 different health-related media campaigns from smoking cessation to AIDS prevention by Leslie Snyder of the University of

Connecticut found that, on average, such campaigns caused 7 to 10 percent of those exposed to the campaign to change their behavior (relative to those in a control group). As with community-based programs, media campaigns vary enormously in their effectiveness and need to be designed with care. But existing evidence suggests that they are a good way to reach large numbers of teens inexpensively.

> *As with community-based programs, media campaigns vary enormously in their effectiveness and need to be designed with care. But existing evidence suggests that they are a good way to reach large numbers of teens inexpensively.*

Are Efforts to Reduce Teen Pregnancy Cost-Effective?

At first appearance, the finding by Rebecca Maynard that each teen mother costs the government an average of $3,200 per year suggests that government could spend as much as $3,200 per teen girl on teen pregnancy prevention and break even in the process. But, of course, not all girls become teen mothers and programs addressing this problem are not 100 percent effective so a lot of this money would be wasted on girls who do not need services and on programs that are less than fully effective.

Here is a simple but useful method to estimate how much money could be spent on teen pregnancy prevention programs and still realize benefits that exceed costs. If we accept Maynard's estimate that reducing teen pregnancy saves $3,200 per birth prevented (in 2001 dollars), the question is how much should we spend to prevent such births? We first have to adjust the $3,200 estimate for the fact that not all teen girls will get pregnant and give birth without the intervention program. We know that about 40 percent of teen girls become pregnant and about half of these (or 20 percent) give birth. This adjustment yields the estimate that $640 (20 percent multiplied by $3,200) might be saved by a universal prevention program. (If we knew how to target the young people most at risk we could save even more than this.) However, a second adjustment is necessary because not all intervention programs are effective. Based on data reviewed by Douglas Kirby and by Leslie Snyder, a good estimate is that about one out of every ten girls enrolled in a program or reached by a media campaign might change her behavior in a way that delayed pregnancy beyond her teen years. This second adjustment yields the estimate that universal programs would produce a benefit of 10 percent of $640 or about $64 per participant. As the Wertheimer survey showed, actual spending on teen pregnancy prevention programs in the entire nation now averages about $8 per teenage girl. If the potential savings are $64 per teenage female while actual current spending is only $8 per teenage female, government is clearly missing an opportunity for productive investments in prevention programs. In fact, these calculations—while rough—suggest that government could spend up to eight times ($64 divided by $8) as much as is currently being spent and still break even.

Implications for Welfare Reform Reauthorization

Research and experience over the last decade suggest several lessons for the administration and Congress as they consider reauthorization of the 1996 welfare reform legislation.

First, the emphasis in the current law on time limits, work, and child support enforcement should be maintained. The 1996 welfare reform law included a set of very important messages. To young women, it said "if you become a mother, this will not relieve you of an obligation to finish school and support yourself and your family through work or marriage. And any special assistance you receive will be time limited." To young men, it said "if you father a child out-of-wedlock, you will be responsible for supporting that child." Although opinions vary as to whether these messages have had an impact, in my view the decline in teen pregnancies and births together with the leveling off of the non-marital birth ratio and of the proportion of children living in single parent homes all suggest such an impact. These messages may be far more important than any specific provisions aimed at increasing marriage or reducing out-of-wedlock childbearing, and their effects are likely to cumulate over time.

Second, the federal government should fund a national resource center to collect and disseminate information about what works to prevent teen pregnancy. Until recently, little information was available about the best ways to prevent teen pregnancy. States and communities had no way of learning about each other's efforts and teens themselves had no ready source of information about the risks of pregnancy and the consequences of early unprotected sex. Some private organizations have attempted to fill the gap without much help from public sources.

Third, Congress should send a strong abstinence message coupled with education about contraception. Surveys of both adults and teens reveal strong support for abstinence as the preferred standard of behavior for school-age youth, and they want teens to hear this message. At the same time, a majority is in favor of making birth control services and information available to teens who are sexually active. In addition, few expect all unmarried adults in their twenties to abstain from sex until marriage. And since a large proportion of non-marital births occurs in this age group, and a significant number of teens continue to be sexually active, education about and access to reproductive health services remains important through Title X of the Public Health Service Act, the Medicaid program, and other federal and state programs.

Fourth, adequate resources should be provided to states to prevent teen pregnancy, without specifying the means for achieving this goal. In addition, states that work successfully to reduce teen pregnancy should be rewarded for their efforts. A strong argument can be made that the federal government should specify the outcomes it wants to achieve but not prescribe the means for achieving them. This is especially important given some uncertainty about the effectiveness of different programs and strategies, and the diversity of opinion about the best way to proceed. It suggests the wisdom of retaining a block grant structure for TANF and avoiding earmarks for specific programs. This does not mean the federal government should not reward states that achieve certain objectives, such as an increase in the proportion of children living in two-parent families, a decline in the non-marital birth ratio, or a decline in the teen pregnancy or birth rate. Reducing early childbearing may be one of the most effective ways of increasing the proportion of children born to, and raised by, a married couple. But states should decide on the best way to achieve these outcomes, subject only to the caveat that they base their efforts on reliable evidence about what works. The evidence presented above suggests that states should be spending roughly eight times as much as they are now on teen pregnancy prevention.

Fifth, the federal government should fund a national media campaign. Too many public officials and community leaders have assumed that if they could just find the right program, teen pregnancy rates would be reduced. Although there are now a number of programs that have proved effective, the burden of reducing teen pregnancy should not rest on programs alone. Rather, we should build on the fledgling efforts undertaken at the state and national level over the past five years to fund a broad-based, sophisticated media campaign to reduce teen pregnancy. These funds should support not only public service ads but also various nongovernmental efforts to work in partnership with the entertainment industry to promote more responsible content. These media efforts can work in tandem with effective sex education and more expensive and intensive community level programs targeted to high-risk youth.

Conclusion

These steps have the potential to maintain the progress made over the past decade in reducing teen and out-of-wedlock pregnancies. There are only two solutions to the problem of childbearing outside marriage. One is to encourage early marriage. The other is to encourage delayed childbearing until marriage. Although commonplace as recently as the 1950s, early marriage is no longer a sensible strategy in a society where decent jobs increasingly require a high level of education and where half of teen marriages end in divorce. If we want to ensure that more children grow up in stable two-parent families, we must first ensure that more women reach adulthood before they have children.

Additional Reading

Henshaw, Stanley. 2001. *U.S. Teenage Pregnancy Statistics.* New York: Alan Guttmacher Institute.

Kirby, Douglas. 2001. *Emerging Answers: Research Findings on Programs to Reduce Teen Pregnancy.* Washington, D.C.: National Campaign to Prevent Teen Pregnancy.

Ku, Leighton, and others. 1998. "Understanding Changes in Sexual Activity Among Young Metropolitan Men: 1979–1995." *Family Planning Perspectives,* 30(6): 256–262.

Lichter, Daniel T., Deborah Roempke Graefe, and J. Brian Brown. 2001. *Is Marriage a Panacea? Union Formation Among Economically Disadvantaged Unwed Mothers.* Columbus: Ohio State University.

Maynard, Rebecca A., ed. 1997. *Kids Having Kids: Economic Costs and Social Consequences of Teen Pregnancy.* Washington, D.C.: Urban Institute.

National Campaign to Prevent Teen Pregnancy. 2001. *Halfway There: A Prescription for Continued Progress in Preventing Teen Pregnancy.* Washington, D.C..

National Center for Health Statistics. 2000 and 2001. *National Vital Statistics Reports,* 48 and 49, various issues. Hyattsville, Md.: Department of Health and Human Services.

Sawhill, Isabel. Forthcoming. "Welfare Reform and the Marriage Movement." *Public Interest.*

Snyder, Leslie B. 2000. "How Effective Are Mediated Health Campaigns?" In *Public Communication Campaign,* edited by Ronald E. Rice and Charles K. Atkin. Thousand Oaks, California: Sage.

Wertheimer, Richard, Justin Jager, and Kristin Anderson Moore. 2000. "State Policy Initiatives for Reducing Teen and Adult Non-Marital Childbearing." *New Federalism: Issues and Options for States* (No. A-43). Washington, D.C.: Urban Institute.

PART VII

RELATED PROGRAMS

MICHAEL WISEMAN

Food Stamps and Welfare Reform

Executive Summary

The Food Stamp Program (FSP) is the nation's nearly universal anti-poverty initiative, providing support to a broad range of low-income households. This brief summarizes FSP operations, program issues, and options for better meeting the program's objectives. A distinction is drawn between the food stamp safety net function and the program's role in supplementing the resources of low-income working families. Food stamps have attracted attention because of a decline since 1994 in take-up rates (the percentage of eligible families that actually receive benefits), a decline that accelerated following national implementation of welfare reform in 1996. Factors contributing to the decline include problems with assessing eligibility and benefits for the working poor and with ensuring that families leaving cash welfare for work continue to receive the food stamp benefits for which they are eligible. There are three overarching issues in food stamps policy discussions: defining what the program is intended to do, structuring the relationship between food stamps and cash welfare, and defining the terms of the federal-state partnership required for achieving food stamps goals. Welfare reform reauthorization offers an opportunity for progress on all three fronts. Options for reform include relaxing eligibility criteria, altering procedures for delivering benefits, and changing the focus of state performance assessment.

In a typical month in 2001, 17.3 million people in 7.5 million households received food stamps at an annual cost of $20 billion. Current Food Stamp Program (FSP) appropriations expire September 30, 2002, coincidentally with the expiration of authorization for Temporary Assistance for Needy Families (TANF). The 1996 legislation that created TANF included food stamp provisions, and the close connections between TANF and the FSP mean that the welfare reform reauthorization debate involves both.

For low-income families with children, the FSP shares some characteristics with both TANF and the Earned Income Tax Credit (EITC). On the one hand, TANF dollars provide a general time-limited income floor for needy families that lack other means of support. On the other, the EITC bolsters the income of those who have jobs but work at low wages. The FSP supplements both TANF benefits and the incomes of the working poor and near poor while ensuring access to a necessity: food. And unlike the EITC, which is usually received annually as a lump sum, food stamp benefits are received monthly.

Evidence has accumulated over the past decade that the FSP is not functioning well as a support for working families. Some reforms have been implemented, and many others have been proposed. But before analyzing these reforms, this policy brief reviews the basic features and problems of the program.

How the Food Stamp Program Works

Food stamps help people buy food. Over 80 percent of recipients receive food stamp assistance by using special ATM-like debit cards in grocery stores. The basic benefit is adjusted annually for changes in food costs.

To be eligible for food stamps, households must have gross (before tax) monthly incomes of less than 130 percent of federal poverty guidelines (in 2001 the guideline was $1,219 for a family of three) and few assets. Certain adults are required to register for work, and some adults without dependents are required to work or to participate in training as a condition of assistance. Families receiving TANF benefits and persons receiving Supplemental Security Income are in most circumstances automatically eligible for food stamps if they live alone.

In fiscal year 2001, the maximum monthly food stamp benefit for a household of three was $341. Beyond a standard deduction and certain other allowances, benefits are reduced by $0.30 for each dollar of income from sources other than earnings and by $0.24 for each dollar of earnings. In fiscal year 2000, households with children received an average monthly food stamp benefit of $234.

While the federal government pays most FSP costs and sets most of the regulations, the program is operated by states, generally through local welfare offices. Management is evaluated annually by a joint federal/state review of a sample of cases drawn from each state's recipients list. This quality control sample is sufficiently large to provide reliable information on the people receiving food stamps, the rate at which administrators make errors in benefit determination, and the amounts of payments involved. States can be charged for the benefit cost of error rates in excess of national averages. In practice such penalties are often waived; when enforced, states pay by investing the fine in programs to improve performance.

Food Stamps Play Two Roles

Food stamps both help protect household access to a necessity and provide income support. The safety role is reflected in the program's focus on monthly income and on adjusting benefits relatively quickly when income changes. Beyond the safety net, food stamps help fill long-term gaps between the income people need, at least for nutrition, and what they have. The food stamp benefit serves as a supplement to a family's other resources, usually Supplemental Security Income, TANF, or earnings. In at least fourteen states, TANF families receive more each month in food stamps than in TANF cash.

In its income support role, the FSP is an important contributor to the well-being of the working poor and near poor who are not TANF recipients. In 2001, a single mother with two children who worked thirty hours a week at $8 an hour earned about $950 a month after social insurance deductions—less than the poverty standard of $1,219 for a family this size. But when she files her federal income tax return, she will get almost $4,000 ($324 per month worked) from the EITC. In addition, she is eligible each month for at least $134 in food stamps. While for most working households the EITC benefit is greater than the food stamps benefit, EITC income is usually not available to meet ongoing expenses until the end of the year.

From the perspective of welfare policy, TANF, the FSP, and the EITC should work together: TANF gives states program flexibility for addressing general family needs and moving people into the workforce; the FSP provides a real-time income supplement; and at tax time, the EITC provides a special cash bonus for families working at low wages and contributing to Social Security. Combined, these programs bring most low-wage families that work full-time above the poverty level. Thus, the idea of food stamps as a bridge from welfare to work is attractive. But recent data suggest that the bridge may not be working as well as it should.

The Big Decline in Participation

As illustrated in figure 1, between 1993 and 2000 the number of persons counted as poor fell by 21 percent, from 39 million to 31 million. The number of children living in poor households declined as well, by 26 percent, to 12 million. These trends would normally be expected to reduce food stamps usage. But especially after 1995, the number of FSP participants fell by considerably more than would seem warranted by the observed reduction in poverty. Since most poor families are eligible for food stamps, the implication is that the percentage of eligible families that actually received the benefit fell.

It is difficult to estimate take-up rates with precision, because available household surveys do not provide the detail on assets and monthly income necessary to simulate reliably FSP eligibility determination procedures. Nevertheless, the best available estimate is that food stamp take-up fell by 24 percent between 1993 and 1999, and the decline accelerated following welfare reform. Consequently, by 1999 as many as 4 million children were living in households eligible for, but not receiving, food stamp assistance. The decline appears particularly pronounced

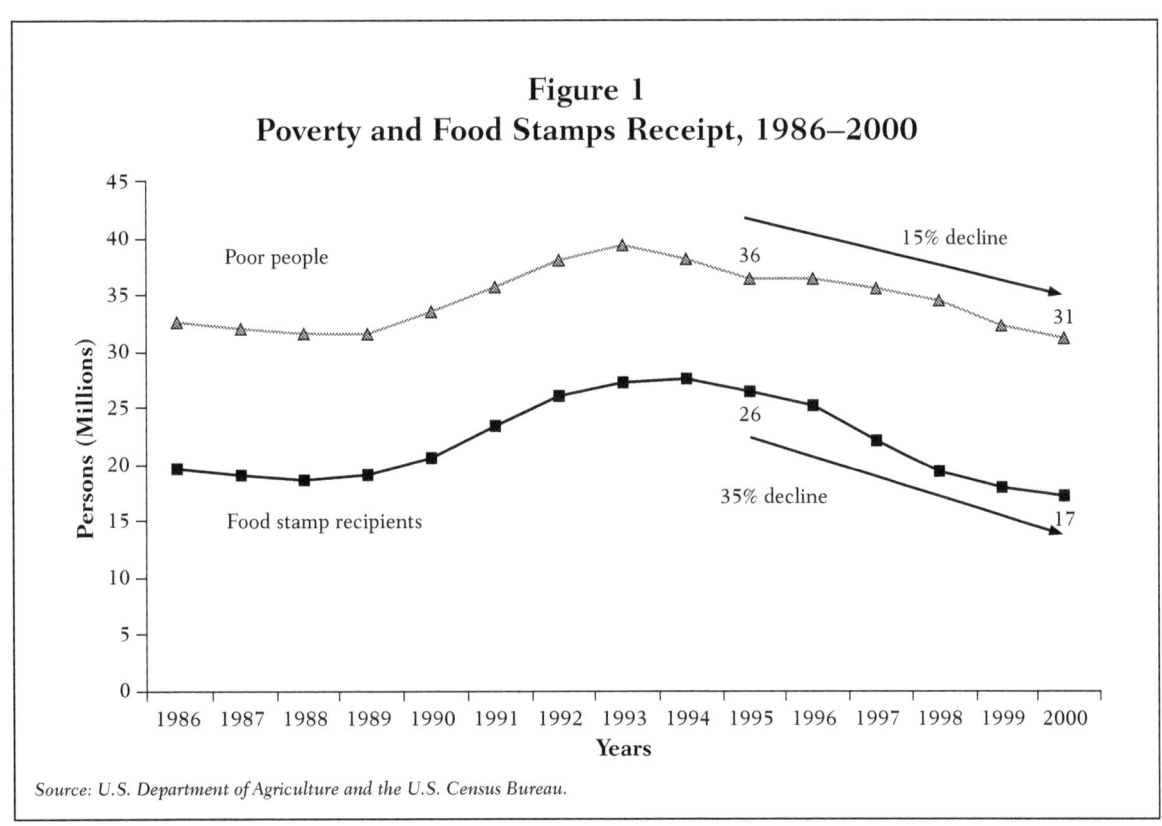

Figure 1
Poverty and Food Stamps Receipt, 1986–2000

Source: U.S. Department of Agriculture and the U.S. Census Bureau.

among both single-parent and married-couple families with earnings. Given that a major objective of welfare reform is to encourage work and to promote marriage, these changes are of special concern.

Why has this occurred? Many analysts point to the administrative tension between TANF and food stamps as a factor in at least the early decline. Food stamps are a federal entitlement, while the 1996 reforms made eligibility for TANF a matter principally of state policy. States often attempt to avoid establishing new cases for TANF applicants by meeting particular one-time needs or by rapid job placement. Given such "diversion" strategies, application for food stamps, if not discouraged, was often not promoted. In response to studies by the U.S. General Accounting Office and efforts by both the Food and Nutrition Service of the Department of Agriculture (which runs the FSP) and by advocates, states eventually moved to clarify the distinction between food stamps and TANF and to make more information about food stamps available to all persons seeking assistance.

Administrative problems also arise in the case of families leaving welfare. It appears that many families leaving TANF have been unaware of the possibility of continued eligibility for food stamps assistance. States have responded with efforts to better inform families about the FSP, and states may now allow food stamp benefits to continue automatically for three months after TANF benefits cease in order to facilitate transition.

The last decade saw a substantial increase in employment among low-income families, especially among single parents. Somewhat paradoxically, this desirable development may have contributed to the decline in food stamp take-up. More earnings means lower food stamp benefits. At the same time, working takes time, making it more costly to come into welfare offices to review the food stamps application. This apparently leads some families to give up food stamps even when still eligible for significant benefits.

In some instances state policy may have added to the difficulty families encounter in trying to sustain food stamps eligibility. Working households generally have more variable incomes than do households dependent on other sources of income. Accordingly, benefit computation errors tend to be more common for working families. States have apparently responded to this hazard by increasing food stamp reporting requirements for workers, thereby raising the "hassle factor" even further for households facing the greatest time constraints. To offset this development, the Department of Agriculture has changed program regulations so that states can reduce the reporting burden without generating errors that will lead to federal penalty.

There is some evidence that efforts to streamline the program since 1996 and more aggressive outreach efforts have increased utilization: participation began to rise in early 2001. However, the near-simultaneous economic slow-down confounds the interpretation of such changes. What is clear is that making work pay is central to national welfare strategy, and if, for whatever reason, eligible working people lose access to food stamps, reform belongs on the agenda for reauthorization.

Policy Opportunities

The core objective of the FSP is to provide nutrition support for people in need. The central question for reform is how to find efficient ways to improve access to the program's benefits for those it is intended to serve without compromising other national objectives such as fraud reduction and promotion of self-support.

Working Families For working families, the options for food stamp reform most commonly cited involve changing rules and administrative procedures. More ambitious possibilities include changing the way the benefit is delivered.

It is possible that estimates of low FSP take-up are exaggerated because families qualified for food stamps on the basis of income do not apply, or are determined ineligible, because of their assets. The liquid assets maximum ($2,000) was set in 1985; the maximum automobile value ($4,650) was set in 1996. The assets maximum could be increased by over 60 percent without exceeding amounts equivalent in purchasing power to those used in the past; the automobile maximum is obviously too low for households that need a reliable vehicle for commuting. Under regulations established by the Department of Agriculture in 2000, states are now allowed to align the FSP vehicle maximum to the limits in their TANF programs—if these limits are higher—and a majority of states have done so. Updating and increasing both the vehicle and liquid asset limits nationally would be consistent with other efforts to promote saving and self-sufficiency, since households that save create their own safety nets. Current proposals in both the House and Senate farm bills generally leave vehicle policy to the states; the administration's proposal calls for exempting one vehicle per adult.

Turning to procedural issues, the FSP requires regular "recertification" of individual and family need. In most jurisdictions, recertification is done at quarterly intervals for families with earnings, which is a burden for working families. The obvious solution is to fix benefit values over a longer period of time. Regulatory changes made by the Department of Agriculture in late 2000 give states the option of setting benefits semi-annually for earners while allowing households to apply for a benefit adjustment if income falls. Senate farm bill proposals call for extending this option to virtually the entire caseload.

Frequent recertification is costly, both for agencies and for clients, especially those clients who are working. The problem is one of conflict between the requirements of a safety net program—meeting the nutrition needs of the moment—and the longer-term perspective appropriate for supplementing the low, and sometimes unsteady, incomes of working families. A system that fixes benefits for an extended period on the basis of current income increases the gain from applying for food stamps when income is low, even when recovery is imminent. In principle, this issue might be addressed by reconciliation of benefits with actual income at, say, income-tax time. But to do so would require more elaborate income reporting than is now done and possibly integrating the food stamps program with the income-tax reporting system. Given such integration, consideration might be given to converting the food stamp benefit to cash, at least for working families.

But taking this step of converting food stamps to cash would seem to contradict the fundamental orientation of the FSP toward nutrition. Evidence exists that providing aid in the form of food stamps does in some cases lead households to purchase more food than they would if the benefit were provided in cash. However, this does not mean that the Electronic Benefit Transfer (EBT) card, which is now used by most states, is the best way of distributing FSP benefits. Payment through EBT is most likely to effect consumption for those with the lowest incomes—the families for whom the program's safety net function is most important. For those families with benefits that are small in comparison with overall expenditures—typically families with earnings—the FSP principally provides the equivalent of more income. In such cases both the nutrition and the income support function might be served equally well by depositing the benefit in a bank account. Without experimentation, it is not clear how much this shift would raise FSP participation.

Some food stamp applicants and recipients do cheat. Suppressing fraud is important to maintaining the FSP's political viability, and regular assessments of eligibility and review with recipients of their obligations contribute to the program's integrity. Nevertheless, the gains from using an expanded horizon for eligibility assessment and simplified processes for recertification appear substantial. Rather than introduce such changes by directive, as the Department of Agriculture has done for some features, it might be better to undertake careful experimentation in order to determine the best among a number of options for modification of income assessment and reporting procedures. Current food stamp proposals in both the House and Senate include provisions for funding of demonstrations intended to test alternatives for FSP regulation and operation.

Integration with TANF Problems with integration of food stamps with TANF arise in three ways. One, mostly resolved in the 1996 welfare reform law, concerns sanctions. When adult TANF recipients lose benefits due to failure to comply with TANF rules, their income falls. Without adjustment, a fall in income would produce an increase in the food stamps benefit, offsetting the sanction. Current regulations allow states to preempt such adjustment for the adult portion of the food stamp benefit.

A second TANF integration issue involves assets. States have in many instances adopted more generous assets restrictions for TANF than for food stamps. This does not pose a problem for TANF recipients, since TANF receipt automatically qualifies families for food stamps. However, it is possible for a working family to leave assistance and lose food stamps not because of application of the income test but because of more stringent FSP vehicle or savings restrictions. This inconsistency has been addressed by giving states a variety of options for relaxing federal rules. The result is a hodgepodge.

The pressure to adapt FSP rules to state TANF choices has occurred in part because of failure to adjust the federal food stamp limits upward. If federal policy were consistent with the support role the FSP is expected to play for working families, it would be reasonable to expect states to adapt their TANF policies to the federal program. But when the federal government is not actively involved in program review and improvement, it is not surprising that pressure mounts for accommodating national policy to the varied strategies, wise and otherwise, of the states.

A third integration issue is related to closure of TANF cases. It is awkward and possibly counterproductive to immediately conduct a new eligibility determination for food stamps as families are leaving TANF. Current regulations allow states to treat the value of the benefit at closure as transitional assistance, and to sustain the payment for three months before undertaking recertification. This transition could be lengthened:

extension to six months would be consistent with current practice in Medicaid and could be linked to a more general policy of extended benefit determination like that outlined earlier. Food stamp proposals in both the House and Senate include provisions for extending the transition benefit, although details differ.

Federal Oversight Because states bear a substantial share of FSP administrative costs but pay nothing for benefits, fiscal incentives for careful administration are diminished. States contribute to the increased management costs often required for raising efficiency and participation, but they gain nothing from savings generated by reducing inappropriate payments or successes achieved in raising participation. The quality control system, which imposes careful checks on state administration, is the federal government's attempt to deal with this dilemma. There is little doubt that states improve their performance when problems are revealed by quality control assessments. But auditors focus on rules, and rules make systems inflexible.

Proposals for change tend to be of four types: to eliminate or weaken the quality control system, to change what is considered an error, to change the state reward structure, or to assist states with error rate reduction. The desire to eliminate the quality control system is understandable; the FSP is one of the few government programs where comparative performance by states is assessed and publicized. Nevertheless, there are other options for addressing shortcomings of the program.

State liability for errors is currently based on comparison of state error rates to national averages, something that can be known only after the fact. An alternative procedure, helpful to state planners, would be to fix national targets for error rates and to assess rewards and penalties relative to these rates. Such target rates could be adjusted to reflect special circumstances. In 2000, the Department of Agriculture introduced adjustments in its liability assessment procedures to offset the potential cost to states of errors generated by increases in working family FSP participation. However, instead of adjusting fiscal liability to reflect state caseload or population characteristics, it would be better to adjust the targets themselves. Current House and Senate farm bills call for adjusting procedures for error determination and penalty assessment, but retain focus on average error rates.

Accuracy in food stamps benefit determination is surely not the only objective of national food stamps policy, yet current quality procedures focus virtually all attention on such considerations. Recent changes in recertification requirements and other administrative procedures clearly promote access by making outreach to working families less risky. But if access is important, performance assessment should be expanded beyond issues of computation and documentation to include, for example, measures of state provision of opportunity for food stamp application and recertification when and where they are most useful to working families.

Conclusion

There are three overarching issues in food stamps policy discussions: defining what the program is intended to do, structuring the relationship between food stamps and cash welfare, and defining the terms of the federal-state partnership required for achieving food stamps goals. Reauthorization presents an opportunity for progress in all three areas. What seems most important is a new approach to the partnership itself, one that recognizes the unique national character of the Food Stamp Program but seeks ways to more systematically integrate state experience and capacity in the process of national program improvement and evolution. Thinking this way might move the debate from reauthorization to revitalization.

Additional Reading

American Public Human Services Association. 2001. *Crossroads: New Directions in Social Policy.* Washington, D.C.

Brown, Rebecca. 2001. "Reauthorizing the Food Stamp Program." *Reauthorization Notes,* (Vol. 1, No. 4). Washington, D.C.: Welfare Information Network.

Center on Budget and Policy Priorities. 2001. *The Food Stamp Program Can Be Improved for Working Families.* Washington, D.C.

Super, David, and Kathy Patchan. 2002. *The Food Stamp Program: Important Sources of Information on the Program and Policy.* Washington, D.C.: Center on Budget and Policy Priorities.

U.S. Department of Agriculture. 2001. *Characteristics of Food Stamp Households: Fiscal Year 2000* (Report No. FSP-01-CHAR).

U.S. Department of Agriculture. 2001. *The Decline in Food Stamp Participation: A Report to Congress* (Report No. FSP-01-WEL).

Zedlewski, Sheila, and Amelia Gruber. 2001. "Former Welfare Families and the Food Stamp Program: The Exodus Continues." *New Federalism/National Survey of America's Families* (Series B, No. B-33). Washington, D.C.: Urban Institute.

Helpful comments and corrections were received from Joe Richardson at the Congressional Research Service and various people at the Food and Nutrition Service of the U.S. Department of Agriculture.

ALAN WEIL AND JOHN HOLAHAN

Health Insurance, Welfare, and Work

Executive Summary
Congress included provisions in the 1996 federal welfare reform legislation to preserve existing Medicaid eligibility even as it introduced major changes in welfare. Despite these provisions, Medicaid enrollment fell quickly and dramatically in the early years after the 1996 reforms were enacted. Quantitative analysis shows that these declines were in part due to welfare policies and resulted in an increase in the number of people without health insurance. Subsequent actions by states and the federal government reversed these trends. Even so, many families leaving welfare continue to lose health insurance, despite the fact that the families—or at least their children—remain eligible for coverage. Future steps to improve the relationship between health and welfare must complete the "de-linking" of these programs, with effective outreach and administrative systems providing coverage to all who are eligible for Medicaid. The federal government should retain and expand incentives for states to expand coverage and simplify systems, although this policy will leave considerable interstate variations in place.

The 1996 welfare reform law included provisions specifically designed to prevent major changes in the welfare system from leading to the loss of Medicaid health insurance for low-income children and adults. Despite these provisions, Medicaid enrollment among this group fell in the first few years after welfare reform, leading many to conclude that something had gone wrong. In recent years, Medicaid enrollment has begun to climb again. As the federal welfare law comes up for reauthorization in 2002, policymakers may want to consider changes in the law that would increase Medicaid coverage for low-income families.

Medicaid and Welfare Eligibility Policy
Since its enactment in 1965, the primary path by which low-income parents and their children have become eligible for Medicaid is through receipt of cash welfare, in particular, the Aid to Families with Dependent Children (AFDC) program. AFDC was only available to families that met a "deprivation" standard, meaning the death, continued absence, incapacitation, or unemployability of at least one adult in the family. Maximum income standards for eligibility varied across states, with the median state (on the eve of the 1996 welfare reform law) restricting eligibility to families with income no greater than 36 percent of the federal poverty level.

Expanding Medicaid Eligibility Prior to Welfare Reform More than a decade ago, the Medicaid and welfare eligibility paths began to diverge. During the late 1980s, a series of laws created two new eligibility categories for Medicaid: children under age 6 and pregnant women with incomes below 133 percent of poverty (with a state option to go as high as 185 percent); and children under age 19, born after September 30, 1983, from families with incomes below the federal poverty level. Another Medicaid provision allowed states to set their own income disregard policies, effectively permitting them to expand eligibility beyond these levels.

Three other eligibility policies are relevant to the relationship between Medicaid and welfare. First, the Family Support Act of 1988 created Transitional Medical Assistance (TMA), which required states to extend Medicaid coverage for 12 months to families that lose AFDC eligibility because of earnings. Second, "medically needy" programs are a state option and permit some people with incomes above welfare eligibility standards, or with substantial health care costs, to obtain Medicaid coverage. Third, states may obtain research and demonstration waivers in their Medicaid and welfare programs, which can include expanding coverage to new groups.

These policy changes started a process of what has come to be known as the "de-linking" of Medicaid eligibility from welfare eligibility. These new "non-cash" or "poverty-related" eligibility groups consisted of people eligible for public health insurance coverage, even though their families were not necessarily receiving cash assistance. In 1996, as welfare reform was being implemented, 53 percent of Medicaid-enrolled children and 59 percent of Medicaid-enrolled adults fell into this non-cash category.

Protecting Medicaid Eligibility during Welfare Reform The federal welfare reform law of 1996, which replaced AFDC with the Temporary Assistance for Needy Families (TANF) program, was written with an eye toward assuring continued Medicaid coverage for all eligible groups. The Medicaid-related provisions of the welfare law are complex, but in general they:
- freeze Medicaid eligibility standards as they existed on the date of the law's enactment;
- provide states with flexibility to expand coverage to all members of a family in which at least one child meets Medicaid eligibility standards, and give states new flexibility in how they count income;
- narrow children's eligibility for Supplemental Security Income, which is accompanied by Medicaid coverage; and
- limit or eliminate Medicaid eligibility for many legal immigrants.

One year after welfare reform, Congress passed the State Children's Health Insurance Program (SCHIP), which provides states with new federal funds to expand health coverage for children, either by developing new or expanding existing state-funded programs, or extending Medicaid eligibility to more children.

Medicaid in the Wake of Welfare Reform

TANF and Medicaid have different objectives. TANF is designed to be temporary and transitional and is targeted at only the poorest families. Medicaid benefits, by contrast, are not time-limited and aim to assist a large number of low-wage working families that are not offered coverage through their employer. How do these two systems work together?

Medicaid caseloads peaked in 1995 after

Table 1
National Medicaid Enrollment Levels, 1995 to 1998

Enrollee Group	Enrollment Levels (thousands)				Percent Change 1995–98	Average Annual Change 1995–98
	1995	1996	1997	1998		
All Enrollees	41,677	41,295	40,591	40,381	-3.1%	-1.0%
Cash Assistance	23,507	22,515	20,157	18,323	-22.1	-8.0
Other Enrollees	18,170	18,779	20,434	22,057	21.4	6.7
Adults	9,600	9,255	8,583	8,643	-10.0%	-3.4%
Cash Assistance	5,399	4,934	4,082	3,452	-36.0	-13.8
Other Enrollees	4,202	4,321	4,501	5,190	23.5	7.3
Children	21,630	21,259	21,058	20,665	-4.5%	-1.5%
Cash Assistance	11,236	10,474	8,931	7,640	-32.0	-12.1
Other Enrollees	10,393	10,785	12,127	13,025	25.3	7.8
Aged	4,115	4,117	4,114	4,090	-0.6%	-0.2%
Cash Assistance	1,847	1,840	1,813	1,783	-3.5	-1.2
Other Enrollees	2,268	2,278	2,301	2,306	1.7	0.6
Disabled	6,333	6,664	6,836	6,984	10.3%	3.3%
Cash Assistance	5,025	5,268	5,331	5,448	8.4	2.7
Other Enrollees	1,308	1,396	1,505	1,536	17.4	5.5

Source: HCFA 2082 data from the Centers for Medicare and Medicaid Services, Department of Health and Human Services, as edited by the Urban Institute. Enrollment is defined as the unduplicated number of people signed up for Medicaid at any time in the federal fiscal year.

several years of growth, then fell until 1998, when a slow turnaround began in most states. Enrollment began falling prior to federal welfare reform, presumably because of the strong economy and state welfare reform efforts that preceded the federal law. Table 1 shows that the number of people who were enrolled in Medicaid at any point in a given year fell from 41.7 million in 1995 to 40.4 million in 1998. The number of children and non-disabled adults each fell by about 1 million, with the percentage reduction for adults roughly twice that of children (10 percent vs. 4.5 percent). These declines are attributable to reductions in the number of Medicaid enrollees eligible by receipt of cash welfare. The number of adult and child cash welfare enrollees fell by 1.9 million persons and 3.6 million persons, respectively, between 1995 and 1998.

While the number of Medicaid enrollees eligible by receipt of cash welfare decreased, the number of non-cash enrollees increased significantly. Adult non-cash enrollees increased by 1 million while child non-cash enrollees increased by 2.6 million. The increases in non-cash enrollees were no doubt partially in response to the reduction in cash enrollees, as many of the latter (particularly children) remained on Medicaid through eligibility pathways other than cash welfare.

Declines in Medicaid enrollment began

to turn around in 1998. A study of state Medicaid enrollment data by the Kaiser Commission on Medicaid and the Uninsured showed that after average monthly enrollment declined between June 1997 and June 1998,

> *Medicaid enrollment of immigrants fell as new immigrants were made ineligible by the 1996 welfare reform law.*

it then increased between June and December 1998. A year later Medicaid enrollment had increased again, by 3.6 percent over the previous year.

Why Did Medicaid Enrollment Fall? Four factors played a role in the falling Medicaid caseloads. First, the strong economy was increasing people's earnings: higher earnings means fewer people are eligible for Medicaid. Second, many people were leaving welfare and losing Medicaid coverage as well. Despite the fact that most of these families were eligible for Transitional Medical Assistance for up to a year, and, given their low earnings, their children continued to be eligible for Medicaid even longer, many faced administrative or other barriers to retaining Medicaid enrollment as they left welfare. Third, welfare rolls were falling as families faced more significant hurdles to obtain benefits. Most states adopted either formal diversion programs or added steps (such as job search or an orientation meeting) that had to be completed before a cash assistance application would be accepted. These policies diverted or discouraged families from applying for Medicaid, even if they were eligible.

Finally, Medicaid enrollment of immigrants fell as new immigrants were made ineligible by the 1996 welfare reform law and some eligible immigrants left the rolls due to confusion or concerns that participating in Medicaid would affect their immigration status.

Two recent studies have attempted to sort out the effects of welfare reform and the economy on Medicaid enrollment. The first, by Amy Davidoff and her colleagues at the Urban Institute in Washington, D.C., simulated the impact on eligibility of changes in Medicaid eligibility rules and changes in the economy. This study found that if eligibility rules had not changed, rising incomes would have decreased the number of children eligible for Medicaid to 20.5 million in 1997, down from 22.9 million in 1994. In fact, 24.1 million children were eligible in 1997, meaning broader eligibility rules—such as expanded income disregards, expansions to older children, and expansions through waivers—increased Medicaid eligibility by 3.6 million children. Similarly for adults, the improved economy would have reduced eligibility from 7 to 6 million adults, but expanding rules added back 500,000 adults, leaving 6.5 million eligible.

The authors then analyzed changes in actual Medicaid enrollment to determine the effect of changes in administrative practices, diversion efforts, and other aspects of welfare reform. This analysis demonstrated that, while economic and eligibility changes subsequent to federal welfare reform should have yielded greater Medicaid enrollment, Medicaid rolls fell after welfare reform. This was entirely due to lower enrollment among those eligible, presumably due to behavior changes and more restrictive state administrative practices.

A second study, conducted by Bowen Garrett

and Alshadye Yemane of the Urban Institute, used an econometric model to examine the relative impact of welfare reform and the economy on caseload declines. Using data from 1991 to 1998, they concluded that both welfare reform and the growing economy contributed to the decline in Medicaid enrollment, though welfare policies played a larger role.

Did Those Leaving Welfare Become Uninsured? Bowen Garrett and John Holahan of the Urban Institute used data from the National Survey of America's Families to analyze whether those who left welfare retained insurance coverage (through Medicaid or privately) or became uninsured. They found that, one year after leaving welfare, 22 percent of the women and 47 percent of the children retained Medicaid, while 49 percent of the women and 29 percent of the children became uninsured. Those who left welfare and obtained jobs were more likely to obtain private coverage and less likely to become uninsured. Yet even among those who left welfare and obtained employment, 34 percent of adults and 24 percent of children were uninsured a year after leaving welfare.

In another study of changes in insurance coverage, Holahan and Johnny Kim of the Urban Institute found that 8.4 percent of the non-elderly population was on Medicaid in 1998 versus 10 percent in 1994, a drop of 3.1 million people. Of those below 200 percent of poverty, the percentage on Medicaid dropped from 24.9 to 22.5, a decline of 3.3 million people. Although employer-sponsored coverage for low-income people increased somewhat, there was a net increase of 800,000 in the number of uninsured people. This number would have been much larger if the expanding economy had not shifted so many people into higher income groups.

The rate of employer-sponsored health coverage continued to increase between 1998 and 1999. As a result an additional 500,000 people gained coverage. But unlike previous years when Medicaid declined, the percentage of people on Medicaid remained relatively constant. Because Medicaid enrollment stabilized, the increase in employer and individual coverage translated into a reduction of 1.2 million people among the low-income uninsured.

Responses to Falling Enrollment Falling Medicaid caseloads were universally interpreted as a sign of failure, which prompted a flurry of activity. Some states responded on their own. The federal government stepped into the fray with a letter from the Department of Health and Human Services instructing states to make sure that Medicaid eligibility was redetermined when people left cash assistance. Advocates pointed out that states had made limited use of a $500 million allocation in the welfare reform law specifically designed to assist states in improving their Medicaid eligibility systems.

Taking De-Linking Seriously The story of falling Medicaid rolls reveals the complications involved in de-linking Medicaid from welfare. As a practical matter, most states had simply added new eligibility categories to the Medicaid program while continuing to administer it in the same way. Eligibility continued to be determined by traditional welfare agencies using rule-based systems administered by eligibility technicians.

Recent policy changes have given states two new opportunities to fundamentally alter the relationship between Medicaid and welfare, and go beyond simply fixing the administrative systems that determine Medicaid coverage. These opportunities came in the form of the new SCHIP program enacted in 1997, and through increased flexibility in Medicaid program design given to states in 1996 by Section 1931 of the Social Security Act.

SCHIP offers states the opportunity to design entirely new eligibility and enrollment systems for health insurance that operate apart from the old welfare system and its emphasis on fraud prevention and error reduction. Under SCHIP, states may simplify their eligibility categories, measures of income, and required documentation to apply for and prove eligibility. States may develop new eligibility systems (separate from welfare agencies and offices) that accept electronic, telephone, or mail-in applications, or rely on private vendors to conduct enrollment functions. States have great flexibility in defining the benefits provided under SCHIP, the cost sharing provisions, and the networks of providers they will use. Much of what states have done with their flexibility in SCHIP they can also do in Medicaid—and some already have.

Section 1931 of the Social Security Act offered states a different opportunity to address the issue of family fragmentation that existed in prior Medicaid policy. The practical effect of de-linking Medicaid eligibility from welfare was to make a large number of children eligible for Medicaid coverage even though their parents were ineligible. Prior to welfare reform, in most states, different members of the same family were likely to have different insurance status, with Medicaid eligibility based on income as well as age. Section 1931 gave states the option of covering all members of a family in which the children met Medicaid eligibility standards. This provision, combined with the flexibility in measuring income noted above, allows states to greatly expand their Medicaid coverage to families of almost any income.

It is too early to tell if simplified eligibility

The goal should be to create health insurance programs that serve the needs of all who are eligible, whether they are currently on welfare, recently left the rolls, or have never had any contact with the welfare system.

---

rules and more complete family coverage will yield significant increases in participation by otherwise uninsured people who are eligible for public insurance coverage. Setting aside the specific effects of particular policies, these changes demonstrate the potential of de-linking Medicaid and welfare. It is possible to develop separate systems for the two programs, encouraging enrollment in Medicaid while operating a welfare system that emphasizes work.

Policy Implications

The Medicaid provisions of the 1996 welfare reform law led to unintended declines in Medicaid enrollment by adults and children. Although states and the federal government responded to remedy the problem, many observers think that too many adults and children still lose Medicaid coverage when they make the transition from welfare to work. In the context of welfare reform reauthorization, Congress may be tempted to focus public policy on assuring that families retain their Medicaid coverage when they leave welfare. States could be given performance targets to assure that a high percentage of those who leave welfare have either private or public coverage. While such policies would certainly benefit some people, we consider this approach to designing the Medicaid-welfare interaction too narrow.

Rather, public policy should emphasize the complete de-linking of Medicaid and TANF eligibility. The goal should be to create health insurance programs that serve the needs of all who are eligible, whether they are currently on welfare, recently left the rolls, or have never had any contact with the welfare system.

We recommend three steps to accomplish this goal. First, federal policies should continue to encourage states to expand coverage as they have done in recent years. SCHIP increased the average eligibility level for older children from 76 percent to 208 percent of the federal poverty level (about $11,000 to $30,500 for a family of three in 2001). Several states, including California, New Jersey, and Connecticut, have adopted significant Section 1931 expansions. Other states, including Massachusetts, New York, and Rhode Island, have used waivers to substantially expand coverage.

Second, federal and state policy should build on practices that simplify Medicaid eligibility. Many states have already taken significant steps in this direction. Yet participation rates for those not receiving cash assistance remain in the 50 percent to 60 percent range and vary considerably among states. Eliminating asset tests, simplifying eligibility categories, reducing documentation requirements, minimizing cost sharing, and adopting longer periods of eligibility can all make the program more supportive of working families.

Third, Congress and the states should continue adopting incremental expansions of coverage while acknowledging that reaching new populations requires new funding. Among the many ideas being considered, two proposals warrant mention. The FamilyCare Act of 2001, introduced by chairman Ted Kennedy in the Senate, would not increase matching rates for current Medicaid populations, but would extend coverage to parents of Medicaid and SCHIP children at the higher SCHIP matching rate. The Bush administration has proposed tax credits for the low-income uninsured ($1000 for single adults and $2000 for families) to allow them to buy private coverage. While neither of these proposals is directed at families leaving welfare, they have the potential to reduce work disincentives by expanding coverage opportunities as people take jobs and their incomes increase.

The federal government can provide incentives or mandate that states expand coverage or change administrative systems. In recent years, the federal government has relied primarily on financial incentives, and there has been progress under this model. But progress is uneven, with only 15 states extending coverage to parents with income above the federal poverty level and just 10 states covering non-parent adults at all. In addition, financial incentives may be insufficient if state fiscal conditions continue to deteriorate, making the state share of program costs harder to cover. Still, the federal government should retain and expand financial incentives for states, although this policy will leave considerable interstate variations in place.

The best way to make Medicaid and SCHIP operate as effective work supports for families leaving welfare is to make sure that all families eligible for these programs actually receive the benefits. Despite bumps along the road, the nation has made good progress in de-linking these programs from welfare and recognizing that public health insurance programs meet needs well beyond the welfare population. The future success of welfare reform is dependent in part on building health programs that support all low-income families that do not have cover age through their job and that cannot afford insurance on their own.

Additional Reading

Davidoff, Amy, and others. 2000. "Medicaid Eligibility, Takeup, Insurance Coverage and Health Care Access and Use Before and After Welfare Reform: National Changes from 1994 to 1997." Washington, D.C.: Urban Institute.

Ellis, Eileen R., and others. 2000. "Medicaid Enrollment in 50 States: June 1997 to December 1999." Washington, D.C.: Kaiser Commission on Medicaid and the Uninsured.

Garrett, Bowen, and Alshadye Yemane. 2001. *National Trends in Medicaid Enrollment and Expenditures* (Unpublished Manuscript). Washington, D.C.: Urban Institute.

Garrett, Bowen, and John Holahan. 2000. "Health Insurance after Welfare." *Health Affairs,* 19(1): 175–184.

Holahan, John, and Johnny Kim. 2000. "Why Does the Number of Uninsured Americans Continue to Grow?" *Health Affairs,* 19(4): 188–196.

A version of this chapter appeared in *Welfare Reform: The Next Act,* edited by Alan Weil and Kenneth Feingold, which was published by the Urban Institute in March 2002.

GINA ADAMS AND MONICA ROHACEK
Child Care and Welfare Reform

Executive Summary
Child care assistance is a key element of welfare reform because many low-income working parents, including most single mothers leaving welfare for work, need help paying for child care. Consequently, child care was an integral part of the 1996 welfare reform debate. Since then, states have received additional federal funding for child care through the Child Care and Development Block Grant (CCDBG). States are also using significant amounts of Temporary Assistance for Needy Families (TANF) funding for child care. Despite these increases, there is still inadequate funding to provide child care to all eligible families. As a result, states formally and informally ration child care subsidies. Low-income working families that have not recently received welfare are less likely to receive assistance than those leaving welfare. This approach favors mothers who have been on welfare over equally poor mothers who have not. The role of subsidies in affecting the quality of care is also important given evidence that quality affects children's development. The 2002 reauthorization of the CCDBG and TANF presents an opportunity for policymakers to address three important issues: funding levels, who should get subsidies, and the quality of care.

Child care is an essential part of federal and state welfare policy because it allows low-income families to move from welfare to work and to stay employed. Because the two primary sources of federal funding for child care subsidies, the Child Care and Development Block Grant (CCDBG) and the Temporary Assistance for Needy Families (TANF) Block Grant, are scheduled for reauthorization in 2002, child care will be a vital part of the welfare reauthorization debate. Child care subsidies, which are usually provided as vouchers that parents can use to purchase any type of child care, have primarily focused on helping low-income parents work. But because child care also affects children's development, policy and funding decisions about the CCDBG and TANF have implications for the development and safety of millions of low-income children.

The Child Care Context
Child care subsidy policies operate within a larger context that frames the current debate, one element being the dramatic increase in maternal employment rates, particularly among single mothers. Between 1996 and 2000, the proportion of single mothers who were employed rose from 66 to 76 percent. At least partially due to this trend, non-parental child care has become a reality for millions of American families. The 1999 National Survey of America's Families, conducted by the Urban Institute in Washington, D.C., found that a majority of children under age 13 with an employed primary caretaker were regularly placed in a non-parental child care arrangement. The over 20 million children

in this group were cared for in a range of settings, including centers, family child care homes (care in the home of an unrelated adult), nannies or babysitters, and relatives.

For many families, cost is an important factor in their choice of child care. In fact, child care expenses can take up a large share of the family budget, often coming right after housing and food. About half of all working families with children younger than age 13 paid for child care in 1997, spending an average of 9 percent of their earnings. While poor working families were somewhat less likely to pay for care, those that did spent an even larger portion of their earnings—23 percent—for child care.

The quality of care also is important. There is evidence that, in addition to being influenced by their home environments, children's development is related to the quality of their non-parental care. Despite the importance of quality care, however, studies show that many child care arrangements across a range of settings do not adequately support children's development. Research also shows high turn-over rates among child care staff (related to low wage and benefit levels), which limit children's ability to develop stable relationships with nurturing caregivers. In addition, state licensing laws, which are designed to protect children from harm, have gaps in coverage, standards, and enforcement. Finally, although low-income children can see some of the largest benefits from participation in high quality programs, low-income families face particular challenges in obtaining high quality care.

Child Care Policy and Funding Under Welfare Reform

Recent Developments Federal funding for child care was a major part of the 1988 Family Support Act (FSA). The FSA created two new entitlement programs, Aid to Families with Dependent Children Child Care and Transitional Child Care, which combined federal and state funds to provide guaranteed subsidies to families leaving welfare. Congress passed two additional child care initiatives in 1990: the CCDBG and At-Risk Grants to States.

These four federal programs were overlaid upon a diverse landscape of state child care funding, policies, and programs. Some states had a long history of significant investments in child care while others had virtually no subsidy programs for low-income working families. In fact, when FSA was implemented, average annual child care funding ranged from 24 cents per child in Idaho to $152 per child in Massachusetts.

In 1996, welfare reform made three major changes to federal child care funding and related policies. First, the four existing programs were combined into a single federal child care program, also called the CCDBG, which gave states greater flexibility in designing their subsidy systems (this program is sometimes referred to as the Child Care and Development Fund). Second, the federal legal guarantee of child care support to current and former welfare recipients was eliminated, thereby increasing state discretion in determining priority groups for subsidies. Third, overall child care funding was increased by directly increasing the funding for the CCDBG above the combined total for the previous programs and by allowing states to use TANF block grant funds for child care.

These changes, combined with subsequent funding increases, resulted in a significant increase in federal child care funding. In fiscal year 2000, for example, $7.4 billion in federal funding was allocated to child care through the CCDBG and TANF, compared

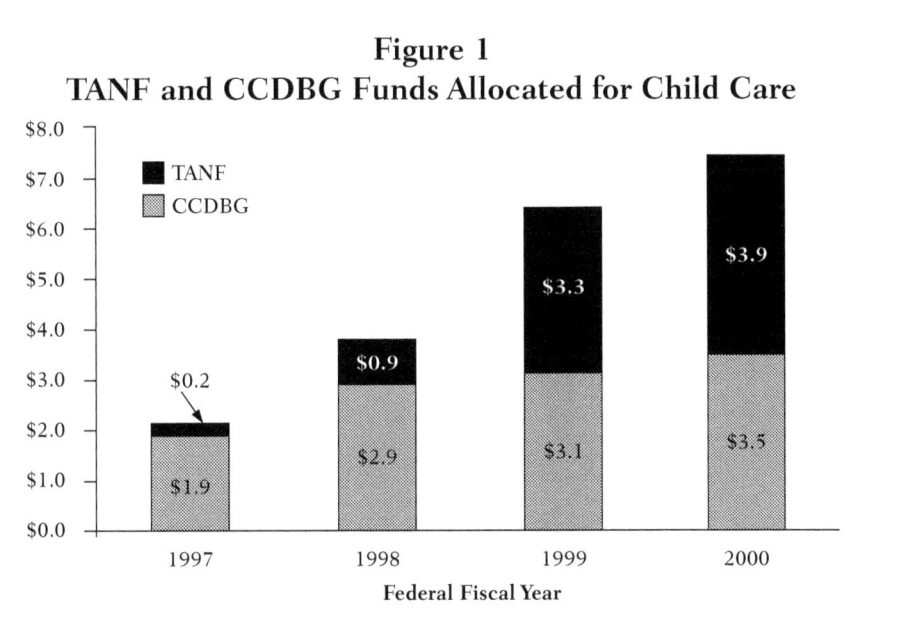

**Figure 1
TANF and CCDBG Funds Allocated for Child Care**

Note: Temporary Assistance for Needy Families (TANF) allocations include funds states transfer to the Child Care and Development Block Grant (CCDBG) as well as TANF funds that states spend directly on child care.

Source: Schumacher, Greenberg, and Duffy. Center for Law and Social Policy, 2001.

to $2.1 billion in FY 1997. (Head Start, a comprehensive program for poor 3-4 year olds that has also experienced recent funding increases, is not included in this analysis because it is not aimed at the child care needs of working families).

Total funding levels, however, tell only part of the story. Examining CCDBG and TANF funding separately provides further insight into the commitment to funding child care at both the federal and state level. Figure 1 shows the growing federal investment in child care through the CCDBG, under which allocations to states rose from $1.9 billion in FY 1997 to $3.5 billion in FY 2000. Similarly, CCDBG funding reflects state commitment to child care, as almost every state has consistently met or exceeded federal CCDBG requirements for state child care spending (totaling $1.8 billion in FY 2000). In addition, states have chosen to spend significant portions of their TANF block grant on child care. In FY 2000, 44 states transferred $2.4 billion from TANF into the CCDBG and 35 states spent $1.5 billion in TANF funding directly on child care. In fact, TANF now surpasses the CCDBG as the primary source of federal child care funding.

Who Is Getting Served and What Are They Getting? Not surprisingly, the growth in child care funding has resulted in significant growth in the number of children served. Through the CCDBG alone, states provided subsidies to an estimated monthly average of 1.9 million low-income children under age 13 in fiscal year 2000, compared to an estimated 1 million served in 1996. Research suggests that subsidies generally go to the lowest-income families within eligible populations.

Child care subsidies are usually administered through vouchers that help parents access any legally operating child care provider who is willing to serve subsidized children. CCDBG administrative data for 1999 show

> **Table 1**
> **Consistent Themes in Federal and State Child Care Subsidy Policy**
>
> **Supporting parent choice.** Since 1988, the federal and state child care subsidy system has been predicated on a concept of parent choice that allows families to use any legal provider that accepts the subsidy—whether licensed or legally unlicensed, and ranging from relatives to child care centers.
>
> **Supporting parents' work.** The child care subsidy system focuses primarily on supporting work among low-income parents, and far less on ensuring that parents are able to access good quality care that supports their children's development.
>
> **Prioritizing assistance to families working to leave welfare.** Prior to 1996, states were required to give subsidies to current or former welfare recipients, while low-income working families that had not received welfare were served at state discretion. Though this requirement was eliminated in 1996, most states continue to prioritize current and former welfare recipients over other low-income working families, at least in part to meet federal TANF work requirements and to support families subject to these requirements and time limits.
>
> **Allowing for state diversity and variation.** States have always had significant latitude in how they set up, administer, and fund their child care subsidy systems. Consequently, state variation is a hallmark of child care subsidy policy and is seen in funding levels, program structure and administration, the proportion of eligible families served, and other policies such as eligibility, parent fees, and reimbursement rates. States also have complete discretion over child care licensing and regulation.

that about 71 percent of subsidized children were in regulated settings (child care centers or licensed family child care homes) and 29 percent were in legally unregulated child care arrangements (relatives or non-relatives in the child's or the caregiver's home).

What Has Changed and What Is the Same? As Table 1 shows, state and federal child care policy has consistently followed four themes over the past decade: support for parents' choice of child care provider, support for parents' work, priority assistance to families leaving welfare for work, and latitude for state diversity and variation.

During this time, however, state subsidy systems also have undergone tremendous expansion and evolution. While all states have responded to increased funding by serving additional children, there is substantial variation in other policy areas. For example, although a number of states have reduced parent co-payments, raised income eligibility limits, raised reimbursement rates, or funded quality enhancement initiatives, other states have moved in the opposite direction on each of these dimensions.

There has also been variation among states in changes to service priorities. Though most states continue to give current and former welfare recipients higher priority for subsidies, a few states—including Illinois, Rhode Island, Vermont, and Wisconsin—have moved toward creating a single system that gives all low-income families equal priority. These states base eligibility solely on income and work status rather than welfare status and invest sufficient funds to serve all low-income families that apply.

Challenges Remaining

Are Low-Income Families that Need Subsidies Getting Help? Despite major increases in funding for child care subsidies since the 1996 reforms, research suggests that many low-income families are still not getting help. One study of sixteen states found that no state was serving more than 25 percent of the families who would qualify for subsidies under federal income limits (85 percent of state median income, which varies across states but averages about $38,000), and some were serving less than 10 percent.

While some eligible families may not want or need subsidies, two recent multi-state studies found that states use a variety of formal and informal methods to ration child care subsidies, primarily because of insufficient funds. One rationing approach is to limit access by setting eligibility requirements below the federal maximum. In 2000, forty-seven states set their income eligibility limits below the federal limit, with some states as low as 40 to 45 percent of the state median income. In twenty-two states, a family of three earning $25,000 did not qualify for assistance in March 2000.

Most states also ration services, albeit indirectly, by limiting outreach efforts. As a result, many eligible low-income families (particularly families that never received welfare) do not know that subsidies are available. Finally, some eligible families make it past these barriers and apply, but are denied subsidies due to inadequate funds. In these cases, states ration funds through waiting lists and prioritizing categories or by freezing program intake. Seventeen states had waiting lists or had frozen intake as of March 2000 because they had insufficient funds to serve those that were eligible, knew about subsidies, and applied. Typically in these cases, current and former TANF recipients are given higher priority and get served, while non-TANF families are denied service.

How Well Is the Subsidy System Working for Families? Another reason low-income families may not get child care subsidies is that administrative policies and practices can create barriers that make it difficult for families to complete the application process or meet all of the requirements for retaining the subsidy. A study conducted in twelve states by Gina Adams and her colleagues at the Urban Institute showed that some parents have to repeatedly take time off work to apply for benefits or to prove their continuing eligibility by reporting all changes in work status, work schedule, income, or provider. Taking time off work to make office visits is difficult for entry-level workers and undercuts the subsidy program's goal of supporting work. These challenges also particularly affect parents who most need support, including parents with barriers to employment, parents who experience many job changes, and parents who receive TANF and must navigate both the TANF and child care systems.

These challenges varied across and within states, and were caused both by policy and implementation. When combined with reports of problems dealing with caseworkers and multiple agencies, these barriers may help

> *Although funding levels have increased significantly since 1996, current funding is not sufficient to help families access quality child care and serve all eligible families that want services.*

explain recent evidence of low usage rates and short spells of subsidy use, even among families that are a high priority for service. One five-state study found that the average length of subsidy receipt was three to seven months. The research by Adams and her colleagues suggests that to better support low-income working families, states should focus more attention on eliminating barriers to subsidy access and retention. However, improving access and retention without investing additional resources may simply increase the number of eligible parents who end up not getting served.

Does the Current System Help Families Get Quality Care? Rising concerns about the importance of early learning and literacy, school readiness, and youth development underscore the importance of child care subsidies in affecting the quality of care received by the 1.9 million low-income children served by CCDBG funds. The quality of child care for low-income families was a major topic in the 1996 welfare reform debate, and states must now spend at least 4 percent of their CCDBG funds to improve the quality and supply of care. However, the CCDBG places a higher priority on supporting work than on supporting access to good quality child care, and states must trade between quality and subsidy access in allocating child care funds. In particular, while a cornerstone of the CCDBG is to give low-income families "equal access" to the kinds of choices that higher-income families have, there are several ways in which CCDBG subsidies are administered that can make it difficult to realize this goal.

First, vouchers funded by the CCDBG help low-income families gain access to the child care available in their communities. But research suggests that low-income communities tend to have a lower supply of regulated care than higher-income communities. In addition, the non-center-based care used by low-income families tends to be of lower quality than similar care used by higher-income families. Consequently, while subsidies are likely to broaden the child care choices available to low-income families, parents are still limited by what is available in their communities. Furthermore, current subsidy policies do little to expand good quality options in low-income areas.

Second, families served with CCDBG funds are unlikely to have access to the full range of providers in their communities. The CCDBG encourages states to set maximum reimbursement rates for child care providers at least at the seventy-fifth percentile of current market rates, which ensures that parents have access to all providers except those whose fees fall in the top 25 percent of local market rates. However, nearly half the states set their reimbursement caps at lower levels, thus restricting access to an even smaller pool of less costly providers.

Third, the Urban Institute case studies suggest that the implementation of subsidy payments to providers may further undercut payment levels. Miscommunications about when families are authorized or terminated, delays in payments, and policies that directly undercut the payment amount (such as partial subsidies or not paying for sick days), may mean that subsidized providers receive less than the rate set by reimbursement policies. The extent of these problems varies across local sites, but they appear to make some providers unwilling to serve subsidized children, and can affect the quality of care providers can offer, thereby further limiting the choice of quality child care for subsidized families.

Issues for Reauthorization

Funding There are three major funding issues that are likely to be part of the reauthorization debate. First, although funding levels have increased significantly since 1996, current funding is not sufficient to help families access quality child care and serve all eligible families that want services. This situation is likely to worsen as state budgets become tighter with the economic downturn. Some states have already begun reducing child care spending.

Second, much of the recent funding increase occurred because states have used large amounts of TANF funding for child care. The ability to use TANF for this purpose was an important provision of the 1996 reforms and was designed to help states meet their unique child care needs. However, there is a risk that comes with using the flexible TANF funding; namely, that TANF funds available for child care could diminish either because of an economic downturn or because of a reduction in TANF funding by Congress. Thirty-one states drew more than one-third of their combined federal CCDBG and TANF child care funds from TANF in 2000, showing that any threat to TANF funding is also a threat to child care funding. If states are to take additional steps to improve the subsidy system, they are likely to require some assurance that child care funding will be stable.

Third, an ongoing challenge facing policymakers is the difference in funding levels across states. This situation reflects the classic tradeoff between devolution and equity. It is likely that some states have invested more money and developed more innovative child care models than they would have under a single national approach. However, funding for and access to child care subsidies remains fundamentally inequitable across states.

Who Should Get Child Care Subsidies? There is widespread consensus that subsidies are important both to prevent welfare receipt by low-income parents who never received welfare and to support work by current and former welfare recipients. However, despite increases in the numbers of non-welfare families receiving subsidies, the current reality in many states is that families receiving TANF are still more likely to get subsidies. And in the seventeen states with waiting lists, a low-income working parent who urgently needs child care assistance can be most certain of getting it by quitting work and applying for TANF. This perverse incentive undercuts the fundamental premise of welfare reform. If Congress and the states want to build a child care subsidy system that effectively supports work for all low-income families, it will be necessary to appropriate additional funds. States must also eliminate administrative barriers that prevent low-income families from obtaining and keeping subsidies, and conduct outreach to ensure that eligible families know they can get help.

Should Child Care Subsidies Support Child Development? There has recently been a convergence of opinion about the importance of the preschool years for early learning, early literacy, and school readiness, and about the importance of after-school time for the education, development, and safety of school-age children. Nonetheless, there continues to be a disconnect between this set of concerns and the way subsidy funds are spent.

As a consequence, quality of child care is likely to be part of the reauthorization debate; i.e., the extent to which the nation's child care subsidy system should support child development and school readiness as well as parental work. In order to meet this goal, policymakers would need to make several adjustments to current policy. These include increasing the funding dedicated to improving the quality and supply of care providers in low-income communities; increasing the reimbursement rates to allow families to access all the providers in a community; eliminating subsidy policies and practices that undercut payment levels and stability; allocating resources to recruit and retain providers through compensation and education initiatives; and funding strategies to upgrade the quality of unregulated settings.

Additional Reading

Adams, Gina, Kathleen Snyder, and Jodi Sandfort. 2002. *Getting and Retaining Child Care Assistance: How Policy and Practice Influence Parents' Experiences* (Occasional Paper No. 55). Washington, D.C.: Urban Institute.

Collins, Ann, and others. 2000. *National Study of Child Care for Low-Income Families: State and Community Substudy Interim Report.* Cambridge: Abt Associates.

Giannarelli, Linda, and James Barsimantov. 2000. *Child Care Expenses of America's Families* (Occasional Paper No. 40). Washington, D.C.: Urban Institute.

Schulman, Karen, Helen Blank, and Danielle Ewen. 2001. *A Fragile Foundation: Child Care Assistance Policies.* Washington, D.C.: Children's Defense Fund.

Schumacher, Rachel, Mark Greenberg, and Janellen Duffy. 2001. *The Impact of TANF Funding on State Child Care Subsidy Programs.* Washington, D.C.: Center for Law and Social Policy.

Vandell, Deborah, and Barbara Wolfe. 2000. *Child Care Quality: Does It Matter and Does It Need to be Improved?* Washington, D.C.: U.S. Department of Health and Human Services.

A version of this chapter appeared in *Welfare Reform: The Next Act,* edited by Alan Weil and Kenneth Feingold, which was published by the Urban Institute in March 2002.

REBECCA SWARTZ AND BRIAN MILLER

Welfare Reform and Housing

Executive Summary

Housing plays a central role in the lives of families; it is the largest single cost for most families, and its location determines a parent's access to employment and a child's access to education. Despite the impact housing can have on the lives of low-income families, government housing programs are often overlooked as a work support for low-income families. Although the number of households that met the government's definition of "worst case housing needs" decreased from 1997 to 1999, 4.9 million very low-income renter households continue to spend at least half their income on housing or live in severely substandard housing without receiving government housing assistance. Housing problems continue, or even intensify, as families leave welfare for work. This policy brief examines how the federal government intervenes in housing markets and analyzes the important housing reforms currently under discussion. These include changing the administration of housing vouchers, imposing work requirements and time limits on families receiving housing benefits, converting housing subsidies to a cash benefit, and others. Although answers to the nation's housing challenges are not obvious, the connections between housing stability and work are. These connections should spur more discussion and creative action on housing reforms during the upcoming welfare reform reauthorization debate.

Housing is more than bricks and mortar. It is a key factor in determining a family's access to economic and educational opportunities, exposure to violence and environmental hazards, and ability to accumulate financial assets. Too few low-income families reap the positive benefits of living in stable and reasonably priced housing, and many frequently move in and out of undesirable or unsustainable housing. This lack of stable housing can create difficulties for parents trying to retain employment and can increase the likelihood that their children will have problems in school.

Despite being the single largest cost for most families, housing receives little attention in welfare reform debates. A recent report from the U.S. Department of Health and Human Services found that, although around 80 percent of families leaving welfare participate in the workforce to some degree, roughly 25 percent have trouble paying rent. The fact that low-income families have housing difficulties is not new, and housing experts have long cited the need for more affordable housing. What is new is the growing recognition that housing assistance can be an important support for working families, joining the battery of other work support programs such as food stamps, child care, Medicaid, child support enforcement, the Earned Income Tax Credit, and the child tax credit. Moreover, the greater flexibility in use of federal funds under the Temporary Assistance for Needy Families (TANF) program means that TANF funds can be used to help low-income families with their housing costs— although providing on-going housing assistance with federal TANF funds does count toward the maximum of five years that a given family can receive benefits from the TANF program. Yet debates over welfare reform and low-income housing are rarely joined together because the programs are under the jurisdiction of different agencies and congressional committees and have different funding cycles.

In this policy brief, we provide an overview of the current state of housing for low-income families, describe some current government interventions, and analyze a range of proposed housing reforms that Congress should consider as it debates reauthorization of the 1996 welfare reform law.

Housing Needs of Low-Income Families

Roughly 20 percent of all middle- to low-income households in the U.S., over 13 million in all, live in substandard housing or pay more than half of their income in housing costs, well above the affordability standard of 30 percent of gross income established by the U.S. Department of Housing and Urban Development (HUD). Whereas housing quality was the major housing problem in the decades leading up to the 1970s, today the leading problem for low-income families is affordability. While it is no surprise that poor families are disproportionately unable to afford housing, it may be surprising that more than 85 percent of renter households with incomes below 30 percent of area median income (AMI) spend more than 30 percent of their income on housing, with well over half of them spending more than 50

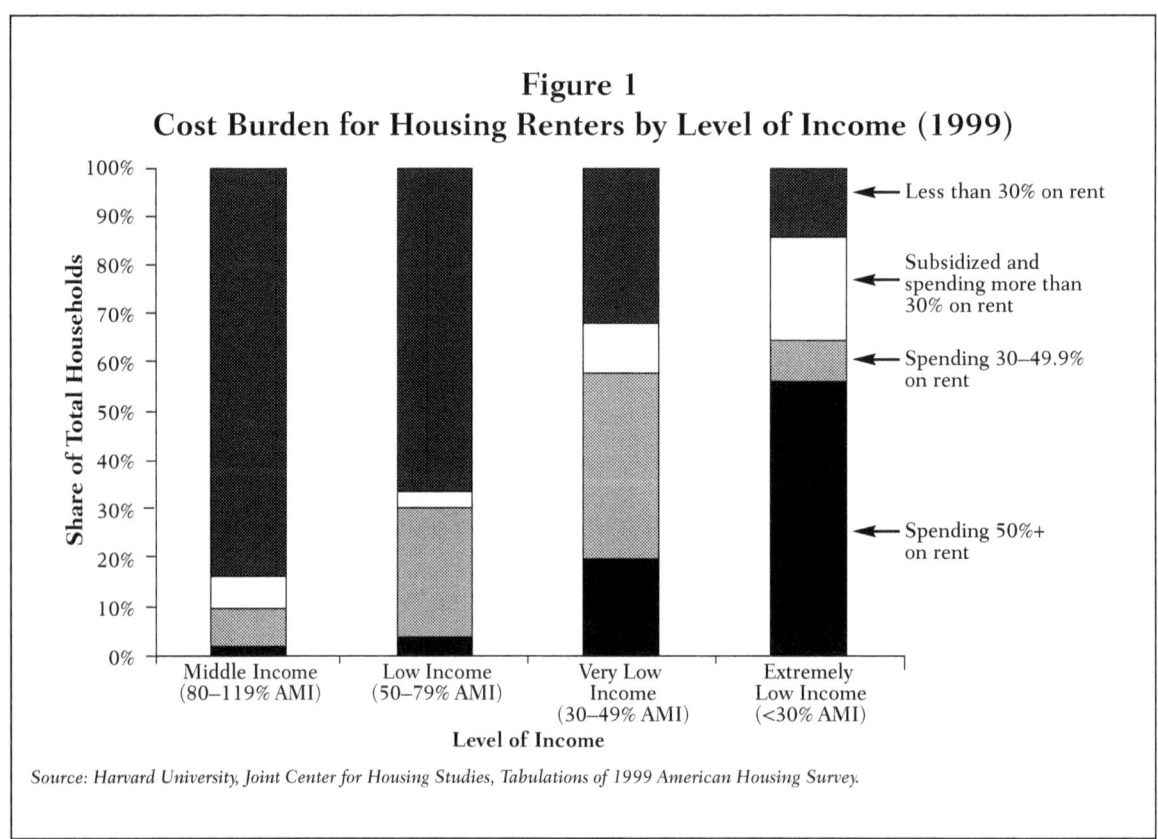

Figure 1
Cost Burden for Housing Renters by Level of Income (1999)

Source: Harvard University, Joint Center for Housing Studies, Tabulations of 1999 American Housing Survey.

> ### Area Median Income
> Welfare programs generally use the federal poverty level as the primary measure for income eligibility. In contrast, housing programs use a locally calibrated measure—the percentage of the area median income (AMI). While the national average AMI was $52,500 in 2001, AMI ranged from $16,300 in Starr County, TX to $109,800 in Fairfield County, CT.
>
> Using the national average:
> 30% of AMI = $15,750
> 50% of AMI = $26,250
> Poverty line = $17,650 (family of 4)

percent of their income on housing (figure 1, bar graph on far right).

To track the needs of poor families, every two years HUD publishes a report on renters without housing assistance who live in substandard housing or who pay more than half of their income in rent. This "worst case" housing report is a good proxy for the housing problems of current and former welfare recipients. Unlike studies that include households from all income levels, the worst case report limits the analysis to households with incomes under 50 percent of AMI defined as "very low-income". In 1999, the latest year available, 4.9 million households had worst case housing needs.

The story in the worst case housing report is a straightforward one: in much of the country, there are more very low-income households than there are affordable housing units available to them. This shortfall affects renters with incomes less than 30 percent of AMI ("extremely low-income") the hardest. The shortfall in the number of units affordable to these households is made worse by the fact that almost half of units affordable to the poorest households are rented by households with higher incomes. As a result, for every one hundred extremely low-income renters in the nation, there are only thirty-nine units that are both affordable and available. The housing shortage particularly impacts renters in the western part of the U.S., where only twenty-five units are available and affordable for every one hundred extremely low-income renters.

Over the past eight years, the number of affordable rental units nationwide has declined. These decreases in the housing stock result primarily from rent increases that have pushed existing units out of the affordable range, rather than from demolition or other physical changes. Such rent increases are not universal. Rent increases were less than general inflation in twelve of the twenty-six largest metropolitan areas between 1997 and 2000. But affordability has reached very serious proportions in some housing markets such as San Francisco and Boston. To make matters worse, several factors may lead to a greater shortage of affordable housing in the future— these include rapidly increasing land costs, an aging stock, and a host of expiring federal arrangements, among them many properties that received federal subsidies in exchange for offering low-rent apartments that will reach the end of their 15-year affordability periods.

While the supply of affordable housing shrank in some parts of the nation, the number of working families increased. The share of worst case renters with children whose income derives primarily from earnings increased from 49 percent in 1993 to 68 percent in 1999.

Despite having jobs and earnings, many families continue to have trouble paying for their housing. The inability of working households to find available housing in a location and at a cost that permits self-sufficiency and stability poses a challenge both for those families and for the general objectives of welfare reform.

Government Housing Assistance Programs

Federal policies and programs influence both the supply of and demand for housing. In fiscal year 2001, the federal government dedicated $155 billion to housing assistance with about one-quarter of those funds targeted to low-income individuals. The remaining funding was provided in the form of tax breaks, the largest of which is the mortgage interest deduction, which cost $63 billion in 2001. HUD administers most of the funds targeted to low-income families. In this section, we divide federal housing programs into two groups: direct housing assistance designed to help individual families with their housing costs, and indirect housing programs designed to affect the housing markets in which low-income families live.

Direct Housing Assistance At a cost of $24 billion in 2001, 4.2 million low-income renters received assistance through public housing and Section 8. Roughly 1.3 million of those renters are tenants in public housing, 1.6 million receive vouchers to rent private market units of their choosing (known as Section 8 vouchers), and 1.3 million live in privately owned buildings with subsidies tied to the properties (known as project-based Section 8).

Public housing and Section 8 vouchers are operated through a decentralized network of roughly 4,000 local Public Housing Authorities (PHAs). Chartered by states and given significant autonomy to issue bonds and enter other long-term financing arrangements, PHAs generally operate at the local municipality or county level, often with multiple PHAs functioning in the same metropolitan area.

Like a lottery, direct housing assistance provides substantial benefits to the few households that receive it. With five- to ten-year waiting lists that are sometimes closed to new applicants, only one-fourth of those eligible for housing assistance actually receive it. Families receiving assistance pay about 30 percent of their adjusted gross income in rent, while the government pays the remainder. Although 1998 federal legislation gave local PHAs more authority to give preference to working families and required that PHAs disregard earnings in rent calculations for the newly employed, most PHAs have not yet taken full advantage of these work-support policies. As a result, every new dollar earned by low-income adults can mean an increase in rent of 30 cents as well as a potential loss in benefits from other work supports.

PHAs have little incentive and few resources to encourage or prepare their clients to move off direct housing assistance. Although HUD offers three such programs (Family Self-Sufficiency, Moving to Work, and homeownership options), these programs come with little or no additional funding and are only an option for local PHAs. Under Family Self-Sufficiency, families voluntarily sign a five-year contract during which they work toward specific employment goals. Increased rent due to increased earnings is saved in an escrow account designed to help participants buy a home or otherwise move off housing assistance, although there is no requirement to do so. The Moving to Work demonstration gives high-performing PHAs the opportunity to design and test innovative practices that promote self-sufficiency. Only twenty PHAs, however, are currently participating in the program. Likewise, few PHAs take advantage of their new authority to use the Section 8 voucher program to expand homeownership options and to sell all, or a portion of, a public housing development to eligible residents or resident organizations.

In addition to programmatic challenges, direct housing assistance programs face structural challenges. High maintenance and operating costs coupled with their reputation for fostering social problems have led policymakers to decrease public housing projects and, in many cases, to tear them down. Although HUD's HOPE VI program has successfully revitalized some public housing projects in the past five years, the unfunded backlog of needed repairs in HUD's public housing inventory averages $20,000 per unit. According to a report by the Joint Center for Housing Studies at Harvard, there is also concern about the potential loss of Section 8 units as the contracts of one million units expire by the year 2004, thereby allowing project owners to opt out of affordability agreements and to raise rents to market levels. And families receiving Section 8 vouchers who live in tight housing markets often have difficulty finding landlords who will accept their vouchers. Despite the voucher program's goal of encouraging residential mobility, most Section 8 families do not move into low-poverty neighborhoods unless explicitly required to do so by program rules. As a result, these families make short-distance moves, remaining in or near their original high-poverty neighborhoods, which are often characterized by high crime rates and a lack of job opportunities.

Indirect Housing Assistance Federal and local governments influence housing markets indirectly through a range of funding, taxing, and regulatory activities. HUD's largest production programs for increasing the supply of affordable units are the Community Development Block Grant (CDBG) and HOME, costing $4.8 billion and $1.7 billion respectively in 2001. For both of these programs, HUD allocates funding to a range of state and local jurisdictions, which then allocate resources to communities and housing producers. CDBG assists approximately 185,000 housing units annually, most for rehabilitation of existing owner-occupied homes. Since 1990, HOME program funds have been used to acquire, rehabilitate, or build over 500,000 housing units. These and other HUD funding streams are granted to local communities based on much-debated formulas that take into account housing stock, income levels, and unmet housing needs. Because each source of capital has its own affordability standard, rent ceiling, targeted population, and compliance mechanism, the use of CDBG and HOME funds can be complicated and multi-layered, at times causing difficulties for the direct-service agencies and developers who must layer the subsidies to reduce housing costs for tenants.

Another indirect program not administered by HUD is the Low-Income Housing Tax Credit, which cost $3.3 billion in 2001. With oversight from the U.S. Department of Treasury and state housing finance administrations, this program generates 60,000-80,000 new affordable apartments annually by providing tax credits to each state based on population. States distribute the tax credits to qualified developers who sell them to investors and use the capital generated by the transaction to pay part of the capital cost of the housing. The investor receives the federal subsidy only over time and through tax relief, after having proven that the project remains high in quality and available to low-income renters. While some states target their tax credits to lower-income families, without these targets developers are likely to serve only the upper limit of eligible renters (50-60 percent AMI) and gain the financing benefits of the program without offering units accessible to extremely low-income families.

Housing Reform Proposals

Given the dramatic decrease in the number of families receiving cash welfare and the resulting increase in the number of working low-income families, Congress has an opportunity to carefully examine federal housing policy to determine how best to accommodate the needs of the growing number of low-income working families. While there is widespread agreement that both direct and indirect housing assistance programs need improvement, there is little agreement on what those changes should be. Below are five of the most interesting proposals that Congress should consider.

Regional Administration of Section 8 Vouchers Recent reports on the Moving to Opportunity five-city demonstration project, which encourages Section 8 voucher families to move into low-poverty neighborhoods, have shown that such families see positive impacts on their health and safety as compared to families remaining in high-poverty neighborhoods. Proponents argue that regional administration of Section 8 vouchers would facilitate portability by reducing the number of Section 8 jurisdictions in a metropolitan area and by providing better housing counseling and search assistance. Under this proposal, HUD would select the administering agencies through a competitive process, potentially opening up the administration of vouchers to a wider variety of public, for-profit, and non-profit entities. Given the current difficulty finding landlords willing to accept Section 8 vouchers, some opponents argue that large-scale portability is not feasible without significant additional funds for housing search assistance. Others disagree with the very concept of integrating the poor into higher income neighborhoods, asserting that portability may weaken the important informal support that poor families must leave to move to higher-income neighborhoods.

Work Requirements and Time Limits A proposal that is sure to generate controversy is the establishment of mandatory work requirements and time limits on housing assistance for families headed by an able-bodied adult that live in public housing. Like recent efforts in welfare reform, time limits would change direct housing assistance into a transitional benefit by adding a sense of urgency for both the participants and for housing agencies. To be successful, however, PHAs would either have to provide augmented case management and employment services themselves or coordinate with local job programs, probably through the one-stop centers established under the Workforce Investment Act. In either case, additional funding would be required. Time limits are being tested in nine Moving to Work demonstrations, although these evaluations have not yet had enough time to produce results.

Convert Housing Aid to Cash The most radical proposal for housing reform is to eliminate federal housing initiatives altogether and provide direct housing assistance only through cash transfer programs such as the Earned Income Tax Credit. One approach would be to cover one-half of housing costs in excess of 30 percent of income, capped at the fair market rent of the jurisdiction. Determining and administering the adjustable housing add-on could become very complicated, although a similar adjustment is made in the food stamp program. Another administrative issue with an EITC-like approach would be working out a mechanism to provide housing subsidies on a monthly basis. The Department of Treasury, which now makes EITC payments almost exclusively on an annual basis, is ill-equipped to handle monthly payments. In addition, PHAs and other housing assistance providers will likely fight any proposal that eliminates the long-standing role of the federal government and local housing authorities in owning and operating housing for the poor.

Housing Trust Fund A coalition of organizations and elected officials is endorsing the establishment of a national trust fund to build and preserve 1.5 million rental units affordable to extremely low-income families over the next 10 years. Like state and local trust funds, the national trust fund would use on-going revenues from dedicated sources of funding such as the excess Federal Housing Administration (FHA) and Government National Mortgage Association revenue derived from lower than expected home loan default rates. Trust fund proponents argue that the excess revenue, which is normally returned to the federal treasury, should go to support the nation's affordable housing goals, whereas critics want to return the surpluses to low- and moderate-income FHA-insured homeowners as a rebate or reduction in their premiums. Critics also challenge the effectiveness of yet another source of capital layered upon many existing—and complicated— funding streams.

Deter Exclusionary Zoning Many local governments set zoning rules in ways that discourage reasonably priced housing. Minimum lot-size requirements, square-footage standards, prohibitions on accessory housing units, and occupancy standards that ban non-related households all conspire against a diverse, affordable housing stock. Congress could create incentives to influence local governments to be less parochial in their zoning decisions. Because local governments have almost complete control over zoning rules, designing these incentives in ways that are palatable to affluent areas is difficult, but not impossible.

Connecting Housing and Welfare

Most of the housing policy options described in this brief are long-term solutions. In the interim, welfare agencies, PHAs, and other housing providers and developers can work together to address the more immediate housing concerns of low-income working families as they transition from welfare to work. Some short-term changes include:
- enforcing the housing earned income disregard requirement created in 1998;
- expanding Individual Development Accounts to help families save for a down payment on a home;
- removing the barriers to housing assistance for two-parent families;
- providing housing advice and search assistance, as well as stop-gap housing

assistance through local one-stop job centers to help families avoid homelessness; and
- changing the TANF program so that housing assistance paid for by TANF funds does not count against a family's five-year time limit.

The coming year provides an opportunity to bring together two currently unconnected debates in the halls of Congress—reauthorization of welfare reform and publication of the bipartisan Congressional Millennial Housing Commission report on improving federal housing policy. The Bush administration and the leadership in both houses of Congress should use these two events to stimulate a thorough examination of the federal role in helping low-income families obtain decent housing while maintaining and further promoting work incentives. At the very least, the administration and Congress should fund experiments to test many of the proposals reviewed here. Improving the coordination between housing, cash welfare, and work programs should be high on the public policy agenda for 2002.

Additional Reading

Advisory Commission on Regulatory Barriers to Affordable Housing. 1991. *Not In My Back Yard: Removing Barriers to Affordable Housing*. U.S. Department of Housing and Urban Development.

Dolbeare, Cushing. 2001. "Housing Affordability: Challenge and Context." *Cityscape*, 5(2): 111–130.

Joint Center for Poverty Research. 2001. "Moving to Opportunity." *Poverty Research News*, 5(1).

Katz, Bruce, and Margery A. Turner. 2000. *Who Should Run the Housing Voucher Program? A Reform Proposal*. Washington, D.C.: Brookings.

Millennial Housing Commission. 2001. *Housing Program Tutorial*. Washington, D.C..

Sard, Barbara. 2001. *Outline of How Federal Housing Programs Can Help Provide Employment and Training Opportunities and Support Services to Current and Former Welfare Recipients*. Washington, D.C.: Center on Budget and Policy Priorities.

Swartz, Rebecca J., and Brian Miller. 2001. *Making Housing Work for Working Families: Building Bridges between the Labor Market and the Housing Market*. Indianapolis: Hudson Institute.

U.S. Department of Housing and Urban Development. 2001. *A Report on Worst Case Housing Needs in 1999: New Opportunity Amid Continuing Challenges*.

MICHAEL FIX AND RON HASKINS

Welfare Benefits for Non-citizens

Executive Summary
Substantial cuts in public welfare benefits for non-citizens were a major feature of the 1996 welfare reform law. Although the cuts were legally complex, one sweeping new rule governing welfare for immigrants emerged: non-citizens who legally enter the country after 1996 are subject to a five-year ban on some public benefits and permanent bans on others, including Supplemental Security Income and food stamps. The dramatic reforms have led to very large reductions in the receipt of most public benefits by non-citizens. These reductions extend even to citizen children of non-citizen parents and to refugees, two groups that maintain their eligibility for welfare benefits. There is evidence of increased hardship among non-citizen families. This increased hardship may well be caused in part by the 1996 benefit cuts. Although complete restoration of welfare benefits to their pre-1996 level is unlikely because of high costs, there are already several proposals in Congress and a recent proposal from the Bush administration to restore some benefits to some groups of non-citizens. Given both the changes in the politics of welfare benefits for non-citizens and the recent proposals, this year's reauthorization of the 1996 welfare reform law will probably result in some reversal of the benefit cuts for non-citizens.

One of the more contentious issues in the 1996 welfare reform debate was whether the federal government should provide welfare benefits to non-citizens who are legal residents of the United States. The sometimes bitter debate revealed a fundamental divide in how advocates, analysts, and policymakers think about welfare for non-citizens. On the one hand, those who support welfare benefits for non-citizens point out that at the time of the 1996 reforms, legal non-citizens enjoyed access to a wide range of welfare benefits. This access was based on the principle that non-citizens come to America to participate in the full range of American social, economic, and political life and that, with modest exceptions, they should be treated like other Americans. The children of non-citizens, the vast majority of whom are American citizens, are especially deserving of the safety net provided by welfare programs. Supporters believe that to deny non-citizens and their children welfare benefits is to leave them outside the protective sphere of social welfare guaranteed to the disabled and destitute by federal and state government policy. Moreover, like other Americans, non-citizens pay taxes, and unlike non-citizens in many other countries, can be drafted in time of war.

By contrast, those who oppose benefits for non-citizens argue that restricting their access to welfare has been a principle of American domestic policy since colonial times. The federal law, established in 1882 and strengthened in the early twentieth century, was that immigration officials should refuse entry to any non-citizen who appeared likely to become a "public charge" and should deport those who did, although actual deportations of public charges have been rare. Those supporting the 1996 reforms also point out that, both in statutory law and in the minds of American citizens as revealed in polls, welfare for non-citizens has always been suspect. The congressional prohibitions from the late nineteenth century have already been mentioned, but more recent restrictions are also notable. Specifically, in 1993 the Democratically controlled Congress extended from three to five years the period that immigrants entering the country had to wait before they could qualify for the Supplemental Security Income (SSI) program. Thus, the principle that non-citizens do not have the right to benefits on the same basis as citizens has long been established and maintained by the Congress. Finally, those in favor of benefit cuts for non-citizens have been strongly motivated to save taxpayer dollars and balance the budget.

In 1996, those who supported reduced welfare for non-citizens, primarily Republicans, had the upper hand in both houses of Congress. The reforms they enacted were sweeping in both their intent and effect. As the 2002 reauthorization debate begins, those opposed to the 1996 reforms and those in favor of them are preparing for another lively debate on both the fundamental principles and the specific provisions of federal law on welfare for non-citizens. There is a good chance that Congress will enact some benefit expansions.

Overview of 1996 Provisions

The 1996 reforms changed almost every aspect of non-citizen eligibility for welfare benefits. Although the provisions are exceedingly complex, a rough general principle provides useful guidance. With some exceptions, non-citizens entering the United States after August 22, 1996, the date of enactment of the welfare reform legislation, are not eligible for most welfare benefits, including Temporary Assistance for Needy Families (TANF), SSI, Medicaid, and the State Children's Health Insurance Program (SCHIP), until they have been in the U.S. for at least five years. Keeping this general principle in mind, a more thorough review of the 1996 provisions reveals both their complexity and breadth.

In determining welfare eligibility for non-citizens, two broad criteria are taken into account. The most general screen is the concept of "qualified" and "not qualified" alien. Generally, qualified aliens are non-citizens who have been permitted to reside permanently in the United States. They include legal permanent residents (LPRs), refugees, asylees, Cuban/Haitian entrants, and a few other categories. Qualified immigrants may be eligible for federal and state benefit programs that aim to help families with limited income and resources. Not qualified aliens (mostly illegal and temporary immigrants), by contrast, are ineligible for all except emergency benefits—a policy that was largely in place even before the 1996 reforms.

The second factor is date of entry into the United States. Specifically, qualified immigrants who entered after August 22, 1996 are barred from SSI and food stamps until they become citizens and from TANF, Medicaid, and SCHIP for five years after entry. Qualified immigrants, who entered before August 22, 1996, have wider eligibility for these benefits, in part because states have elected to pay for the benefits and in part because federal legislation enacted since 1996 restored some benefits for those already in the United States. As a result, many immigrants who entered before 1996 are eligible for TANF, Medicaid, SCHIP, and SSI. Eligibility for food stamps is more restricted.

In addition to the two broad criteria, there are several other factors that condition non-citizens' eligibility for welfare benefits. Children born to either qualified or not qualified non-citizens after they have entered the United States are citizens and are therefore eligible for benefits on the same basis as native citizens. Refugees and asylees are eligible for all welfare benefits for the first seven years they reside in the U.S., after which their eligibility is greatly reduced. Non-citizens who have worked for ten years and armed forces personnel and their dependents are eligible for all benefits. Finally, some emergency benefits—especially Medicaid—are provided to all non-citizens.

A major provision of the 1996 legislation required that most legal immigrants have sponsors with incomes over 125 percent of the federal poverty line. The provision also required the income of sponsors to be deemed as available to the immigrants when calculating eligibility for welfare benefits, which usually has the effect of disqualifying them from benefits. The sponsor was also held liable for the costs of any welfare benefit used by the immigrant. The purpose of these requirements was to ensure that sponsors assume financial responsibility for newcomers, thereby reducing the potential burden on taxpayers.

These provisions constitute a revolution in welfare policy for non-citizens. But there is widespread disagreement about their fairness. The fairness issue will be a major part of the

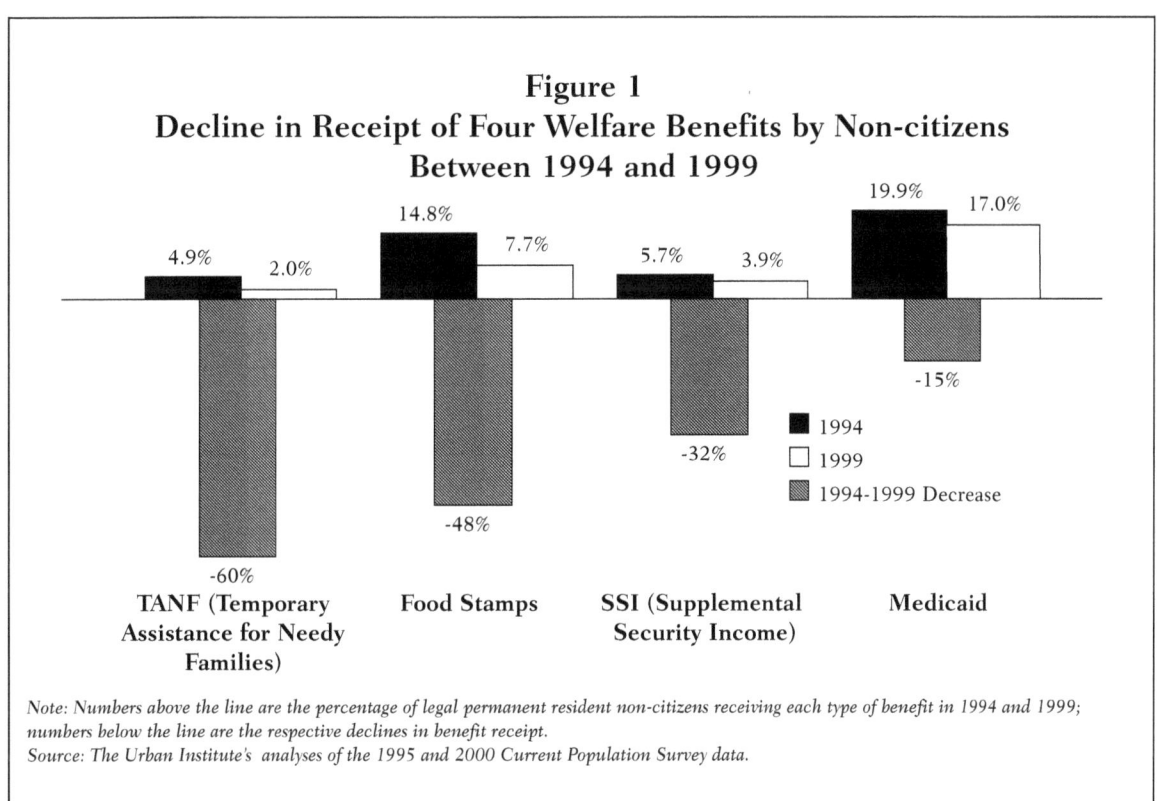

Figure 1
Decline in Receipt of Four Welfare Benefits by Non-citizens Between 1994 and 1999

Note: Numbers above the line are the percentage of legal permanent resident non-citizens receiving each type of benefit in 1994 and 1999; numbers below the line are the respective declines in benefit receipt.
Source: The Urban Institute's analyses of the 1995 and 2000 Current Population Survey data.

reauthorization debate over welfare for non-citizens. But the debate will also be informed by the actual effects of the 1996 changes, a topic to which we now turn our attention.

Effects of the 1996 Reforms

Declining Use of Public Benefits by Type of Family The intent of the 1996 reforms was to reduce the use of welfare by non-citizens. Studies by Michael Fix, Jeffrey Passel, and Wendy Zimmermann at the Urban Institute show that use of public benefits by LPRs not only declined sharply, but did so at a faster rate than use of benefits by citizens (the 1996 reforms also reduced eligibility for many benefit programs among citizens).

Data for 1999 from the Current Population Survey conducted by the U.S. Census Bureau show that there has been a sustained decline in legal non-citizens' use of TANF, SSI, food stamps, and Medicaid or SCHIP from 1994 through 1999. As shown in Figure 1, the sharpest decreases occurred in TANF (60 percent) and food stamps (48 percent) and the lowest in Medicaid (15 percent). The declines in participation rates for LPR families exceeded the declines experienced by citizen families for TANF, SSI, and food stamps, but not Medicaid (not shown).

Fix and Passel have tried to disentangle the effects of the law's immigrant restrictions on different types of low-income families with children: those headed by LPRs, those headed by refugees, and those headed by citizens. The trends in benefit receipt by low-income LPR families with children reveal that they experienced large declines in use of TANF (53 percent) and food stamps (38 percent) between 1994 and 1999. But their participation in Medicaid and SCHIP remained essentially unchanged. Over the period, poor LPRs and poor citizens' use of most benefits declined at about the same rate. By 1999, poor LPR families were less likely to use TANF and food stamps than citizens were, while they were slightly more likely to use Medicaid.

The benefit cuts not only led to reduced benefit use among the LPRs who had been the principal targets of reform, but also spilled over to U.S.-born citizen children who live in families in which one or both parents is a non-citizen. These children, who are fully eligible for benefits, constitute a surprisingly large group. Roughly three quarters of all children living in immigrant families with non-citizen parents are citizens. Moreover, 10 percent of all children and 15 percent of poor children in the United States live in mixed status families. These families have substantially lower participation rates in benefit programs than citizen families for TANF (7.8 versus 11.6 percent) and food stamps (19.8 versus 27.9 percent). For both programs, mixed status families experienced significant declines in participation from 1994 to 1999.

There have also been striking declines in benefit use among refugees. Refugees are a protected population under welfare reform, retaining their eligibility for federal benefits for seven years after entry. Nonetheless, between 1994 and 1999 steep declines occurred in use of TANF (78 percent), food stamps (53 percent), and Medicaid (36 percent) by low-income refugee families with children. Before welfare reform, refugee families had use rates that were more than double those for either citizen or LPR families. However, by 1999 the rates for refugee families had fallen to levels roughly equal to those of citizens.

As noted, there was no change in receipt of Medicaid (including SCHIP) among low-income LPR families with children between 1994 and 1999. There are a number of explanations for these stable Medicaid use rates. These include the introduction of expanded health care coverage under SCHIP, stepped up state and local outreach for child health insurance, and the impact of new federal guidelines clarifying that use of health benefits would not be a bar to obtaining a work permit ("green card") or citizenship. In addition, the doctors, hospitals, and clinics that provide health care have a strong incentive to keep both immigrants and natives enrolled in government health programs to ensure the payment of medical bills. Other welfare programs do not have third parties who have such direct incentives to make sure low-income families are signed up for welfare benefits. Another possible explanation for the relatively modest decline among LPR families with children may be increased use of emergency Medicaid by legal immigrants.

Despite the lack of decline in Medicaid use between 1994 and 1999, the percentage of LPR children who are uninsured remained higher than that of other children. Less than 20 percent of poor citizens' children were uninsured in 1999, while the rate among citizen children of LPRs was 27 percent and the rate for non-citizen children of LPRs was 39 percent.

Declines in immigrant use of benefits are evident nationwide, but they are especially pronounced among the states that offer the least generous safety nets such as Texas and Florida. As a group, the thirty least generous states experienced rapid growth in their immigrant populations between 1995 and 2000, with the number of foreign born families with children rising by 31 percent—more than four times the rate of the remaining twenty states. TANF participation among low-income LPR families with children dropped 73 percent in the least generous states between 1994 and 1999 as compared with 45 percent among the more generous states. As might have been predicted, the 1996 reforms, which gave more discretion to states in determining non-citizens' eligibility

The 1996 reforms have led to substantial differences across states in benefit eligibility and benefit use.

for welfare benefits, have led to substantial differences across states in benefit eligibility and benefit use.

Taken together, these migration and policy trends cast doubt on the welfare magnet theory, which holds that immigrants are drawn to places with generous welfare benefits. These trends also raise the concern that low-income LPR families will find themselves outside increasingly localized safety nets as the labor market tightens.

Explaining the Trends How do we explain these declines in benefit use among non-citizens? Increased naturalizations could reduce the number of non-citizens receiving benefits if the immigrants who become citizens do so to continue receiving welfare benefits. Between 1994 and 1999, the number of non-citizen families that naturalized did increase rapidly. These increases were the product of a number of demographic and policy shifts that include, but go beyond, welfare reform. For example, increased naturalizations also resulted from the fact that 2.7 million immigrants acquired legal status around 1990 under the 1986 Immigration Reform and Control Act and thus became eligible to become citizens in the mid-1990s.

This rise in the number of naturalizations, however, can account for only a small proportion of the drop in benefit receipt by non-citizens. While the number of families containing a naturalized citizen grew by 1.5 million between 1994 and 1999, the number of such families participating in welfare programs rose by only 170,000. At the same time, the number of LPR families on welfare dropped by 480,000. Thus, increased naturalizations fall well short of offsetting decreases in benefit use among non-citizens.

If naturalizations account for only a fraction of the decline in LPR use of welfare, perhaps increased income—which would lower benefit eligibility—can explain the decline. However, Urban Institute analyses reveal that only about one-quarter of the reduction in TANF and food stamp participation rates for both citizens and LPR families is explained by changes in income. Thus, rising incomes also explain only a fraction of the decline in welfare use.

Research by Wendy Zimmermann and Karen Tumlin at the Urban Institute shows that, while fewer immigrants are joining TANF, non-citizens are having a difficult time leaving. They find that legal immigrants make up a significant share of the remaining caseload in several major cities and that, as compared with native American TANF recipients, immigrants in these cities face a number of barriers to entering the workforce, including limited English proficiency, less education, and less recent work experience than native workers. The researchers also found that the programs needed to help potential non-citizen workers overcome these barriers were often not available.

To sum up, welfare reform's immigrant restrictions have led to a rapid decline in TANF and food stamp use among LPR families with children, citizen children in mixed status families, and refugees. There have also been declines in the use of Medicaid among legal, working-age adult immigrants, but not among poor non-citizen families with children or children themselves. Increased naturalization rates and higher incomes contributed to the declines in benefit receipt by non-citizens, but they fall well short of accounting for the entire decline. We are left to conclude that the benefit cuts of 1996 directly contributed to the decline in welfare use by non-citizens.

Hardship Among Non-citizens Whatever the cause, there is some evidence that declining welfare use by non-citizen families may be associated with increased hardship. Randy Capps at the Urban Institute found that roughly one half of all immigrant families with children had incomes below 200 percent of poverty and that the children of immigrants were more likely than the children of natives to have no health insurance (22 versus 10 percent) and to have some difficulty getting enough food to eat (37 versus 27 percent). Similarly, George Borjas of Harvard has produced strong evidence that the exclusion of immigrants from food stamps is leading to rising food insecurity among non-citizen households.

The Policy and Politics of Reauthorization

The reauthorization debate will feature proposals by both the Bush administration and by members of Congress to expand welfare benefits for non-citizens. The most important proposals will be those that expand benefits for non-citizens who arrived after 1996 because the distinction between pre-1996 and post-1996 entrants constitutes something like a line in the sand for policymakers. Although there have already been several changes in the 1996 reforms, no legislation has been enacted that moved benefits for non-citizens across the 1996 line of demarcation. Given what is known about human longevity, if benefits are not extended to post-1996 entrants, there will eventually be very few non-citizens receiving welfare benefits.

In penetrating the 1996 line in the sand, it is unlikely that there will be serious attention to proposals that attempt a complete restoration of benefits for non-citizens. The major reason is that a complete restoration of food stamp, TANF, SSI, and Medicaid benefits would be very expensive. According to the Congressional Budget Office, just restoring SSI and Medicaid to non-citizens who qualify for SSI would cost nearly $25 billion over five years. Under congressional budget rules, increased spending must be offset either by equivalent cuts in other programs or by tax increases, neither of which is feasible in this case. Thus, proposals are likely to be more modest than complete restoration of benefits.

In recent months, the president and members of the House and Senate have offered several proposals that would expand the benefits of several groups of non-citizens including children, the elderly, and the disabled. The Senate Farm Bill included several provisions expanding food stamp benefits for children, working non-citizens, refugees, and the disabled that would cost around $1.1 billion over ten years. President Bush recently proposed extending food stamps to post-1996 immigrants who have been in the country for five years, essentially applying the same five-year ban on food stamps now imposed on TANF and Medicaid. Proposals to expand post-1996 immigrants' eligibility for Medicaid, TANF, and, on a more restricted basis, SSI for the disabled are also likely. One legislative proposal already advanced would expand Medicaid coverage for immigrant children and pregnant women. When fully implemented, Medicaid proposals of this type would cost around $2 billion over five years.

The politics of these proposals are fascinating. It is useful to recall that the original sweeping changes in welfare policy for non-citizens were enacted as part of the most comprehensive welfare reform legislation since the New Deal of 1935. Thus, many individual provisions of the immense bill, including the cuts in benefits for non-citizens, were swept along with the overall package and did not receive extensive scrutiny from Congress. Nor were there separate votes on many of these provisions on the floor of either house of Congress. It is not clear, then, whether the non-citizen reforms would have passed if a separate vote had been required. Moreover, in 1995 and 1996, when Congress shaped and then approved the final welfare reform package, the overriding goal of Congress and President Clinton was saving money so that the federal government could reach a balanced budget. Over half the savings in the 1996 welfare reform legislation were in the cuts for non-citizens (although Clinton did not support them).

Conditions in 2002 are sharply different than those in 1996. There is less pressure to achieve budget cuts and there are no prominent proposals to deepen the cuts in welfare for non-citizens. Democrats now control the Senate, and a Republican president has proposed to partially reverse the cuts in food stamps for non-citizens. These shifts respond, in part, to a changing electorate. The Census Bureau reported last year that Hispanics had moved ahead of African Americans as the nation's largest minority population. Cuts in non-citizens' benefits are opposed by ethnic groups that count substantial numbers of immigrants among their number, making many politicians reluctant to support cuts. This is especially the case for Republicans, the party that proposed and enacted the 1996 cuts in welfare benefits for non-citizens. Because many Republicans are trying to improve their image among minority groups—especially Hispanics—it may not be surprising that the president has taken the lead in proposing an expansion in non-citizen benefits in his 2003 budget. Finally, many states believe they have been forced to spend more money on non-citizens due to their loss of federal benefits. Especially given the pressure on state budgets caused by the recession, states can be expected to support all proposals that restore federal benefits to non-citizens.

The bottom line is that at least some modest restoration of benefits, including some that provide eligibility to post-1996 entrants, seems destined to have major support from Congress and the Bush administration. Thus, if Congress finds a way to finance a moderate expansion of non-citizen welfare benefits, the legislation has a good chance of becoming law. A modest restoration would then leave the door open to future expansions.

Additional Reading

Borjas, George J. 2001. *Food Insecurity and Public Assistance.* Cambridge: John F. Kennedy School of Government, Harvard.

Fix, Michael, and Jeffrey S. Passel. 2001. *The Scope and Impact of Welfare Reform's Immigrant Provisions* (Assessing the New Federalism: Discussion Paper No. 02). Washington, D.C.: Urban Institute.

Fremstad, Shawn. 2001. *Immigrants and Welfare Reauthorization.* Washington, D.C.: Center on Budget and Policy Priorities.

U.S. House of Representatives. 2000. "Appendix J: Welfare benefits for non-citizens." In *2000 Greenbook: Background Material and Data on Programs within the Jurisdiction of the Committee on Ways and Means.*

Zimmermann, Wendy, and Karen C. Tumlin. 1999. *Patchwork Policies: State Assistance for Immigrants under Welfare Reform* (Assessing the New Federalism: Occasional Paper No. 24). Washington, D.C.: Urban Institute.

Most of the data analysis presented here is drawn from a paper by Michael Fix and Jeffrey S. Passel that appeared in *Wefare Reform: The Next Act,* edited by Alan Weil and Kenneth Feingold, and published by the Urban Institute in March 2002.

Contributors

Gina Adams is a senior research associate at the Urban Institute.

Rebecca M. Blank is the Dean of the Gerald R. Ford School of Public Policy at the University of Michigan and a former member of the Council of Economic Advisers in the Clinton Administration.

Dan Bloom is a senior research associate at the Manpower Demonstration Research Corporation.

Nancye Campbell works in the Office of Planning, Research, and Evaluation at the Administration for Children and Families, U.S. Department of Health and Human Services.

Greg J. Duncan is a professor of education and social policy at Northwestern University and the director of the Northwestern University/University of Chicago Joint Center for Poverty Research.

Michael Fix is the principal research associate at the Urban Institute's Population Studies Center.

Thomas Gais is the director of the Federalism Research Group at the Nelson A. Rockefeller Institute of Government.

Irwin Garfinkel is the Mitchell I. Ginsberg professor of contemporary urban problems at the Columbia University School of Social Work.

Judith Gueron is the president of the Manpower Demonstration Research Corporation.

Gayle Hamilton is a senior research associate in the Manpower Demonstration Research Corporation's Work, Community, and Economic Security Department.

Ron Haskins was a senior fellow at the Brookings Institution and a co-director of the Welfare Reform & Beyond initiative when the policy briefs were written. He is now a guest scholar at the Brookings Institution and a senior consultant with the Annie E. Casey Foundation.

John Holahan is the director of the Health Policy Center at the Urban Institute.

Andrea Kane is a visiting fellow at the Brookings Institution and the outreach director of the Welfare Reform & Beyond initiative.

Irene Lurie is a professor of public administration and policy at the Rockefeller College of the State University of New York at Albany and a research associate at the Rockefeller Institute of Government.

John K. Maniha works in the Office of Planning, Research, and Evaluation at the Administration for Children and Families, U.S. Department of Health and Human Services.

Sara McLanahan is the director of the Center for Research on Child Wellbeing and a professor of sociology and political affairs at Princeton University.

Brian Miller is the executive director of Community Housing and Services, Inc.

Ronald B. Mincy is the Maurice V. Russell professor of social policy and social work practice at the Columbia University School of Social Work.

Robert A. Moffitt is a professor of economics at Johns Hopkins University.

Pamela A. Morris is a senior research associate at the Manpower Demonstration Research Corporation.

Paul Offner is a research professor at the Institute for Health Care Research and Policy at Georgetown University.

LaDonna Pavetti is a senior fellow at Mathematica Policy Research, Inc.

Wendell Primus is the director of income security at the Center for Budget and Policy Priorities.

Monica Rohacek is a research associate at the Urban Institute.

Howard Rolston works in the Office of Planning, Research, and Evaluation at the Administration for Children and Families, U.S. Department of Health and Human Services.

Isabel Sawhill is a senior fellow at the Brookings Institution and a co-director of the Welfare Reform & Beyond initiative.

Rebecca Swartz is a research fellow with the Hudson Institute's Welfare Policy Center.

R. Kent Weaver is a senior fellow at the Brookings Institution and a co-director of the Welfare Reform & Beyond initiative.

Alan Weil is the director of the Urban Institute's Assessing the New Federalism Project.

Don Winstead was the welfare reform administrator at the Florida Department for Children and Families when the policy brief was written. He is now the deputy assistant secretary in the Office of the Assistant Secretary for Planning and Evaluation, U.S. Department of Health and Human Services.

Michael Wiseman is a research professor of public policy and economics at George Washington University and a visiting scholar at the National Opinion Research Center.